lenry James

F. W. DUPEE

study of James that
ted considera-

The American Men of Letters Series

The American Men of Letters Series

Henry James from a painting by Jacques Emile Blanche

Henry James

F. *Frederick* W. *Wilcox* Dupee

The American Men of Letters Series

WILLIAM SLOANE ASSOCIATES

The author wishes to make the following acknowledgments for permission to use quoted material:

Appleton-Century-Crofts, Inc., for quotations from *A BACKWARD GLANCE*, by Edith Wharton, Copyright 1934 by D. Appleton-Century Co., Inc.

Jonathan Cape Limited, for Canadian rights to use quotations from *THE DESTRUCTIVE ELEMENT*, by Stephen Spender, London, 1935.

Harper & Brothers, for quotations from *THE AMERICAN SCENE*, by Henry James, 1907; and from *A WRITER'S RECOLLECTIONS*, by Mrs. Humphry Ward, 1918.

Harvard University Press, for quotations from *THE THOUGHT AND CHARACTER OF WILLIAM JAMES*, by Ralph B. Perry, 1935.

Houghton Mifflin Company, for quotations from *THE DESTRUCTIVE ELEMENT*, by Stephen Spender, 1936; and from *WATCH AND WARD*, by Henry James, 1886.

John Murray, for Canadian rights to use quotations from *MEMORIES AND FRIENDS*, by A. C. Benson, London, 1924.

Oxford University Press, Inc., for quotations from *THE NOTEBOOKS OF HENRY JAMES*, edited by F. O. Matthiessen and K. B. Murdock, Copyright 1947 by Oxford University Press, Inc.

G. P. Putnam's Sons, for quotations from *MEMORIES AND FRIENDS*, by A. C. Benson, 1924.

Paul R. Reynolds & Son, for quotations from *THE JAMES FAMILY*, by F. O. Matthiessen, 1947.

Charles Scribner's Sons, for quotations from *A SMALL BOY AND OTHERS*, by Henry James, 1913; from *NOTES OF A SON AND BROTHER*, by Henry James, 1914; and from *THE LETTERS OF HENRY JAMES*, 1920.

Copyright, 1951, by

WILLIAM SLOANE ASSOCIATES, INC.

First Printing

Typography and format designed by

LEONARD W. BLIZARD

Manufactured in the United States of America

Published simultaneously in Canada by

George J. McLeod, Ltd., Toronto

Contents

Acknowledgments

EVEN today, when Henry James is more widely appreciated than ever during his lifetime, his readers are seldom agreed as to what he is distinguished for, which are his best books and periods, whether he is more profitably studied in relation to American or to English traditions, and finally just how great a writer he really is. He remains a figure of mysteries and problems, and it is no doubt a tribute to this fact that the recent criticism of him, extensive as it is in amount, is in substance extremely detailed, concerned as a rule with the single work, period, theme, relationship, or issue. I have believed it worth while to attempt to portray him in the wholeness of his life, mind, and work; but I think I have been aware of the difficulties of doing this. And my indebtedness to the recent criticism is so large that I can discharge only a small part of it here. Most of us who endeavor to write about authors in the atmosphere of their lives and times owe much to Edmund Wilson, and I am indebted as well to his writings about Henry James. T. S. Eliot, Philip Rahv, and Lionel Trilling are three other critics on whose interpretations of James I have drawn heavily. My account of *The Golden Bowl* could not have been written without Stephen Spender's perfect pages on that novel in his *The Destructive Element*. I have likewise profited from conversations with many others, including Mr. Morton D. Zabel, Mr. Victor Wolfson, and Mr. Quentin Anderson.

In regard to the biographical side of the present book, I have also to acknowledge certain difficulties and many debts. James has never been the subject of one of those detailed and scholarly narratives called "standard biographies," and this is a fact I have had constantly to reckon with. Mr. Leon Edel, who shares with Miss Edna Kenton the distinction of knowing more about James than anyone else knows, is now at work on what promises to be such a biography; and I have had the privilege of his kindly encouragement and expert assistance. He has read the manuscript, made detailed criticisms, and suggested lines of thought which proved fruitful. I am further indebted to his published writings on James, in particular to those studies of his which culminated in his monumental volume, *The Complete Plays of Henry James*. My remarks on James's experience in the theater frequently echo Mr. Edel's. My next largest debt of this kind is to Simon Nowell-Smith's *The Legend of the Master*, an invaluable collection of data on the later Henry James. Much of the material in my chapter "The Lion of Lamb House" is taken from Mr. Nowell-Smith's book. The work of Mr. Edel and Mr. Nowell-Smith is chiefly concerned with James's life in England; and this large phase of his career happens to be the one most neglected by other scholars. The chief primary sources for it are: *The Letters of Henry James*, edited by Percy Lubbock, whose introduction and commentaries are very helpful; *The Notebooks of Henry James*, edited by F. O. Matthiessen and Kenneth B. Murdock, and again with useful comment; and James's own prefaces written for the New York Edition of his selected tales and novels. On James's early life there is comparatively a great deal of material, or at any rate of material more thoroughly ordered by scholarship. James himself ordered his early experiences in his two autobiographic volumes, *A Small Boy and Others* and *Notes of a Son and Brother*; and I found both books to be of fundamental value. An equally important source for the story of James's youth is *The Thought and Character of William James*, by Ralph Barton Perry. This book is remarkable not only because it prints so many family documents but because Mr. Perry's interpretations of the members of the family are so substantial. *The James Family* by F. O. Matthiessen, which is of course another great source of this kind, did not appear until my early chapters were already outlined; and so, although I read and used it, I am perhaps more indebted to such studies in the subject as C. H. Grattan's *The Three Jameses: A Family of Minds*; Austin Warren's *The Elder Henry James*; and *Alice James: Her Brothers—Her Journal*, edited by Anna Robeson Burr. I have also consulted and used some of the unpublished papers of the James family in the Harvard Library. Cornelia Pulsifer Kelley's *The Early Development of Henry James* was helpful on the subject of James's early stories and reviews. A work of another kind on which I have also drawn is "The Ghost of Henry James," a psychiatric study of James's personality by Dr. Saul Rosenzweig. My own sense of James's psychology was clarified and extended by the work of this expert witness; and although I have dealt with the topic in no more than a very general way, what I do say about it implies an agreement with Dr. Rosenzweig's findings.

I want to thank a number of persons for special assistance of various kinds. The editors of the American Men of Letters series have all been encouraging; and Mr. Trilling in particular has read my manuscript and discussed it with me at length. The late F. O. Matthiessen generously talked over the subject with me at an early stage and helped me to get access to the materials in the Houghton collection of the Harvard Library. The late Henry James, nephew of the novelist, kindly gave me permission, in the name of the family estate, to inspect those materials; and Mr. K. D. Metcalf of the Harvard Library has authorized my use of certain passages from James's unpublished letters. I am grateful to Miss Helen Stewart of William Sloane Associates, not only because she is a patient publisher but because she is a sympathetic reader of Henry James. I owe a great deal to Mrs. Elizabeth C. Moore for her editorial work on the manuscript, and to Miss Ruth Montgomery for highly intelligent secretarial assistance. My two final chapters were written at Yaddo; and for the pleasure of staying there I wish to thank the members of the Yaddo corporation and in particular the director, Mrs. Elizabeth Ames.

Finally I must say a word on the subject of texts and dates. James usually revised his work from printing to printing; and when late in his life he got out the *New York Edition of the Novels and Tales of Henry James*, he thoroughly revised a large portion of it once for all. I have used the text of the New York Edition except in two instances: when I have referred to works not included in that edition; and when I have quoted from or alluded to a passage in support of some contention of mine concerning James's mind or style at the time of his writing the work in question. In dating his works I have followed LeRoy Phillips's *A Bibliography of the Writings of Henry James*. Much of his fiction was serialized in magazines, and occasionally a work would run from one year into the next. The dates I give are those of the appearance of the first installment.

Henry James

The Dream of the Louvre

ALTHOUGH Henry James was born in New York City in 1843, and died in London in 1916 an English citizen, his career was less expansive than these facts would suggest. A true Odyssey, it was concerned equally with exploring the antipodes and with putting the house in order. In all but physical adventure and sexual passion his was an eventful life. He lived long, wrote much, traveled extensively, enjoyed as large an acquaintance as any writer of his time, and responded to the literary currents of three nations. Meanwhile he also desired a quite different experience, which may be defined as a feeling for the limits of life. This does not come easily to Americans and it did not come easily to James. The romantic disposition, enhanced by his native idealism, exacerbated by the shabbier facts and interdictions of native life, was his as much as it was Whitman's or Melville's. He too cherished his eternal metaphor of ineffable bounty. Where they dreamed of sea or river or prairie or forest, he dreamed of Europe: "vast, vague, and dazzling—an irradiation of light from objects undefined." But Europe stood for much more than a light that never was. It was also an inescapable witness to the failings and greatnesses of men. It implied that the past was highly relevant to the present, the old world to the new. "Democracy shuts the past against the poet, but opens the future before him," wrote Tocqueville, who cared so much for continuity as a principle that he gave too little weight to it as a fact. That it would assert itself most insistently in the newest of nations and purest of democracies he was unable to foresee. He reckoned without the Whitman who would excel in the elegy; most of all he reckoned without Hawthorne and Henry James.

Past and present, power and innocence, experience and vision, freedom and responsibility, Europe and America— on such antitheses James's mind was nourished. It was not, however, a philosophic mind and systematic irony was foreign to it. It preyed, T. S. Eliot observes, "not upon ideas, but upon living beings." And upon beings no longer living, it should be added, for he was peculiarly open to the play of semiconscious associations, including ancestral ones. Few American writers have had so exceptional a past or one that was so vividly American. It was true, as his brother William said, that he was a "native of the James family"; but it did not follow that he had "no other country." He had a country precisely in having such a family. They were an especially reliable conductor of indigenous sentiment in that they represented it with so refined a passion, humor, and eloquence. Never conspicuous in national affairs, the Jameses were prompt to fill the private roles offered by American life, not excluding those of the invalid, the eccentric, and the waster. The varieties of defeat were familiar to Henry James; in his past they mingled with the still bolder instances of success to compose a formidable picture of the mixed possibilities of life.

His grandfather, the first William James, was a success

in the more obvious sense. A vivid young man of small means, he emigrated from the north of Ireland about 1789, settled in Albany, New York, and rapidly made himself at home in the newly constituted nation. In time thirteen children were borne to him by three successive wives, the last of whom, Catharine Barber, of a notable pre-Revolutionary family, was the placid joyless grandmother of James's childhood recollections. Her husband, who died before his grandson's birth, was energetically Irish, a man of immense character and enterprise, and at length a veritable *novus homo* among the long-established patroons of the upper Hudson country. Beginning as a modest retailer of tobacco and dry goods, he presently organized a savings bank; and when he died his fortune was reputed to amount to three million dollars. But he reached beyond business into public life, and was active in Presbyterian affairs, in the founding of Union College, and in the planning of the Erie Canal. When the Canal was opened he addressed the inaugural crowd, reminding them of "the special intervention of Providence in protecting our national honor and greatness." Little is known about his private character, but he appears to have been swayed by feelings beyond his requirements as a practical man. Each winter he laid by stocks of food which his wife was expected to dispense, with her own hands, to those in need. Any aberrations on the part of his family seem to have made him frantic; his son Henry, future father of the writer, was especially troublesome. Once, as a Union undergraduate, he found himself in debt and obliged to run away from his creditor. He "has so debased himself," his father informed a friend, "as to leave his parent's house in the character of a swindler . . . a fellow from Schenectady was after him today for 50 to 60 drs . . . for segars and oysters." A strict Calvinist, the first William James consorted with clergymen, enforced what his son called "the paralytic Sunday routine," and generally brought the reality of hell into the parlor. But he was not, it appears, an automatic believer; there were depths in his religiousness as well as in his paternal sentiments. He had the domestic sensibility, which passed to his descendants. On occasion his tenderness towards his children was such that the elder Henry James described it as "excessive."

He died in 1832, and his children found that he had provided for them after a fashion which they regarded as excessive in a different sense. Believing sudden wealth to be dangerous to inexperienced heirs, he left a provocative will. They were not to get their share of the estate until the youngest grandson had come of age; certain of the less stable among them were required to prove themselves by practicing a trade; and his son Henry, who had passed from spendthrift to heretic, was cut down to a small annuity until he should become a more reliable Christian. It was a curious testament; did it anticipate the highly experimental spirit of some of his descendants? If so, the experiment was in this case a failure. The will was broken in court, the eager heirs coming into their portions at the usual age. Furthermore, as James was to write, "the rupture with my grandfather's tradition and attitude was complete; we were never in a single case, I think, for two generations, guilty of a stroke of business." Were they guilty of worse things? His grandson would have us believe that many, by no means all, of the immediate descendants of the first William James more than confirmed his fears, talking and traveling and drinking themselves into a tragic if engaging aimlessness.

Whatever the literal truth of this picture, the elder Henry James was an exception to it; and it was by way of him that a confirmed dread of aimlessness was transmitted from the Calvinist grandparent to the cosmopolitan grandson. Indeed, after his erratic youth, and despite his father's censure of him, the elder Henry appears to have succeeded to the paternal authority among his relatives. He was, as his son wrote, "the person in all his family most justly appealed and most anxiously listened to." But he exerted this influence in a manner very different from his father's; for apart from their common drive towards distinction in life, the two resembled each other as little as did the historical periods of which each was in a sense typical. As the father had contributed to an age of large material development, so the son, as an intellectual and a friend of Emerson, played a part in the spiritual reformation of the '40's and '50's. His part was not a conspicuous one in regard to the public force of his thought and his writings. So happily did he embody his ideas in his own personality that he was under small pressure to disseminate them by way of a literary career. He was, nevertheless, among the notable private persons of the age, as is attested by his several books and essays, his numerous letters, the photographs and painted portraits of him, the anecdotes about him that are always cropping up in the writings of his friends, and the admiring memorials of him composed by some of his children. He was a stout, kindly-looking, large-faced man, bearded, spectacled, and bald to the ears: a wit as well as a visionary, a genial fanatic and a man of the world. He had, as Ellery Channing said, "the look of a broker, and the brains and heart of a Pascal." Forever in correspondence with Swedenborgians, Sandemanians, Fourierists, and others of the sectarian underworld, he was likewise known to Carlyle, Mill, and others in England, which he several times visited. Nearly everyone thought him remarkable. "He is," observed Emerson, "the best man and companion in the world."

His ideas, though not very accessible to his contemporaries, were vastly important to the elder James himself, of whom his son William was to observe with literal accuracy that "his truths were his life." Primary among them, indeed, was a belief in the capacity of ideas to become flesh of one's flesh; and however much William and Henry were to smile at "Father's Ideas" in general, they were never to smile at this premise, nor of course at their parent himself unless in tribute to the fact that the all-but-perfect man in an imperfect setting is inevitably comic from certain points of view. For the rest they remained dazzled by the paternal image of human wholeness, as if they had spent their childhood in the company of some sociable saint or domestic Socrates—as in fact they had.

In time a number of family tales came into being which served, like a body of myths, to illuminate and govern the common experience of the Jameses. His sons knew that their father's bliss, far from having come to him as a birthright, was the reward of a hard search. Like so many of his generation, with whom he shared the passion for unity of being, he had been aware of painful incongruities, gross compromises between theory and practice, in the American world of his youth, the same world in which *his* father had thrived. In the elder Henry's case it was principally the religious evils that stood out. What he sometimes called "the old virile religion" of Calvin had become infected with the commercial spirit. God maintained only "a debtor and creditor account" with man, who was thereby reduced to a state of "the most unhandsome mendicancy and higgling"; while the theologian, because he was "personally mortgaged to an *institution*," manifested "a fatal professional conscience." It was in his father's house, swarming with clergymen and rank with money, that he first glimpsed these abuses. They were confirmed by the years he later spent (after the too jolly term at Union) at orthodox Princeton. But meanwhile his reflective habit had been quickened by a personal disaster. As a boy of thirteen, he had lost a leg and spent two years in bed as a result of terrible burns suffered when he tried to extinguish a fire in an Albany hay barn. He emerged from this experience with permanent faith in what he was invariably to call "the spirit," and he came in time to conceive the essence of the spiritual life as a tireless process, a habit of converting limitations into virtues, nature into consciousness, evil into good. As this strenuous doctrine assumed a kind of purpose in things, so it rejected the possibility of mere waste. It was therefore very little inclined ever to relax into any attitude of tragic acceptance. And in the family code, adjunct of the family myth, this discipline became central, lending itself very often to a habit of fortitude, sometimes to despairing heroics, depending on the individual or the circumstances. To see a purpose in things was not necessarily to entertain supernatural beliefs; for Henry James junior, to whose morality and morale the conversion philosophy was extremely important, it represented simply a principle of survival and endurance in human life itself.

But for the elder Henry James God was a necessity. Beyond reach of the secular new thought of Boston till his middle age, he cherished many aspects of *his* father's faith and did not pause before he had recaptured it in a new form. After a false start or two, and having meanwhile married Mary Robertson Walsh of New York City, the sister of a Princeton classmate, and witnessed the birth of two sons, William and Henry, he found himself in 1844 in England, temporarily at rest. There, in a rented house adjoining Windsor Forest, his calm was broken by an event known in the domestic annals as "the vastation." As he described it, he had been sitting alone in after-dinner comfort when suddenly he was assailed by "a perfectly insane and abject terror, without ostensible cause, and only to be accounted for, to my perplexed imagination, by some damned shape squatting invisible to me within the precincts of the room, and raying out from his fetid personality influences fatal to life." The terror, enduring for a full hour, reduced him to a state of "almost helpless infancy," till he was fit only for the physician or a major revelation. He tried the former without effect; and then, through a casual acquaintance, heard of Swedenborg. Hastening to London he acquired a couple of Swedenborg's numerous works and finding them almost uncannily to the purpose in his present crisis, soon became another of the remarkable men who were disciples, however independent, of the Swedish prophet.

In the elder James's case, why Swedenborg instead of, say, Spinoza, or Emerson, or simply the Gospels themselves? Beyond remarking that Swedenborg's magic appears to have been that he had everything—science and mysticism, reason and myth, a theory of creation and a flair for psychology—we are not able to pursue the question here or to inquire deeply into the elder James's subsequent beliefs except as they may be said to have clearly influenced his son. Apart from those already mentioned, which may well have antedated his conversion to Swedenborg—his faith in the unified personality, in the spiritual life, in the transmutation process—there now came into being in his mind, with Swedenborg's help, a host of convictions hovering around the words Creation, Selfhood, and Society. Bliss for the elder James originates in despair. "Empirically, we know that we are creatures with a lack, a destitution, a dearth, an ultimate helplessness," for the very fact of our having been created implies our estrangement from the Creator. We know our creature-status for what it is, moreover, by our ineluctable egoism or selfhood, with its passion, at best for mere morality, mere self-gratifying "works," and at worst for unmitigated acquisitiveness. But despair gives way when it is revealed that the creation, far from having been achieved with the making of the cosmos and the Adam of Genesis, is ever in process and driving towards millennium, towards the reunion of creature and creator. As for men, they speed the creative process in the degree that they allow themselves to be inwardly "refined out of that supreme love of self and the world that alone constitutes hell." When, in short, the communal sense has at last replaced egregious selfhood, the Divine Natural Humanity will make its appearance on earth and the creation be done.

It follows that for the reformist agitation of his time, insofar as it was an end in itself, the elder James had but a limited sympathy. If, however, he read Fourier, associated with Greeley, Dana, and Ripley, and wrote for militant publications, it was because reform implied an expanding human solidarity and so portended the millennium. But how literally was he convinced of this? In a letter to Emerson, after relating some depressing item of news, he ends: "What a world! What a world! But once we get rid of slavery and the new heavens and new earth will swim into reality." Of this passage his son Henry wrote:

No better example could there be, I think, of my father's remarkable and constant belief, proof against all confusion, in the imminence of a transformation-scene in human affairs—"spiritually" speaking of course always—which was to be enacted somehow without gross or vulgar visibility, or at least violence, as I have said, but was none the less straining to the front, and all by reason of the world's being, deep within and at heart, as he conceived, so achingly anxious for it. He had the happiness—though not so untroubled, all the while, doubtless, as some of his declarations would appear to represent—of being able to see his own period and environment as the field of the sensible change, and thereby as a great historic hour; that is, I at once subjoin, I more or less *suppose* he had. His measure of the imminent and immediate, of the socially and historically visible and sensible was not a thing easy to answer for, and when treated to any one of the loud vaticinations or particular revolutionary messages and promises our age was to have so much abounded in, all his sense of proportion and of the whole, of the real and the ridiculous, asserted itself with the last emphasis. In that mixture in him of faith and humour, criticism and conviction, that mark of a love of his kind which fed on discriminations and was never so moved to a certain extravagance as by an exhibited, above all by a cultivated or in the least sententious vagueness in respect to these, dwelt largely the original charm, the peculiarly social and living challenge (in that it was so straight and bright a reflection of life) of his talk and temper.

No doubt the elder James's theology was arbitrary and homemade; but these were the very qualities that recommended it to him. He was as little alarmed because it had no deep support in tradition as he was that it did not lend itself to empirical proof. Henry, who was to judge his father's ideas as they colored his father's behavior, believed them to be fantastic in an honorable sense. They brought order and peace to his mind; their very arbitrariness left him immune to the drearier forms of highmindedness; and his feeling for the universal egoism of man made him what we should today call a realistic observer of human nature. The age, Emerson's age as it is sometimes named, may be defined as one in which the chief figures including Emerson were *of* the age in being distinctly *apart* from it. Each had his notably idiosyncratic way of arriving at not dissimilar sublimities. The elder James, a religious mystic in a time of secular mysticism, an intellectual with money, a self-confessed city man among writers who were so often confirmed rustics (he made New York City his residence after marriage, some said because his wooden leg necessarily confined him to city pavements), was indeed a special case. It was less as a seer that he was effective among his contemporaries than as a sceptic, alert, flexible, and with a tongue for satire. He was no Jeremiah; he preserved the affable tone of the period, the amenity of a talkative, sociable, much-traveled man. Still, whether he was assailing what he called the "flagrant morality" of some of his contemporaries, or the mere vacuousness of others, he did so in shrewdly phrased sallies and paradoxes that must sometimes have taxed the prevailing cheerfulness. He was fond of announcing that "religion in the old virile sense has disappeared and been replaced by a feeble Unitarian sentimentality" or by the "cuddling-up to God" of the Evangelicals. Although himself a disciple of Swedenborg, he was on uneasy terms with the organizing, proselytizing, self-confident band of professional New Churchmen, some of whose dogmas were, as he said, fit only "for Barnum's museum of curiosities." Nor did he spare individuals. Of Margaret Fuller he remarked that "she thought herself somebody, and a somebody so large as to attract the gaze of the world, and perhaps bias human destiny." But Margaret Fuller was clearly vulnerable, and so was Bronson Alcott, in whom, as he said, "the moral sense was wholly dead, and the aesthetic sense had never been born." The far less vulnerable Emerson he admired as much as anyone ever has. They corresponded at length, they exchanged visits, and Henry was to recall Emerson as something of a household presence. Still the elder James pronounced him intellectually recessive, even at bottom unconscious; and he apostrophized him as a "man without a handle," remarking that "when you went to him to hold discourse . . . , you found him absolutely destitute of reflective power." On one occasion he scandalized a gathering in Emerson's Concord house by assailing the Moral Law and apologizing for criminals. Writing to Emerson in 1861 he made the following sketches of certain more or less eminent persons present at a dinner of the Saturday Club at the Parker House in Boston:

> Hawthorne isn't a handsome man nor an engaging one anyway, personally: he had the look all the time, to one who didn't know him, of a rogue who suddenly

finds himself in a company of detectives. But in spite of his rusticity I felt a sympathy for him amounting to anguish and couldn't take my eyes off him all the dinner, nor my rapt attention; as that indecisive little Dr. Hedge found, I am afraid to his cost, for I hardly heard a word of what he kept on saying to me, and felt at one time very much like sending down to Mr. Parker to have him removed from the room as maliciously putting his artificial little person between me and a profitable object of study.

Yet I feel now no ill-will to Hedge and could recommend any one (but myself) to go and hear him preach. Hawthorne, however, seemed to me to possess human substance and not to have dissipated it all away as that debauched Charles Norton, and the good, inoffensive, comforting Longfellow. He seemed much nearer the human being than any one at that end of the table, much nearer. John Forbes and yourself kept up the balance at the other end: but that end was a desert with him for its only oasis. It was so pathetic to see him, contented, sprawling Concord owl that he was and always has been, brought blindfold into that brilliant daylight, and expected to wink and be lively like any little dapper Tommy Titmouse, or Jenny Wren. How he buried his eyes in his plate, and ate with such a voracity that no person should dare to ask him a question!

My heart broke for him as that attenuated Charles Norton kept putting forth his long antennae towards him, stroking his face, and trying whether his eyes were shut. The idea I got was, and it was very powerfully impressed upon me, that we are all of us monstrously corrupt, hopelessly bereft of human consciousness, and that it is the intention of the Divine Providence to overrun us and obliterate us in a new Gothic and Vandalic invasion of which this Concord specimen is a first fruits.

The elder James was prompt to detect flagrant morality even in his sons. When Henry, already a young man and himself touched by the Moral Law, wrote admiringly of Turgenev while at the same time objecting to his "wanton melancholy," the elder James, by way perhaps of implied dissent, delivered himself of one of his characteristic gestures. To Turgenev, personally unknown as yet to any of the family, he addressed across the Atlantic, as from one man of letters to another, a spirited appreciation that referred to Homer and quoted Horace; expressed the hope that the Russian would sometime "come to Cambridge, and sit with us on the piazza in the evening"; and remarked that "you sink your shaft sheer through the world of outward circumstance, and of social convention, and shew us ourselves in the fixed grasp of fate, so to speak, or struggling vainly to break the bonds of temperament. Superficial critics revolt against this tragic spectacle, and pronounce you cynical. They mistake the profound spirituality of your method."

He was impatient of other people's absolutes, even their absolutes of personal anguish and elation. In his old age he carried on a strange correspondence with his youngest son, Robertson, then grown from unhappy child to unhappy man. When Robertson complained of his failures, the elder James briskly prescribed sympathy with "the Divine purpose" and generally took so high a teleological line that William, who was following the correspondence, could remind Robertson that "Father's religious optimism has, I think, a tendency to make him think too lightly of anyone's temporal troubles, even to neglecting to look into them at all." When, for a change, the moody Robertson wrote in a self-confident vein, his father replied: "I

lose no time in saying that you must be on your guard. Your sense of power is very likely illusory. I do not say that is so necessarily; but it is very likely to be so, because it is a judgment about oneself, and there is nothing we are so liable to be mistaken about as ourselves. . . . Our judgments are always dictated by feeling—a feeling of undue elation or undue depression, and the verdict we come to is apt to be preposterous in either case alike."

The fascination of the man remains, unthinkable as he perhaps is apart from his time and place. Nor was he merely a "personality"; as his contemporaries knew, he was a formidable stylist and humorist. It is true that his savor is mainly in the dashing phrase or figure, the long sentence that runs extravagantly on through hazards of grammar and sense to its triumphant conclusion. He was a natural writer, with a natural abundance of language and command of tone, able to jeer or caress at will and to turn from the amiable to the horrible. He was a more human Emerson, a less truculent Carlyle—or would have been had he possessed the artist's patience and urgency along with his artist's gifts. He knew some of that urgency; he was forever writing long books; and he was not without remorse when they failed, as they usually did, to reach more than a few dozen readers. He was at his best on some particular figure—Emerson or Carlyle—or some issue of the moment. His longer efforts were usually expositions of his philosophy and they could not help revealing it all on nearly every occasion. They were too general and diffuse; and good as the detail was, the comprehensive image refused to materialize. His longer books seem to have been written out of a feeling of duty to his ideas rather than to his audience. Financially secure, notably happy and fulfilled

in his position as husband, father, and friend, he felt no great impulse to make himself relevant to others; and the prevailing disdain of professionalism that marked the age of Emerson was to him only too compatible. So too with its prevailing cheerfulness, although on this point it is easy to misjudge him. He never seems to be whistling in the dark; Emerson's interesting note of half-acknowledged misgivings is rarely the elder James's. His cheerfulness is of his entire being, a being which knew perfectly well the other side of life but which could only express truthfully its own preponderantly joyous experience. If there is a sense in which events may be said to have made him look foolish, it is a superficial sense. To be sure, he hailed American institutions as the work of God, spoke of the crowded horsecar as heaven on earth, insisted—and on the very eve of the Civil War—that "an immense deal of imprudence may yet be transacted in America with the happiest social and individual consequences." No doubt, too, his children were to owe to his domestic experiments and inescapable presence many of their troubles in life. Still, those experiments and that presence, like his religious optimism and political hyperboles, can be interpreted as the conscientious rashness of a man who knew perfectly what he was about. They were so interpreted by his children, who rejected a great deal of him but not his habit of feeling intensely, not his fear lest life prove to be without honor or meaning. The despair that was the premise of his philosophy was more than a metaphysical convenience. He could write that "every man who has reached even his intellectual teens begins to suspect this; begins to suspect that life is no farce; that it is not genteel comedy even; that it flowers and fructifies on the contrary out of

the profoundest tragic depths,—the depths of the essential dearth in which its subject's roots are plunged. . . . The natural inheritance of everyone who is capable of spiritual life, is an unsubdued forest where the wolf howls and the obscene bird of night chatters."

His love of life was to descend to his sons; but he knew one sort of experience of which Henry, for one, was to be largely denied and which, perhaps, he was to regret all the more because his father had been such a happy example of it. This was the *shared experience* that the elder James so intensely enjoyed, partly as an American among Americans, partly as lover, husband, and father. His patriotism was not quite a simple and inevitable identification with an expansive and hopeful civilization. However effervescent, it had its reasons, connected with his system, and its limits. There were no such reserves in his domestic feeling, although this too was supported philosophically by his belief that the human family at its best was a paradigm of the Divine Natural Humanity of the future. He confessed to an "ineffable delight in the marriage sentiment," to an "infinite and exquisite tenderness and peace" in the presence of his wife and children. And for all his odd ways, his union with Mary James was a pure domestic idyl, even to the fact that husband and wife, unable to endure separation, eventually died within the same year.

Mrs. James was a dim but far from insignificant figure; indeed, in such a vivid and assertive family group as presently surrounded her, her very dimness came to be a value, above all to her painfully passive son Henry. Coming of an orthodox and hardheaded New York family, she was held to be more "conventional" than her husband (she could not easily have been *less* so), and this too doubt-less recommended her to her son. But it was her selfless-ness and her genius for endurance that meant the most to him. "Her sweetness, her mildness, her great natural benef-icence were unspeakable," he was to write, and these traits seem to have contributed essentially to the solidarity of the family. "She was our life, she was the house, she was the keystone of the arch. She held us all together." As his father suggested to him the expansive virtues, so his mother stood for the necessary drawing-in and continuity. She it was, perhaps, who best represented that sense of the in-evitable, that feeling for the limits of life, which was to distinguish his mind and work. To her were born five children: William (1842), Henry (April 15, 1843), Garth Wilkinson (1845), Robertson (1846), and Alice (1848).

The elder James's dislike of convention exploded in sheer physical restlessness. He was forever hunting improved quarters for the family and better teachers for the chil-dren; perhaps he believed that a state of permanent do-mestic revolution, in addition to fostering their independ-ence of local prejudice, would help to keep his family from hardening into an aggressive social group—in short into the usual family. They spent some time in Albany; but New York City was the main scene of their movements for the first twelve years of Henry's life. Sharing his father's urbanity, he was to recall with some pride that the young Jameses were town-bred. William and he were born in a house, which has since disappeared, on Washington Place, between the quiet Square and noisy Broadway. Somewhat later the family lived for a number of years in a large house at 57 West Fourteenth Street, near Sixth Avenue.

"Old New York," as distinguished from the industrial metropolis of later days, remained a genuine point of reference for Henry James. Although it provided only a meager setting for his early novel, *Washington Square*, its tone is happily imaged in his memoirs. Unkempt and planless and full of weed-grown vacant lots, the city advertised its too-close link with a wilderness that was never attractive to the history-loving James. Still, the "solid and honorable dwellings" of the Washington Square neighborhood; the pink of brick and the summer green of ailanthus trees, the pleasant interiors with their parlors front and back, their tall mirrors and marble chimneypieces; the not too cruel or showy wealth of merchant families, who gave friendly dinners and balls and displayed a conscientious pleasure in the arts, implied a kind of peace and a kind of social order—all, to be sure, distinctly prehistoric.

It was first in Albany and then in New York that Henry and William began to attend school—or schools, for there were to be more of them in their lives than they could recall, more even than there were of residences. Their father agreed that some sort of formal training was necessary for them, even at the risk of its somewhat standardizing them, which in his opinion was the reverse of what an education ought to do. By constantly uprooting them, however, he could at least prevent any one teacher or institution from getting too exclusive a hold, and at the same time indulge his own taste for change. In New York they went from tutor to tutor, from private school to private school. "We could n't have changed oftener . . . if our presence had been inveterately objected to, and yet I enjoy an inward certainty that, my brother [William] being vividly bright and I quite blankly innocuous, this reproach was

never brought home to our house." In 1855 the entire
family traveled to Europe, where they lived off and on
for some five years. By turns in London, Paris, Geneva,
Boulogne, and Bonn they set up temporary residences and
engaged once more in fleeting educational ventures. In the
hope of correcting what his father regarded as his one-
sidedness, Henry was even exposed briefly to scientific
training at a Swiss school. "Harry is not so fond of study,
properly so-called, as of reading," observed his father when
the boy was 14. "He is a devourer of libraries, and an
immense writer of novels and dramas. He has considerable
talent as a writer, but I am at a loss to know whether he
will ever accomplish much." The Swiss experiment promptly
failed; Henry's intellectual sloth yielded to no formal discipline. Before the European scene itself, as we shall see,
he gave way almost with violence. But in all the phantas-
magoria of Scottish tutors and French governesses and
pension-schools, he seems to have had only one solid experience so far as his formal schooling was concerned.
That was in Boulogne, the rather dreary seaside town to
which his family went for a time in order to recover from
the effects of the Panic of 1857 at home. There Henry had
a nearly fatal attack of typhoid; and there he read classic
French authors with a robust old tutor; "and though our
mornings were short and subject, I think, to quite drowsy
lapses and other honest aridities, we did scumble together,
I make out, by the aid of the collected extracts from the
truly and academically great which formed his sole resource and which he had, in a small portable and pocketed
library, rather greasily preserved, some patch of a picture
of a saving as distinguished from a losing classicism."

William James was later to complain that this haphazard

schooling had retarded his development as a scientist. Henry was to record only the amusing sides of it. The willing victim of a system which in effect left him to educate himself, by way of endless private reading, he was to have no grounds for regret. We know that he consumed Scott, Dickens, and Thackeray as a boy; it is not certain just when or how thoroughly he read Shakespeare, Cervantes, Goethe, Wordsworth, and the other old authors to whom he makes occasional allusion, modest but often singularly apt, in his mature writings. Nor do we know how he acquired that finesse in the manipulation of ideas which he shows, for example, in a remarkable essay on Epictetus composed in his early twenties. He presently wrote no more in the vein of the Epictetus piece, and in his maturity he developed, in Eliot's phrase, "a mind so fine that no idea could violate it." The stress here should be on the word "violate": he had ideas in abundance and he also had erudition. As a self-taught man, however, and one whose reading, like his observation, was far and away his most vital form of experience—almost, as we shall see, a matter of his personal survival—he was in exceptionally intimate possession of his learning. And such was his "mastery over, his baffling escape from, Ideas" (Eliot again) that no one could possibly wish he had really gone to school—which cannot be said of all literary autodidacts.

If he learned a good deal from the classic authors, he was also in daily contact with what he called his father's "passionate spontaneities." The family worked, traveled, and amused itself as a single unit, a body of equals; homesickness overtook any member of it who was obliged to be absent for very long from the others. Above all they talked and debated together, for the elder James, so articulate himself, encouraged his children to speak their least wish or thought, transforming everything within them into consciousness and sociability. T. S. Perry, a friend of their later youth, remarked on "the joyous chaff that filled the Jameses' house. There was no limit to it. There were always books to tell about and laugh over, or to admire, and there was an abundance of good talk with no shadow of pedantry or priggishness." Once when his father was busy writing one of his esoteric and unwanted books (he worked as a rule in full view of the family), William is said to have designed for the title-page a sketch of a man beating a dead horse. With the exception of Henry, all the children were brilliant talkers and intensely sociable personalities. Even the three of them who were not to become professional writers continued to pour themselves out in long letters and in occasional documents like the journal kept by Alice in her last years. Henry alone resisted, in his passive way, the general outspokenness, just as he withstood all attempts to stir him out of his bookish lethargy. Anything so persuasive as the family code was not to be defied openly; it was only to be combated very quietly and genially and with a good deal of remorse and self-mistrust. Perry added that "H. J.'s spirits were never so high as those of the others. If they had been, he still would have had but little chance in a conflict of wits with them, on account of his slow speech, his halting choice of words." Although his rare remarks were even then admired for their wit, it was only in his letters and subsequently in his literary style that he did justice to the family eloquence, until in middle age fame brought him a degree of assurance and he too emerged at last as a formidable talker.

Whatever else they may have discussed as children, the

subject seems rarely to have been their father's religious opinions. He was far from trying to preach Swedenborg to them. It was not until after his death that William, in assembling his father's *Literary Remains* for publication, became really acquainted with the system; while Henry in turn discovered it by reading the *Remains*. Their father sometimes read to them from the Bible but they attended no church. For the rest he simply taught that the unexamined life is not worth living. Thus they came to exercise their wit on one another's prejudices as well as on those of a self-righteous and deluded world. They came to delight in the ambivalence of things, to feel that evil was more apt to be latent than overt. They looked habitually at "the other side of the medal"—a favorite phrase of Henry's later years; they learned to appreciate an "interesting failure." An experiment in the nurture of a radical morality, the family discipline consisted in cultivating ego and conscience simultaneously.

In all this the elder James was transacting, as he proudly announced, "an immense deal of imprudence." As a private venture in American idealism, the life of the James family is very likely without parallel. And that it frankly required money—money to keep the large circle in motion, money to forestall any merely anxious surrenders to convention—is not the least interesting of its aspects, for money will also be a condition of freedom in the novels of Henry James. Yet neither their father's wealth nor his affection nor his high spirits kept the children from living under a considerable strain. Strain was what he expected them to feel, reasoning perhaps that he could introduce them to transcendent experience only by first making mere existence quite impossible for them. And he did make it impossible for them, though not without assistance from outside events.

Returned from their travels, and settled with the family in New England, the young Jameses came of age in the decade of the Civil War. The America that had seemed to condone imprudence was greatly changed, although to say that the elder James had failed to anticipate this is not to suggest that he would have modified his theories if he had. William and Henry were too unwell at the time to enlist; but the younger brothers, Wilky and Robertson, were in the Union Army and out of it again, Wilky having been gravely wounded in action and Robertson injured by sunstroke, while they were still in their teens. After that they tried various businesses, married and settled in the midwest, where Wilky died in 1883. Robertson, who lived until 1910, was the more vivid and ambitious as he was possibly the more troubled of the two, a cause of concern to his parents, on whose affection and counsel he remained heavily dependent. Henry says in his memoirs that Robertson was "an extraordinary instance of a man's nature constituting his profession." In a letter to William of 1899 he is even franker: "Bob's letters most curious, yet rather comforting, if it be not cynical to say so, as an indication of shrinkage (with the weakening mind) of his terrible 'personality.'" The remarkable Alice also suffered from excess of personality and was the most tragic member of the family. More intelligent than Wilky or Bob, she had the same high expectations of life. With her these failed again to condense into tangible proposals; and it might be said that *her* profession came to be constituted by a long illness. At the age of 19 she suffered a nervous breakdown and was thereafter a constant invalid, dying horribly of a breast tumor in 1892. As for William and Henry, if their father's experiment did at last flower in their great careers, it was not until both had weathered ordeals in their youth. In childhood William seems to have played quite happily his privileged part as oldest son. Not till he was obliged to translate this juvenile advantage into mature action did he come close to breaking down. In his late twenties he was overtaken by something like his father's youthful "vastation." Drained of self-confidence and the will to live, he suffered hallucinations and was for some years familiar with thoughts of suicide and insanity. Unlike his sister and younger brothers, however, he had already settled in a vocation before the collapse occurred; and his powerful mind was even then deeply engaged in philosophy. As Professor Perry observes, what he went through was not only a "psychological seizure" but a "spiritual crisis." The very complexity of the experience was an advantage to him. By clearing up, as he eventually did in part, the metaphysical problems that had come to obsess him as he outgrew his father's optimism, he managed also to restore his confidence in his own powers; and he was presently started on a career that did all honor to the pedagogic theories of the elder James.

Any account of Henry's youthful mind must lean heavily on *A Small Boy and Others* and *Notes of a Son and Brother*, two autobiographic volumes composed by him in his old age. Often described as a reticent man, he was in fact much given to reminiscence; and the two books in question (they are really a single continuous narrative of his life up to about 1865, and there exists the fragment of an unfinished third installment called *The Middle Years*) were simply his most extended effort in that vein. Their qualities

of beauty and insight have never been sufficiently appreciated. No doubt they are slow-paced and too merely
sibylline in their revelations; James himself remarked of the
second installment that it was "vitiated perhaps by the effort
to comprehend more than it contains." Yet they are also
witty and profound; scenes out of the remote past come to
brilliant life in them; and in the pages on the elder James
humor and piety combine to form as remarkable a portrait
as any in the literature of memoirs. They belong with *The
Education of Henry Adams* and they complement it: the
personal as against the public history of an American mind.

Desultory as they at first appear, the memoirs are perfectly distinct as to purpose, method, and theme. For all
his celebrated concern with art as an end in itself, James
shared his century's interest in the artistic personality, the
moral and historical conditions of art. He was the disciple
equally of Arnold and of Sainte-Beuve. His books on
Hawthorne and W. W. Story, studies in two opposite types
of native artist, are merely the longest of his essays in
what he preferred to call "literary portraiture." And it is
with these writings that his memoirs belong, describing as
they do the formation of his own artist-nature among the
phenomena of country and family. If their general purpose
is of the last century, their structure is more of this one. A
kind of organized reverie, they recapture his early life in
its emotional essence, subordinating detail and chronology
to the calling up of experiences which continue to live in
his mind and may in a sense be said to *be* his mind. For
Proust's hero it is always seven o'clock in the Combray of
his childhood memories, meaning of course that his whole
recollection of the place is colored by the ordeal of the bed-
time hour. James's recovery of the past is less exacting and

theoretical than Proust's; however imaginative his grasp, he is writing not fiction but autobiography. Still, a good deal of what he remembers of his early years is the direct emanation of a central recollected experience. What this was becomes clear if the innocent-sounding title, *A Small Boy and Others*, is read literally. He states it directly when, writing of the friends and relatives of those days, he says: "They were so *other*—that was what I felt; and to *be* other, other almost anyhow, seemed as good as the probable taste of the bright compound wistfully watched in the confectioner's window." The rueful feeling of estrangement from his fellows, and his gradual conversion of it into the material of a literary vocation, is the burden of his memoirs.

Independently of his brother, Robertson James confessed to having had a similar sensation in childhood: he had sometimes believed that he was a foundling. And no doubt the small ego led an extremely uneasy existence in that paradoxical family, who expected everything and demanded nothing of each other; who thought so highly of personal vividness that they risked creating in their midst a most intense system of fraternal and filial hostilities; but who, by their mutual affection and solicitude, made any invidious rivalry seem as gratuitous as the original sin of Lucifer. In order that it might survive at all, Henry's ego appears to have gone into hiding, played dead, endured a sort of protective arrest. He tells us that he was early reduced to an envy of others which was as helpless as it was unresentful. *A Small Boy* shows him overwhelmed by superior beings, all of them more active and articulate than himself. Their prototype was his father, who combined those qualities with the still rarer ones of love, intellect, and integrity. Recalling an occasion on which the elder James had happily solved a difficult family situation, he says: "I remember not less what resources of high control the whole case imputed, for my imagination, to my father; and how, creeping off to the edge of the eminence above the Hudson, I somehow felt the great bright harmonies of air and space becoming one with my rather proud assurance and confidence, that of my own connection, for life, for interest, with such sources of light." In Henry's eyes, moreover, his father seemed to confirm his powers by delegating them, so to speak, to his eldest son. It was as if William "had gained such an advance of me in his sixteen months' experience of the world before mine began that I never for all the time of childhood and youth in the least caught up with him and overtook him. He was always round the corner and out of sight." William had the quicker mind, the more competitive nature, the larger capacity to associate with people. He had more interests than his younger brother. His quarters were now a laboratory, now a darkroom, now a theater, now a studio, while Henry's were monotonously the scene of endless reading and writing; his air of having a purpose in life was all the more impressive in that the purpose so often changed. But William and their father were not the only persons to be affectionately envied by Henry. Lower down in the hierarchy of vividness but still very much of it were younger brothers, cousins, friends. His brother Wilky: "his successful sociability, his instinct for intercourse, his genius . . . for making friends." His brother Bob: "the easiest aptitude for admirable talk, charged with natural life, perception, humor and color, that I have perhaps ever known." His cousin Gus Barker: "Ingenuous and responsive, of a social disposition, a candour of gaiety, that matched his physical activity—the most beautifully made athletic little person, and in the highest degree appealing and engaging."

There was a family interdiction on aggressive envy: it was called "spiritual snatching." And James assures us that he felt nothing of the sort, but only "a kind of fatalism of patience." Suspiciously highminded though this sounds, there is no reason to doubt it. He had his resentment but he turned it against himself, deciding that he was ineluctably disabled for active experience; and at last, in his youth, taking advantage of an injury to his back to assert his unfitness once for all. Meanwhile he had other consolations. The envied persons seem to have been exclusively males; and we may speculate that he looked to his mother to sanction a course which he felt to be as unheroic as it was unavoidable. Of them all she was the great case of that renunciation of ego to which he too in part aspired. If she had a right to be quiet in a vociferous family, so had he. If one could not be lively one could at least be "good," as he and his mother were said to be good, both of them having been described as "angels." And the fact that she was more "conventional" than the rest may have influenced him when he came to dissociate himself from his father's radicalism and to assert his pleasure in the decorous and traditional. It was even said that he looked very much like her.

But nothing consoled him in childhood as did the resources of his "visiting mind." The turning of hardship into advantage was, as we have seen, a major family habit. "One may most of all see it—so at least have I quite exclusively seen it, the little life out for its chance—as proceeding by the inveterate process of conversion. As I reconsider both my own and my brother's early start—even his too, made under stronger propulsions—it is quite for me as if the authors of our being and guardians of our youth had virtually said to us but one thing, directed our course but by one word, though constantly repeated: Convert, convert, convert!" So the abject and nearly helpless child transformed himself, very slowly, into a dedicated young artist possessed of a large measure of self-respect and a mind and a style as original as any in American letters.

If the poet is the unacknowledged legislator of mankind, as Shelley said, he is also the story-telling parent or elder. Pride in his more or less exclusive access to a large experience, an experience easily surpassing that of his audience, is a sign of the major writer, especially the novelist, who is like Hamlet in knowing that there is more in heaven and earth than is dreamt of in your philosophy. What surprises us about James—and would surprise us more if we did not know that the same was true of Hawthorne—is the extent to which his career was rooted in the conviction of *in*experience. On this unflattering premise he constructed the whole argument of his remarkable life, enriching his tales with the passions of the state of otherness: the pathos, the comedy, the romantic wonderment, the severe critical detachment. He was to make no bold and direct assault upon experience. He was not so much to annihilate the otherness of things as to put himself more at ease with it, forcing its mysteries in such a way that they ceased to seem malignant and came to seem only "wonderful," a favored word of his later years.

He had as a child an intense curiosity which drove him continually on to the New York streets to walk and gaze— to "gape" as he called it. And thus was established, as he

wrote, using the third person, "the very pattern and measure of all he was to demand. . . . He was to go without
many things, ever so many—as all persons do in whom
contemplation takes so much the place of action; but . . .
he was really, I think, much to profit by it." This last is
understatement. In fact the gaping habit, which his parents
first deplored as the sign of his unfortunate passivity,
was by degrees refined into a mode—*his* mode—of artistic
vision. From city sights he went on to gaze at works of
art and quasi-art, ranging from the mere anomalies on view
in Barnum's "dusty halls of humbug" on lower Broadway;
through the French tightrope performers, half acrobats and
half pantomimists, at Niblo's Garden; to Dickens made
graphic by Phiz and Cruikshank. It was in New York, too,
before he had ever visited the Louvre or the Théâtre
Français, that painting and the stage began to attract
him. The James family attended in a body whatever New
York afforded in the way of drama or exhibitions of the
plastic arts. For Henry it naturally didn't matter whether
the play was *A Midsummer Night's Dream* or *The Cata-
ract of the Ganges, She Stoops to Conquer* or *London Assurance*—framed by the stage walls, picked out by lights,
alternately hidden and revealed by the provocative curtain,
any play repaid his gaping. It represented life as he was
coming to apprehend it—life at several removes from the
spectator, life concentrated and epitomized in vivid images. And what the stage did for plays the "composition"
did for paintings, of which there were occasional exhibits
imported by entrepreneurs whose ways were not unlike
Barnum's. The art was usually "big European art," as the
memoirs express it: "If one wanted pictures, there *were*
pictures, as large, I seem to remember, as the side of a

house." Works by Benjamin Haydon or members of "the Düsseldorf school," Leutze's canvas of Washington crossing the Delaware in what resembled "a wondrous flare of projected gaslight," they were executed in a violently representational style which made their subjects, as a rule literary or historical, inescapable. But he studied them as curiously as he did the plays, and for the same reason. They too were images of life.

The European visit of 1855-60 was crucial, and not only because his taste in the arts underwent refinement. This it certainly did, for he and William trod the museums and learned, under the promptings of a family friend, the American painter William Morris Hunt, to prefer Delacroix to Leutze; and Henry in particular came to feel that great images only crystallized under the pressure of a superior *style*. They did not visit Italy: for him that excitement was reserved for a later trip. Nor did England, where they stayed for some time, impress him very much at this period. It was Paris, he says, that first awoke him to the greatness of Europe, a greatness that transcended its treasures of painting and architecture but to which those treasures were a major clue. With its mythical name and its fabled rows of canvases, the Galerie d'Apollon in the Louvre breathed "a general sense of *glory*. The glory meant ever so many things at once, not only beauty and art and supreme design, but history and fame and power, the world in fine raised to the richest and noblest expression." Uncompromised by the trials of his childhood, and by the still worse trials of his early youth, "Europe" was to become the climactic term in the same series that included "gaping" and "art," his principal touchstone of personal power and salvation.

Many years after his early stay abroad he had a dream which he related at length in *A Small Boy and Others*, where it serves as the supreme clarifying image. It was "the most appalling yet most admirable nightmare of my life. The climax of this extraordinary experience—which stands alone for me as a dream-adventure founded in the deepest, quickest, clearest act of cogitation and comparison, act indeed of life-saving energy, as well as in unutterable fear—was the sudden pursuit, through an open door, along a huge high saloon, of a just dimly-descried figure that retreated in terror before my rush and dash (a glare of inspired reaction from irresistible but shameful dread,) out of the room I had a moment before been desperately, and all the more abjectly, defending by the push of my shoulder against hard pressure on lock and bar from the other side. . . . Routed, dismayed, the tables turned upon him by my so surpassing him for straight aggression and dire intention, my visitant was already but a diminished spot in the long perspective, the tremendous, glorious hall, as I say, over the far-gleaming floor of which . . . he sped for *his* life, while a great storm of thunder and lightning played through the deep embrasures of high windows at the right. The lightning that revealed the retreat revealed also the wondrous place and, by the same amazing play, my young imaginative life in it of long before, the sense of which, deep within me, had kept it whole, preserved it to this thrilling use; for what in the world were the deep embrasures and the so polished floor but those of the Galerie d'Apollon of my childhood? The 'scene of something' I had vaguely then felt it? Well I might, since it was to be the scene of that immense hallucination."

Newport and Cambridge

WHEN James was 18 or so he sat to John La Farge for his portrait. The result is a mystifying likeness. A handsome world-weary youth with an elegant large nose, full lips and a brooding shadow around his eyes, he might already be the well-known author of a distinguished tragedy in verse, preferably in French alexandrines. Perhaps at that age he did really look like an Alfred de Musset, or it may be that La Farge with his French associations saw people in that style. There is also a photograph of James, taken at about the same age, that shows him as much more youthful. Swarthy-looking, somehow exotic, he has the same full mouth that La Farge observed; the frank stare in his eyes, however, is that of some well-bred young immigrant disembarked in an unfamiliar and intriguing land; and he gives the impression, for what it is worth, of an abundant vitality.

Newport, Rhode Island, the cosmopolitan seaside town where the portrait and possibly the photograph were made, was not unfamiliar to him. He had been there for some months in 1858 when the Jameses made a brief return to the United States. Arriving there now with his family as a boy of 17 he was still uncertain as to what he wished to do or to be in the world. Except that he had dreamed vaguely of art and Paris, his world had still the tone and dimensions of his immediate family. When, at 19, he left Newport after two eventful years, it was with a clearer idea of his independent destiny.

That this destiny would involve a profession, even a "career" in the honorable European sense, probably began to dawn on him at this time. Some such idea had clearly occurred to William, who, like Henry, was always to have a high regard for the trained professional, as distinguished from either the journalist or the dilettante. This brought them a little into conflict with their father, who so detested specialization of function that he preferred an "interesting failure" to a narrowing success. Indeed it arrayed them against the portentous universality of the entire older generation, much as the young Jameses also disliked the mere Yankee expertness against which Thoreau and Emerson and the elder James had been protesting. If William was to see this universality as the enemy of science, Henry of course judged it as hostile to art. In an atmosphere where artists were regarded primarily as inspired individuals and representative men, such devoted craftsmen as Hawthorne and Poe had been anomalies; and Henry was never to forget Emerson's having said of the former that his novels were not worthy of him. Wasn't it reported of Emerson, moreover, that he "could see nothing in Shelley, Aristophanes, Don Quixote, Miss Austen, Dickens" and thought Dante "a man to be put into a museum but not into your house"?—to which James was dryly to reply that "the confession of an insensibility ranging from Shelley to Dickens and from Dante to Miss Austen and taking Don Quixote and Aristophanes on the way, is a large allowance to have to make for a man of letters."

These were the comments of a much older Henry James, and one who had been for many years absent from his own and Emerson's country. Meanwhile, warmly though he had responded to Europe during his boyhood visit, it was in America that he took the first serious steps towards becoming a writer. Nor did he see Europe again till 1869. Considering how footloose his family had always been, and how much he too was to wander subsequently, it is a fact of some importance that he nevertheless discovered his vocation in his native country—in, as it happened, a country made tensely self-conscious by civil war. The elder James, facing the fact as a necessary evil, had always thought of William as a potential scientist. During their stay in Europe, however, William had likewise succumbed to the Paris museums and the eloquence of William Morris Hunt; and he had ended by deciding to become a painter. Startled though he was by this announcement, the elder James waived coercion and permitted William to set up as a student of painting. France, where they had lately been in residence, might appear to have been the preferred setting for such a venture; but the elder James, weary of Europe in any case, held out for a return to America. And they therefore settled in Newport, where Hunt maintained a studio. For some months William worked hard under Hunt's instruction; and Henry, though feeling "a helpless outsider" in the studio as in so many other situations, modestly followed suit. Hunt, a lean and dedicated man "with a shade of resemblance, as all simple and imaginative men have, to the knight of La Mancha," impressed Henry with the value of diligence and method in the pursuit of the arts. Another impassioned and erudite member of Hunt's group, in fact "quite the most interesting person we knew," was John La Farge. "I see him at this hour again as that bright apparition; see him, jacketed in black velvet or clad from top to toe in old-time elegances of cool white and leaning much forward with his protuberant and over-glazed, his doubting yet all-seizing vision, dandle along the shining Newport sands in far-away summer sunsets on a charming chestnut mare whose light legs and fine head and great sweep of tail showed the Arab strain." For Henry, La Farge had all the enviable qualities. A cosmopolitan and dandy, he was at the same time extremely serious about painting. His antecedents were intriguingly French and Catholic. He represented what the memoirs call "the principle of the imperturbable," a certain tough serenity of mind and manners which Henry might also hope to achieve if he were to give himself to art.

For painting itself he soon discovered that he had no aptitude, although it was greatly to influence his conception of the novel and add a host of studio terms to his vocabulary. Meanwhile he was having a literary awakening of the sort that is likely to occur when an imaginative young person comes upon some body of literature quite alien to his traditions. Brought up on the early Victorians, he was introduced by La Farge to the recent French novel, with its very different specifications. He began to read Balzac and at the same time he encountered, in the current numbers of the *Revue des Deux Mondes*, the more recent work of Gautier and Mérimée, whose *Vénus d'Ille* he proceeded to translate. Balzac's system and documentation, the story-telling finesse of the other two, strengthened his growing belief in professionalism. Besides, the reading of foreign authors refreshed his own surroundings so that by analogy with Balzac's Maison Vauquer an American board-inghouse, such as he was to know presently in Cambridge, became a fascinating place.

But there was a good deal in Newport besides Hunt's studio. An old white seaside New England town, with beautiful cliffs and a mild climate, Newport was then the refuge of a number of well-to-do families. They were a kind of American aristocracy whose distinction, in those days of limited European travel, was in many cases their mobility, their close ties with the Continent, of which indeed the Rhode Island town was for them an outpost: "its opera-glass turned for ever across the sea." The newly and immensely rich had not yet taken over the place completely, although there is surely some provocation of them in the elder James's oration of July 4, 1861—the dazzling essence of all Independence Day addresses—wherein he spoke against "the rapid accumulation of private wealth," adding that "one likes best to introduce one's foreign acquaintance, not to our commercial nabobs, who aggravate the price of house-rent and butcher's meat so awfully to us poor Newporters . . . but to our, in the main, upright, self-respecting, and, if you please, untutored, but at the same time unsophisticated, children of toil, who are the real fathers and mothers of our future distinctive manhood."

In time of war, naturally, Newport's cosmopolitanism gave way to patriotic feeling. Families huddled together to hear news of battles in which sons and friends were involved; and the great Mrs. Howe, a resident of the town, composed her famous Hymn. With the possible exception of Henry, the Jameses were not in any case tempted by the Newport wistfulness, and Henry himself seems then to have been busy responding, in powerful obscure ways, to literature, friendship, and war. As he had been the shyest of the James children, so he was the first to go through a severe adult crisis, and he was to be the first to settle into a profession.

On the eve of their return to America, his father had written that his children were "getting to an age . . . when the heart craves a little wider expansion than is furnished it by the domestic affections. They want friends among their own sex, and sweethearts in the other; and my hope for their salvation, temporal and spiritual, is that they may 'go it strong' in both lines when they get home." He even dreamed of early marriages for them, mentioning Henry, together with Wilky, as being in special need of all these advantages. And Newport, though it did not bring them wives, did introduce them, or reintroduce them, to a lot of engaging young people, cousins and friends of cousins, including T. S. Perry, the first intimate companion Henry had had outside his family. This group, and above all the delicately eager girls in it, did most to endear America to him. They were the nucleus of what he was proudly to describe in his memoirs as "our circle," observing that they "formed a little world of easy and happy intercourse, of unrestricted and yet all so instinctively sane and secure association and conversation, with all its liberties and delicacies, all its mirth and all its earnestness protected and directed so much more from within than from without, that I ask myself, perhaps too fatuously, whether any such right condition for the play of young intelligence and young friendship, the reading of Matthew Arnold and Browning, the discussion of a hundred human and personal things . . . survives to this more complicated age."

Here was the bright spontaneous American innocence he was to transcribe into his novels; and the center of the circle, "the very heroine of our common scene," was Minny (Mary) Temple, of "the great Albany connection," one of the nine children of the elder James's sister Catharine, who was married to a West Point graduate named Robert Emmet Temple. Since James so often described Minny Temple as a heroine, we may add that, as such, she looked back to Elizabeth Bennet and Dorothea Brooke and forward to the Bessies and Isabels and Millys of James himself. Like all these Anglo-Saxon girls she was thought admirable because she was a rare thing in the modern world—a case of the free spirit, an incarnation of the gratuitous; and, as we shall see, she was doomed. "With all that ethereal brightness of presence that was peculiarly her own," Minny dominated the little circle without ever trying or caring. Spontaneity was so much her way that, unlike the Jameses, she couldn't communicate very well in writing. The animation of her surviving letters is charming because so frankly standard. "Sich is life," she sighs, and, "My dearest Harry what a charming tale is Gabrielle de Bergerac! *Just* as pretty as ever it can be." A great reader, especially of George Eliot, she had opinions without being opinionated. *The Spanish Gypsy* was good but not so good as *The Mill on the Floss*. She wouldn't admit that she was really disappointed by Phillips Brooks, whom she had traveled to Philadelphia to hear preach, and yet "he doesn't, or didn't, touch the real difficulties at all." She studied German, attended the opera in New York, burned to visit Europe, cultivated intense friendships with other girls, preferred to dance at balls with experienced older men, and judged the boys of her own age candidly if quite cheerfully. And she died young—that was what finally confirmed her sacredness for Henry James—died at 24 of a lingering tubercular illness which kept her from ever getting to Europe and made her last years a nightmare of attempted cures, abandoned journeys, sudden collapses, and unpredictable hemorrhages. "Death, at the last, was dreadful to her," James was to write, "who would have given anything to live."

She died in 1870, and Henry, writing to his mother and to William (Henry was then in England), gave way to torrents of sensibility. He was like the rest of the family in never letting pass an opportunity to feel; and on Minny's death he wrote more feelingly than ever before. "Oh dearest Mother! Oh poor struggling suffering *dying* creature!" Half a century later he was to devote the final chapter of *Notes of a Son and Brother* to celebrating her memory.

Did he love Minny Temple in the usual sense and did his illness of those days alone prevent him from trying to marry her? Attempts have been made to refer his lifelong bachelor state to the frustration of an ordinary masculine passion for Minny Temple; but these have run into the same difficulties that confront us whenever we look for some single explanation of his deeper behavior. It is true that in his mourning letter to his mother he writes, "It comes home to me with irresistible power, the sense of how much I knew her and how much I loved her." But his mother might have been expected to understand in what general sense he "loved" her. To William, man and brother, member of the same youthful circle to which Henry and Minny belonged, and like the rest of them at an age when love meant something quite definite, Henry took care to be specific. "Every one was supposed, I believe, to be more or less in love with her: others may answer for themselves: I never was, and yet I had the great satisfaction that I enjoyed *pleasing* her almost as much as if I had been." He may not have loved her in the usual sense but that is not to say that he wouldn't have liked to! "She never knew how sick and disordered a creature I was," he continues to William, "and I always felt that she knew me at my worst. I always looked forward with a certain eagerness to the day when I should have regained my natural lead, and one friendship on my part, at least, might become more active and masculine."

Since there is no conclusive evidence either way, it is just as logical to assume that James's invalidism, instead of preventing his courtship of Minny, was itself the symptom of some fear of, or scruple against, sexual love on his part, which then sharpened his regret. Regret for the so sadly attenuated affair he clearly did feel, and even remorse and guilt. Did the suspicion that Minny had *loved him* contribute to his misgivings? The record is blank as to her earlier feelings; but her last letters to him in Europe do show enough of a special shy tenderness, as if she feared rebuff—"My Darling Harry, (You don't mind if I am a little affectionate now that you are far away, do you?)" —to have planted a suspicion in his mind or confirmed one that was already there. And no doubt remorse was strong in him in proportion as it reached beyond the loss of Minny herself to whatever it was in his nature that made him refuse sex in general, as he appears to have done. We may go even so far as to say that, much as in his way he loved Minny for herself, it was chiefly as a symbol of all kinds of beautiful lost things that he appreciated her first and last. The largely legendary meaning she seems to have had for him is as apparent in the letters mourning her death as in the memoir of her composed forty years later. And while in theory this does not preclude the possibility that he might have loved her romantically as well, it does bring us back to what he actually had to say about her.

What *did* she mean to him? Here are some passages from the letters written to his mother and William: ". . . to the eye of feeling there is something immensely moving in the sudden and complete extinction of a vitality so exquisite and so apparently infinite as Minny's. . . . I feel as if a very fair portion of my sense of the reach and quality and capacity of human nature rested upon my experience of her character: certainly a large portion of my admiration for it. . . . Looking back upon the past half-dozen years, it seems as if she *represented*, in a manner, in my life several of the elements or phases of life at large—her own sex, to begin with, but even more *Youth*, with which owing to my invalidism, I always felt in rather indirect relation . . . her image will preside in my intellect, in fact, as a sort of measure and standard of brightness and repose. . . . Poor little Minny! It's the *living* ones that die; the writing ones that survive. . . . She was a breathing protest against English grossness, English compromises and conventions—a plant of pure American growth . . . she the very heroine of our common scene. . . . Twenty years hence what a pure elegant vision will she be."

Some of these comments are prophetic—uncannily so—of what Minny's image was to signify to a writer who, in 1870 when they were set down, was still so far from having absorbed it into his work that he was as yet pretty much a writer without a theme. In short, it is possible to be sceptical of the romantic element in their relations, and still to insist on her vast importance for his work. She was his great emblem of mortality in general; and she came, in a more particular fashion, to be associated with the "passional death," as it has been called, which he suffered in connection with his invalidism. It was in Newport too that there occurred the injury to which his invalidism was due. Of this no account is known to exist save that given in *Notes of a Son and Brother*, which is so rich in overtones, if not in actual facts, that it had better be quoted at length:

> Two things and more had come up—the biggest of which, and very wondrous as bearing on any circumstance of mine, as having a grain of weight to spare for it, was the breaking out of the War. The other, the infinitely small affair in comparison, was a passage of personal history the most entirely personal, but between which, as a private catastrophe or difficulty, bristling with embarrassments, and the great public convulsion that announced itself in bigger terms each day, I felt from the very first an association of the closest, yet withal, I fear, almost of the least clearly expressible. Scarce at all to be stated, to begin with, the queer fusion or confusion established in my consciousness during the soft spring of '61 by the firing on Fort Sumter, Mr. Lincoln's instant first call for volunteers and a physical mishap, already referred to as having overtaken me at the same dark hour, and the effects of which were to draw themselves out incalculably and intolerably. Beyond all present notation the interlaced, undivided way in which what had happened to me, by a turn of fortune's hand, in twenty odious minutes, kept company of the most unnatural—I can call it

nothing less—with my view of what was happening, with the question of what might still happen, to everyone about me, to the country at large: it so made of these marked disparities a single vast visitation. One had the sense, I mean, of a huge comprehensive ache, and there were hours at which one could scarce have told whether it came most from one's own poor organism, still so young and so meant for better things, but which had suffered particular wrong, or from the enclosing social body, a body rent with a thousand wounds and that thus treated one to the honour of a sort of tragic fellowship. The twenty minutes had sufficed, at all events, to establish a relation—a relation to everything occurring round me not only for the next four years but for long afterward—that was at once extraordinarily intimate and quite awkwardly irrelevant. I must have felt in some befooled way in presence of a crisis—the smoke of Charleston Bay still so acrid in the air—at which the likely young should be up and doing or, as familiarly put, lend a hand much wanted; the willing youths, all round, were mostly starting to their feet, and to have trumped up a lameness at such a juncture could be made to pass in no light for graceful. Jammed into the acute angle between two high fences, where the rhythmic play of my arms, in tune with that of several other pairs, but at a dire disadvantage of position, induced a rural, a rusty, a quasi-extemporised old engine to work and a saving stream to flow, I had done myself, in face of a shabby conflagration, a horrid even if an obscure hurt.

The incident appears to have made little stir at the time. The horrid obscure hurt, perhaps a sacroiliac strain, was so inconspicuous that a Boston physician, whom he consulted a few months later, could feel justified in dismissing it as trifling. Which does not mean that it necessarily *was* trifling, and in fact he later accused the physician of incompetence and himself of neglect. How greatly the strain affected his health and his life may be seen from a letter he wrote as late as 1899 to a young friend who was also unwell: "Only, if you have a Back, for heaven's sake take care of it. When I was about your age—in 1862!*— I did a bad damage (by a strain subsequently—through crazy juvenility—neglected) to mine; the consequence of which is that, in spite of retarded attention, and years, really, of recumbency, later, I've been saddled with it for life, and that even now, my dear Howard, I verily write you *with* it. I even wrote *The Awkward Age* with it."

Painful as it was, James made his disability serve him. He came, as he says, to think of his relation to it "as a *modus vivendi* workable for the time." The pages following his account of his injury are among the most pregnant in his memoirs. In writing of the event he does not, it is true, mention the fact that his father, in circumstances strangely like those of his own accident, lost a leg in boyhood only to hobble brilliantly through life. He ignores the familywide configuration of illness, though he does elsewhere make abundantly clear the family ethic of suffering and redemption. And he writes of the injury and its aftermath as if he were aware of their climactic position in an order of events reaching back to the small outsider of his New York childhood. Owing to his invalid state he now at last actually *is* "other"; and having, as it were, established his difference on a simple palpable physical basis,

* The passage quoted above from *Notes of a Son and Brother* suggests the spring of '61 as the date of the accident, but another passage in the same work would seem to date it some months later. Leon Edel, in his forthcoming biography of James, will give reasons for believing that the real date was the fall of '61.

he is free—indeed by the rule of conversion he is *obligated* —to try to compensate for it in appropriate ways and to return to life by means of his art. Long something of a stranger in his family, and lately a stranger in an America, or at least a North, galvanized and drawn together by war, he begins to know "the honour of a tragic fellowship," a community of suffering with the torn country and harassed soldiers. Going by steamboat to a Rhode Island camp for convalescent troops, he spends a day conversing with the inmates, very much, as he says in the memoirs, like "dear old Walt—even if I hadn't come armed like him with oranges and peppermints." He can only give them money, and listen sympathetically to their tales. Not much of an exploit, as he readily admits, and not without its frankly ludicrous side: he is quite solemn, the soldiers incorrigibly cheerful. Still, sailing exhaustedly back to Newport that night he experiences "a strange rapture of reflection." It is one of those moments of visionary self-communion to which he is so much given. With his disabled back and his general sense of powerlessness, he is, like the soldiers, "engaged in the common fact of endurance." He has somehow contrived to unite the positives and negatives of his experience—the injury, the remorse over his civilian status, the impulse towards literary creation—into a single charge of energy.

It was still under the protective leadership of his older brother that he made his first move towards independence of their family. After some six months in Hunt's studio William decided against art as a career; and, reverting to his original love of science, he left Newport in the autumn of 1861 to attend the Lawrence Scientific School at Harvard. Henry might follow him to Cambridge, as he did the following autumn, but he could hardly accompany him into organic chemistry and comparative anatomy; nor could he become really intimate with the circle of philosophic friends—including Charles S. Peirce, Chauncey Wright, and O. W. Holmes, Jr.,—who presently surrounded William in Cambridge. It was some time, as he said, before he could "accept the strange circumstance of my not invariably 'liking,' in homely parlance, his people, and his not invariably liking mine." But he profited by the fraternal estrangement, slight as it was; he was more on his own than he had ever been. Meanwhile he had enrolled in the Harvard Law School. It was a strange step, his last educational experiment. And whatever his original motives may have been, he gave little time to the law, devoting his leisure, and the privacy of his quarters in a Cambridge rooming house, to writing. In the *North American Review* of October 1864 there appeared the first of his book reviews; and the following March the *Atlantic Monthly* carried the first of his stories.

Assisted by his father's connections, he found a ready hearing and many acquaintances in literary Boston. Boston still clung to its title of intellectual capital of the country; and being in one of its periods of conscientious revival, it welcomed new talent. The *Atlantic Monthly* and the *North American Review*, both of recent founding, were edited there by such local figures as James T. Fields, Charles Eliot Norton, and James Russell Lowell; and Norton and other New Englanders had a hand in *The Nation*, which was started in New York in the same atmosphere of resolute postwar stock-taking and hope. With such narrative artists as Poe, Cooper, Hawthorne, and Melville already dead or passing into oblivion, and with Howells and Mark Twain not yet clearly in view, the scene was pretty much dominated by what we may call the *belles-lettres* mind, the kind of mind that expresses itself best in the essay, the lecture, the sermon, the history, the occasional poem. He was presently to revolt against its ascendancy, believing that it had even rather subdued Hawthorne. But the James who was to insist on the majesty of pure fiction, to imitate the drama as the most objective form of narrative, to inveigh against "the platitude of statement," was still many years in the future. The *belles-lettres* mind, it might be argued, had always a strong hold over him as well. In his youth it certainly had, and if his early stories are insufficiently galvanized by a theme, his essays of the period are almost doctrinaire. In any case, so far as he was concerned, the influential figures in the '60's were Lowell and Norton, and soon Howells, all of whom were to become his friends. Lowell wrote Norton in 1865 that "I shall never be a poet till I get out of the pulpit, and New England was all meeting-house when I was growing up." He was not a first-rate poet, but along with Norton he was engaged in the, to James, useful task of secularizing American letters. Lowell and Norton were scholars of the arts, editors, teachers, political reformers; and Norton held advanced views in religion. Both were at home in Europe, to which Lowell once paid as many as five visits in the course of six years, and where Norton stayed for long periods. Of the two Lowell, whom James came to know better in later years when both were abroad, was probably the more attractive person to him. Like the elder James, Hawthorne, and others of the older generation, he was enviably serene in his unquestioned Americanism; as James wrote, "no part of him was traitor to the rest." To Lowell he owed nothing intellectually, but he may have owed something to Norton. A rather shrill moralistic humanism sounds in his early essays, and unless he was simply born with the wisdom of the ages in his head, Norton may have helped to put it there.

He recalled how, "one day in autumn [of 1864] when, an extremely immature aspirant to the rare laurel of the critic, I went out from Boston to Cambridge to offer him [Norton] a contribution to the . . . *North American Review*," and how "he accepted on the spot, as the visitor still romantically remembers, a certain very awkward essay in criticism, and was to publish it in his forthcoming number." This unsolicited performance was partly a discourse on Scott, partly a review of Nassau Senior's *Essays on Fiction*; and for a haphazardly educated writer of 21 it was sufficiently remarkable. The breadth of historical knowledge, the pride in disciplined thought suggested, if not an older writer, at least one who was aggressively a university graduate. Towards Scott he was genially pious; towards the unfortunate Senior he was almost insolent, in a fashion peculiar to his early reviews. There was a novelist's touch in his portrait of Senior as a type of the " 'confirmed' novel-reader" with "his accurate memory for detail, his patient research into inconsistencies—dramatic, historic, geographic," and there was a humor that seldom got into his early stories. The critic, he said in another early piece, "is in the nature of his function *opposed* to the author"; and for some years he did battle with the authors, assailing them in a style full of epigram and antithesis, exhorting them to improve themselves by reading the right Continental authors, and waving in their faces quite impeccably classical standards. No wonder *The Nation*, for which he reviewed so many volumes, came to be familiarly called "the weekly day of judgment."

Much of this young pedantry James was soon to abandon as by degrees the critical faculty in him coalesced with the imaginative. But it seems not to have been uncongenial to the editors of the time, who continued to publish him. When he was only 25 Norton offered him the editorship of the *North American*, a post he refused because of his bad health. And he wrote well, he was well read, he was witty, and no one in the Anglo-Saxon countries was saying better things about fiction considered as an art. Most important of all, he reported at length on the French realists from Balzac to Flaubert. In some respects they shocked him as they did most Anglo-Saxons; yet he read them, studied their methods, and insisted that as artists they were inescapable. "Among writers called immoral, there is no doubt that he best deserves the charge," he said of Stendhal; yet the *Chartreuse de Parme* was "among the dozen finest novels that we possess."

It was more as an Anglo-Saxon than as an American *pur sang* that James wrote his early criticisms. The United States was not yet the special case it was soon to become for him. Still something of a Boston Brahmin, he felt culture to be a simple good of which Americans stood in need as the poor do of charity. The whole matter was to become more complex as he approached the hour of his own quasi-tragic choice between Europe and America. Becoming identified in his mind with experience itself, culture then emerged as a form of pleasure and a kind of knowledge—knowledge of good and evil. This equivocal view of the "aesthetic crusade," as he was to call Norton's effort, was still as far from him in the '60's as it was from Norton himself, of whom James would remark with mild irony that he had been distinguished by an "unqualified confidence" in his civilizing errand. And there is a good deal of James's early mind, though not the best of it, in a review of 1865 of Whitman's *Drum Taps*. His attack on the subject was purely formal. He was amusing at the expense of Whitman's tumescent egoism, but that was easy. He had only to play up the absurder poems, like "From Paumanok Starting I Fly Like a Bird," and ignore the great descriptive lyrics. As a native phenomenon, even a bad one, Whitman interested him not at all. Here was simply another wartime jingo in verse; his language was crude and it didn't scan. Years later James again wrote about Whitman. He had since come to love him, precisely as a native phenomenon; and he now received him into literature as a case of the "natural" poet. Even as an old man and a deeply compromised classicist, James was never much at home with the category of the "natural," and in the '60's he knew it not at all. Which is the simplest way of saying how poorly equipped he then was to be a critic of the American scene. If he presently became a great critic of the scene, it was by virtue of a point of view acquired in exile.

And not till that point of view began to form, in the early '70's, did he become an interesting writer of tales. But he was an industrious one; and between 1865, when "The Story of a Year" came out in the *Atlantic Monthly*, and 1871, when the same magazine carried "A Passionate Pilgrim," commonly and no doubt correctly regarded as his first really good story, he produced a dozen or so tales of varying length and character. Full of intrigue and surprise and strange human predicaments, they are distinctly *stories*; a primitive curiosity compels us to finish them. For the rest they are like the faint and confused murmurs of a sleeper who has something on his mind and is trying to awake. They were "sub-aqueous," James later said. Nor are his uncertain beginnings to be wondered at. So far, his deepest experience had been notably inward, in some cases, "too fine or too peculiar for notation, too intensely individual and supersubtle," as he observed in his memoirs. Determined though he was "to rinse my mouth of the European aftertaste *in order* to do justice to whatever of the native bitter-sweet might offer itself," he was still, so far as American life was concerned, "a poor uninitiated creature." Nor, apart from Hawthorne, were there any American writers to whom he might look to speed his initiation by giving him confidence in his experience, such as it was, and confidence in his imagination. He knew this, but he knew it without any feelings of self-commiseration. He wrote and wrote and wrote, as if to accomplish his ends by sheer industry. And it is significant of a good deal in his situation that the two writers who were closest to his mind were so dissimilar a pair as Hawthorne and Balzac. He was *influenced* by George Eliot—her heroines, her morality—but the other two represented something larger: two opposing ideas of the artist. The two ideas were in James himself and were permanently to remain in him in uneasy combination. Europe, the world, career, reputation, the power of the real, success by virtue of industry and accumulation, the artist as *Master*—this was Balzac; whereas Hawthorne was for him pretty much the opposite of these things: the contemplative, retiring, and only occasionally successful artist.

To James in his extreme youth Balzac could be no more

than a rather remote ideal. And to be influenced by Hawthorne meant to imitate his very subjects and tone, as in "A Romance of Certain Old Clothes," which begins, "Towards the middle of the eighteenth century there lived in the Province of Massachusetts a widowed gentlewoman," etc. For the rest, he could at least reach back through Hawthorne, as well as Poe, to the Gothic romance and so to a common folklore stock of wonder and terror. This he did, and one group of his early tales is peopled with ghosts, alter-egos, and vampires in human form. Not very remarkable stories, they do nevertheless sound some of his characteristic themes; and he was to return to the Gothic note in the more sophisticated wonder tales of his maturity. Something, too, of the popular impulse survived even in the more realistic of his later novels, where the sudden windfalls of fortune, the initiations, prohibitions, and transformations, are often reminiscent of the fairy tale.

In addition to the wonder tales, there is in the period 1865-71 a fairly distinct group of stories which earned for the young James the title of a promising realist. One of them, "Poor Richard," was the occasion of his meeting William Dean Howells, who was then on the staff of the *Atlantic* and who advised the editor, J. T. Fields, to publish "Richard" as well as "all the stories you can get from that writer." This was in 1866; and Howells and James, becoming good friends, remained so for the rest of their lives. For all their difference of background—Howells, a native of Ohio, had worked in a print shop throughout his boyhood—they had a good deal in common: their Yankee consciences; their desire for a large success on their own terms; their conviction that the American scene, hitherto explored principally from the lyric or the epic point of view, was now ripe for discovery by the literary historian, some local counterpart of a Balzac or a Turgenev. James, observed Howells in 1866, is "gifted enough to do better than anyone has yet done towards making us a real American novel."

This was generous and prophetic. But for a present-day reader there is little in the early tales, even in the ones James and Howells would probably have called "realistic," to justify enthusiasm. If "realism" implies a necessary, or at least highly probable, relation between the elements of theme, character, and setting in a story, then the realism of James's initial efforts was sharply attenuated. His settings, frequently rural New England, consist of a few standard properties—a lake, an elm, a cow—which make brief appearances and then vanish from the scene, leaving it bare not only of such objects but of those evidences of manners and institutions which later served the author so well. Nor do his meanings come through very clearly, though a couple of interesting themes are distinctly broached. One has to do with the New England conscience and its potentialities of good and evil. Another and not unrelated one is the theme of the young man's initiation into life. As these themes have considerable reference to his later work, and possibly to his own state of mind at the time as well, they deserve a little study.

It is the heroine's final injunction to the hero of "A Landscape Painter" (1866) that he "be a man"; and this well-to-do young person, who has disguised himself as a poor artist in the hope of eluding mercenary women, is fairly typical of James's initiates in these early stories. Frequently rich, sometimes ill, they face life with a good deal more of suspicion than of eagerness. Nor, with exceptions to be noted, is there any very clear reason for their misgivings. It simply *is—a priori*, so to speak. Thus in James's first published tale, "The Story of a Year," which takes place in a lightly sketched New England and during a rather spectral Civil War, Lieutenant Ford no sooner becomes engaged to Lizzie Crowe, his mother's ward, than he renounces all claim to her in case he is killed in battle. "What rights has a dead man?" he inquires, and of course his fears are realized. Lizzie, having met a more self-confident lover, proves faithless to Ford, who, wounded at the front, returns home, forgives her, and dies. "A Most Extraordinary Case" (1868), another Civil War story, is a far better performance. Here James's impulse to associate himself with the unhappy war veterans flowers in the tragic idyl of an earlier Lost Generation; and here the theme of initiation, with the attendant hopes and misgivings, is fully clarified. No doubt the invalid Colonel Mason is curiously prim: "a man [he thinks] was not to go a-wooing in his dressing-gown and slippers." Yet he has excellent reasons for feeling forlorn and for hesitating to push his case with the blooming Caroline, who, with her air of expecting great things of life, is a prototype of James's later heroines. Estranged by the psychology of war, he is also convalescing from wounds. And if he fails to recover, if his initiation back into the postwar life proves to be abortive, if he takes a turn for the worse and dies on discovering that Caroline is in love with the vigorous Dr. Knight, his own physician, it all follows naturally enough from his given circumstances.

Not all of these tales end tragically. The rather brutal and hangdog farmer who is the hero of "Poor Richard" does at last force his way into the esteem of the heroine and of himself. "She felt that he was abundantly a man, and she loved him. Richard, on his side, felt humbly the same truth, and he began to respect himself." Nor did James drop the theme when, following a trip abroad in 1869–70, he began to write stories and novels in which the hero's pursuit of his manhood became associated with his discovery of Europe. This larger perspective vastly enriched the theme, but it continued to crop up in a more or less pure form even in the later '70's, when James was happily exploiting his international subject in a parallel group of narratives. Indeed those somewhat anomalous novels, *Watch and Ward*, *Confidence*, and *Washington Square*, are possibly to be seen as belated embodiments of it.

Watch and Ward was his first full-length novel and originally ran as a serial in the *Atlantic Monthly* in 1871. Minutely revised, as were most of his works between one printing and another, it reappeared later in book form, only to vanish at last from the canon as James got into the habit of referring to *Roderick Hudson* as his first novel. *Watch and Ward* deserved its oblivion: very little redeems it except its value as a document. Its main business is nakedly with the initiation theme. A kind of school for wives, wherein the wealthy hero, rejected by a woman of his own class, adopts a poor orphan girl and brings her up as his ward and future bride, *Watch and Ward* presents us with *two* neophytes. One is of course the orphan girl Nora, with "her departing childishness, her dawning tact, her growing freedom with Roger"; while the other is Roger Lawrence himself, with his obscurely motivated fear of life and love. His jealous possessiveness towards Nora begins to chill her as she grows older and is pursued by two other men, both more self-assured than her guardian-lover. But after a good deal of intrigue and a long illness on Roger's part (another

stricken hero!) she finds she prefers him after all. The
happy ending is a patent contrivance. The shrinking
Roger is shown as experiencing a most unlikely access of
self-confidence; while his bolder rivals neatly dispose of
themselves by turning out to be, one a light man, the other a
scoundrel.

It must be confessed that Roger Lawrence is the least
engaging of all these powerless-feeling young men. Un-
touched by any pathos of war, he goes beyond Ford and
Mason in expressing his disquiet through a mere fussiness
of manner. A creature of small rages and jealousies, he
never succeeds in persuading us that he cares more for Nora
than for saving his own face. He should, we feel, be transposed into the key of satire, as such gentlemen occasionally
are in James's later work. Because he isn't so transposed, we
find ourselves sitting in constant irritated judgment of
him. And failing to discover, in the usual way, any clues to
his behavior, we do the forbidden thing and go beyond the
author's avowed knowledge of his character. Our trespass is
only too well rewarded, for it turns out that James's un-
spoken and no doubt unconscious knowledge is strangely
deep. Like all the early stories, *Watch and Ward* is strewn
with images so palpably and irresistibly erotic as to imply a
whole resonant domain of meaning beyond anything he
could have intended. What can the following bit of gratuitous "business" signify except that Roger's discomfiture in
life begins on the sexual level?

> While Hubert's answer [Hubert is one of his rivals]
> lingered on his lips, the door opened and Nora came in.
> Her errand was to demand the use of Roger's watch-
> key, her own having mysteriously vanished. She had
> begun to take out her pins and had muffled herself for

this excursion in a merino dressing-gown of sombre blue. Her hair was gathered for the night into a single massive coil, which had been loosened by the rapidity of her flight along the passage. Roger's key proved a complete misfit, so that she had recourse to Hubert's. It hung on the watch-chain which depended from his waistcoat, and some rather intimate fumbling was needed to adjust it to Nora's diminutive timepiece. It worked admirably, and she stood looking at him with a little smile of caution as it creaked on the pivot.

Yet James was beginning to contend more openly with the initiation theme. While Ford and Mason were satisfied to be doomed, Roger really strives towards experience of the world and belief in himself; and although his effort is much reduced in scale by being made to revolve so consistently around the issue of mere poise; although he is allowed none of the charm, the pathos, the superior insight and intelligence by which James's later heroes of sensibility are commonly transfigured; although unlike so many of them he is not even granted the dignity of failure—he does anticipate them in one respect: his helplessness is associated with sincerities and scruples on his part which make him— or are supposed to make him—the moral superior of his worldly rivals.

Confidence (1879) is as urbane as *Watch and Ward* is rough and labored. It is also more inconsequential; and beyond remarking that it is addressed to our theme in the degree that it is addressed to anything at all—one of its pair of heroes trusts no one, including himself, while the other is an "imperturbable" dandy and artist like John La Farge—we need not linger over it. For an author who had already written such first-rate things as *Daisy Miller* and

The American, Confidence was a regression. It was, however, followed a year later by the wonderful *Washington Square*, which we shall consider at this point because its scene is exclusively American, like that of the early tales, and because it is so good an illustration of how James was to redeem their shortcomings.

It is not essential to *Washington Square* that its scene is American. The Old New York setting is lovely but insubstantial, an atmosphere and no more; and so familiar seems the fable of the girl jilted by her fortune-hunting suitor that we are surprised to learn from James's notebooks that he was following quite closely an actual incident related to him by Fanny Kemble. He chose to treat Catherine Sloper's story more as a family story than as a love story; her aunt and her father are quite as important as her faithless suitor. It is a small subject, and an unmistakably psychological one; and James explores it to perfection, neither slighting his situations as he had done earlier, nor too industriously ransacking them as he was sometimes to do later on.

Catherine Sloper is another case of a person devoured by self-mistrust; but there were advantages in making her a girl and placing her in the New York of thirty years before. She had no obvious resemblance to James himself, as had Roger Lawrence; and we are not obliged to make that choice between conscience and animal energy which, in *Watch and Ward*, strikes us as more relevant to the author's own dilemmas than to our own. On Catherine Sloper he was free to lavish all that he knew of the pathos and terror in the experience of the confirmed outsider, the person who, moreover, is estranged from his own family.

Catherine begins as the victim of what is almost a *system* of inverted family relations. Her proud brilliant father mourns a dead wife, her foolish aunt a dead husband; and both have been denied the sons they longed to have. The affection they might be expected to give Catherine turns, in her father's case, to an almost vengeful contempt, in her aunt's, to a perverse romantic attachment for Morris Townsend, the young man who is trying to marry Catherine for her money. Preyed upon by the very persons who are closest to her, whom she most believes and most needs to love her, she is first seen as a plain, inept, lonely, and dependent girl, setting out for a party in a too gaudy red dress. "Is it possible that this magnificent person is my child?" inquires her father in the ironic tone that is an expression of his fearful power over her. Such is the intensity of *Washington Square* that the whole spirit of the story is present in the least speech or scene; and no passage captures it better than the one in which young Townsend, whom Catherine adores and her father despises, presumes to trespass on the latter's private study in his absence while she stands by divided between love of the bold young man and horror at his profanation. She is allowed a larger measure of personal humiliation than is usually the case with James's protagonists: she is not even intelligent. And not until Townsend crudely deserts her, and the egoism of her father and aunt is inescapable, does she begin to exhibit any signs of independence, and even then it is partly the independence of a person intent on simple survival. Catherine is far from the transfigured victims, the Strethers and Milly Theales, in the later novels. Yet she has something in common with them. She is not, at the end, merely an old maid enveloped in the pathos of her unhappy memories. A small but real triumph has been hers: she has survived and become a person without recourse to the selfishness of her tormentors. Between victim and victimizer there is a human middle ground which Catherine makes her own.

The Great Decision

JAMES'S completed memoirs do not carry his life very far beyond 1865, the year when he had made "the discovery that I could for my own part acceptedly stammer a style." With his next great discovery, the now famous decision that he should live in Europe, the memoirs fail to deal directly. As they well might, considering how vexed were his reasons. He had practically merged his literary with his personal self; and almost any act on his part, because it expressed his entire being, was as cumbrous as it was significant. His self-exile was the supreme act of his life. It was nearly as legendary for him as it has become for us; and neither he nor anyone else has ever been able to sum up the causes in a formula. What the memoirs seem to imply is that a European residence was ultimately in order for one who had suffered so many losses and humiliations in America, who had experienced boyhood ecstasies of recognition in Paris, and who was to dream of personal and artistic power in terms of the Galerie d'Apollon. Thus as an old man James could look back and perceive that he had been obeying inclinations deeper than reason. No doubt he also understood that without the unconscious, the provocative, the shady element in his whole feeling about Europe and America he could hardly have possessed his remarkable imagination for their differences, their rival claims and felicities. This feeling he came at last to describe as the "inward romantic principle."

But what was nonrational was not necessarily unreasonable. There were immediate and practical grounds for his preferring Europe, and it was naturally these of which he was mostly aware at the time and which he discussed in his letters and notebook entries. Nor, broadly speaking, was his literary quarrel with American culture—which is what finally interests us most in his exile—at issue during the years when he was coming to his decision. The United States, he then insisted, was the most challenging kind of virgin soil for a writer; it was only for himself that the soil was so virgin as to be depressing; and he was so far from counseling expatriation for others that he invariably urged American writers to stay at home. That he himself was unable, for whatever reason, to become a strictly indigenous writer; and that in any case he found more pleasure and better company abroad—this was as much as he ever maintained. And then there were reasons of physical convenience which weighed heavily in an age that made much of the travel-cure. Still very far from well, he was to be at first as much a pilgrim of Europe's spas and climates as of its cathedrals and landscapes. The search for health, the search for an atmosphere more to his personal liking, were the reasons urged by James at the time; and he was to prove them good reasons by his subsequent well-being and achievement.

He was later to trace the germ of the "inward romantic principle" to a certain day in August 1866 when he "called in Charles St. for news of O. W. H. [Oliver Wendell Holmes, Jr.], then on his 1st flushed and charming visit to England, and saw his mother in the cool dim matted drawingroom of that house (passed *never*, since, without the *sense*), and got the news, of all his London, his general English, success and felicity, and *vibrated* so with the wonder and romance and curiosity and dim weak tender (oh, tender!) envy of it, that my walk up the hill, afterwards, up Mount Vernon St. and probably to the Athenaeum was all coloured and gilded, and humming with it." And young Holmes's adventures had been preceded by the even more remarkable ones of another member of the Boston circle, Henry Adams, who had been his father's secretary while the latter was minister to England during the strenuous war years, and who was later to assist James in becoming acquainted there. But several years were to pass before James could imitate Adams and Holmes; and when at last he did, it was with the eagerness of a person who had suffered a good deal. Faced by illnesses and decisions, and suddenly cast upon serious Boston, he and William were discovering that life no longer seemed to support their father's theoretical imprudence, his large synthesis of levity and earnestness.

But they were not on their own for very long. Quitting Newport in 1864, their parents followed them, settling first in Boston proper and then in Cambridge, where, in a house on Quincy Street facing the Harvard Yard, they remained for pretty much the rest of their lives. The wanderers became at last sedentary—so much so that following his mother's death James was to complain that "summer after summer she never left Cambridge—it was impossible that father should leave his house." And none of them was ever very much in love with the place. T. S. Eliot's remark that Boston was "refined beyond the point of civilization" was anticipated by many a sigh or grimace in the letters of the James family. "Give me a race with some guts to them, no matter if they do belch at you now and then," William once declared after attending an "aesthetic tea"; and Henry could grumble about "that dry, flat, hot, stale and odious Cambridge." Such as it was, however, the New England metropolis was the one large area of intellectual consciousness in the country. The elder James, who had many friends in the vicinity, was to do some of his best work there. And for William, notwithstanding his grievances, the scene was full of interest. There were at Harvard a number of first-rate scientists who thoroughly appreciated him, including Louis Agassiz, whom he accompanied on an expedition to Brazil in 1865. Moreover the German method and technology, which he was presently to admire on a visit to that country, were being rapidly imported into the United States, and not least to the Harvard of President Eliot. His undoubted love of country apart, William had excellent material reasons for being content with America, and even with Boston.

The American literary atmosphere as represented by Norton, Lowell, and Howells was by no means so promising, as Henry could not but feel, even though he greatly relished his friendships with these men and his small early success with his readers. In time, however, his audience began to accord him little more than a hypercritical attention; and not unnaturally it was his very refinement that his refined local readers could not forgive him, being unable, perhaps, to imagine a great writer formed in something like their own image. It is true that he was not then even a very good writer, but the suspicion persisted after he had become one. And Howells, whose admiration remained constant, was always distressed by this coldness. When he was an old man and James was dead, Howells was to write that "the nearest of his friends in Boston would say they liked him, but they could not bear his fiction; and from people, conscious of culture, throughout New England, especially the women, he had sometimes outright insult." In terms of mere vanity they had reason to be offended with James. Beginning with his first tale, his sharply allusive pictures of New England and New Englanders were to represent a personal animus raised to the level of a general observation. His father's old half-serious feud with the mind of the region, his own misfortunes suffered on the scene, his distrust of the Calvinist strain in himself—these supplied the animus. The general observation was to the effect that New England constituted the dead hand; that America's future, that "life" itself, lay elsewhere. With some notable exceptions, the heroic seekers in his novels are of other origin: New York, the Far West, the South; while his New Englanders are at best rather arid Hamlets and Portias, at worst types of extreme spiritual pride. Their names are "Newsome" and their towns are "Woollett." Naturally the real ones resented James. And in finding his satire of them unendurable they exactly proved its point. Many of them found it so even when it was quite tender, as in *The Europeans*, of which the Boston critic, Thomas Wentworth Higginson, was to write:

> The family portrayed has access to "the best society in Boston"; yet the daughter, twenty-three years old, has "never seen an artist," though the picturesque figure of Allston had but lately disappeared from the

streets, where Cheney, Staigg, and Eastman Johnson might be seen any day, with plenty of others less known. The household is perfectly amazed and overwhelmed at the sight of two foreigners, although there probably were more cultivated Europeans in Boston thirty years ago than now, having been drawn thither by the personal celebrity or popularity of Agassiz, Ticknor, Longfellow, Sumner, and Dr. Howe.

Surely this is one of James's own characters talking: the dry complacence, the dogged cataloguing of local advantages. *And Dr. Howe!*

James had begun his career, as writers traditionally did, in a rooming house; but he and William promptly rejoined the family on their setting up in Boston, as if to do so were the most natural thing in the world. William made his home with them as long as he was unmarried; Henry until, in 1875, he at last retired to Paris. Thus, save for a couple of long European absences preceding his final departure, he had a full decade of family life after he had begun to write. American writers and their families! The Jameses were far more stimulating than most, and they were less manifestly possessive; yet in the mid-sixties they were entering on their great time of troubles. All five of the children were ill in the various ways that have been described, though not of course all at once under the same roof, Bob and Wilky having gone their convalescent ways before either Alice or William was gravely stricken. Still, this serial arrangement must have been harrowing in itself, like waiting for the plague or the family curse to strike. But they were all as reticent as they seem to have been stoical in the common crisis, though Henry once wrote that Quincy Street was "about as lively as the inner sepulchre." We cannot be sure how powerfully his imagination was affected by the years of a "shared experience" in Cambridge; but it is a fact, for whatever it is worth, that once he had settled abroad he remained on his own; and that in his novels the absence of family ties is only less frequently a condition of freedom and experience than is the possession of wealth.

Reviewing the emotions of those days in his notebook several years later, he recalled that "some of my doses of pain were very heavy; very weary were some of my months and years." Yet he also remembered "the visions of those untried years. Never did a poor fellow have more; never was an ingenuous youth more passionately and yet more patiently eager for what life might bring." It was, however, William who first broke through the barriers. In 1867-68 he made a long stay in Europe, principally in Germany, where, with the usual luck of the Jameses, he was well launched into the national life, in this case by Hermann Grimm, to whom Emerson had given him a letter of introduction. William devoured everything in sight—politics, science, novels, paintings, theater—as if out of an acute philosophic hunger. As his letters make clear, he is seeking some account of things that is more compatible with reality, as he sees it, than is his father's visionary optimism. It is obvious, too, that illness and spiritual crisis are already at his heels. His letters are among the most remarkable ever written by a man of his age, even though they are not without a certain uncomfortable swagger as if his father's brilliant manner were undergoing distortions from the effects of a self-conscious vitalism in his son. And William is to project some of this on his brother, who is himself presently to "go abroad." The obstacles were mainly financial. So much money had been spent on physicians and on setting Bob and Wilky up in business that their parents, as it appears, could not easily maintain two traveling sons at once. Nor had Henry, for all his writing, as yet achieved financial independence, though this was his wish. It was not till the winter of 1869 that he at last embarked for Europe, for what turned out to be a stay of some fourteen months.

Over the entire venture hung the shadow of illness, his own and that of William, which broke into full crisis on the latter's return to Cambridge; while the news of Minny Temple's death was to reach Henry in England. From the Alps he wrote his brother of "the deep satisfaction in being able to do all this healthy trudging and climbing. It *is*—it *is* a pledge, a token of some future potency." In Florence only three months later he collapsed and was rather ill for several weeks; still later he retired into an English sanitarium. "For what purpose we are thus tormented I know not," he wrote William. "—I don't see that Father's philosophy explains it any more than anyone else's. But as Pascal says, *'malgré les misères qui nous tiennent par la gorge'* . . ." Still, he was well enough or determined enough to turn his trip into a Grand Tour; and he too despatched long and remarkable letters to his family. They are not so remarkable as William's, mainly because they are too much influenced by William. Tintoretto, Henry wrote, is "the biggest genius (as far as I know) who ever wielded a brush," treating his themes "not as a mere subject and fiction but as a great fragment wrenched out of life and history, with all its natural details clinging to it and testifying to its reality." The hyperbole, the *tranche de vie* conception of art, were never to be Henry's tone and Henry's conception of art; but they were

already and distinctly his brother's. He is even less himself
when he goes on to say, still apropos of Tintoretto, that "I'd
give a great deal to fling down a dozen of his pictures into
prose of corresponding force and colour." That he at-
titudinizes is not surprising. His trip is something of a
public enterprise; he travels as with an invisible body-
guard of solicitous sponsors and connections. His parents
are constantly in touch with him. Shown his letters,
Emerson applauds them from Concord. Ruskin greatly admires one of them which Norton, now in England, gives
him to read. No wonder that Henry is a little self-conscious
and that, for all his candid pleasure in Europe, he also takes
care to preserve the traditional wariness of the confirmed
American in the old world. Indeed, having been introduced
around in London by Norton, he carries the critical spirit
into the heart of Pre-Raphaelitism. "Ruskin himself is a
very simple matter," he writes to his mother. "In face, in
manner, in talk, in mind, he is weakness pure and simple
. . . he has been scared back by the grim face of reality into
the world of unreason and illusion, and . . . wanders there
without a compass and a guide—or any light save the
fitful flashes of his beautiful genius." Had he perhaps found
in Ruskin what he came prepared to find? He does better
with the William Morris household. "After dinner . . .
Morris read us one of his unpublished poems . . . and his
wife, having a bad toothache, lay on a sofa, with a hand-
kerchief to her face. There was something very quaint and
remote from our actual life, it seemed to me, in the whole
scene: Morris reading in his flowing antique numbers a
legend of prodigies and terrors (the story of Bellerophon, it
was), around us all the picturesque bric-a-brac of the apart-
ment (every article of furniture literally a 'specimen' of

something or other,) and in the corner this dark silent medieval woman with her medieval toothache." Morris, he concluded, was an extraordinary example of "a delicate sensitive genius and taste, saved by a perfectly healthy body and temper."

On the attractions of the English at large he is divided, as most Americans were and are, and as he is always to remain. Whereas, "what I have pointed at as our vices are the elements of the modern man with *culture* quite left out," the English, while showing certainly no marked intellectual culture, have a "pleasantness" that "comes in a great measure from the fact of their each having been dipped into the crucible, which gives them a sort of coating of comely varnish and colour. They have been smoothed and polished by mutual social attrition. They have manners and a language." This is as far as James is at present prepared to go in defense of European varnish; and in Italy the poorness of the poor, the ubiquity of the priests, the whole "hideous heritage of the past" offends him as it has offended so many American travelers before him. But this is a small part of his response to Italy. In Rome, he goes "reeling and moaning thro' the streets, in a fever of enjoyment"; and though in the meadow country around Great Malvern he is to be charmed by evidences of "the deepest British picturesque," Italy remains the capital of the picturesque as it does of the arts.

By the spring of 1870 he was back in Cambridge. William's crisis had lately been at its height, though on April 30 he had recorded in his diary the beginnings of a change of heart. "My first act of free will shall be to believe in free will." He was still extremely depressed and Cambridge was dreary. Henry was very quiet there; he saw much of Perry and Howells. If the question of a European residence was then in his mind, he was pondering it very earnestly. "It's a complex fate being an American," he wrote, "and one of the responsibilities it entails is fighting against a superstitious valuation of Europe." No doubt he fought hard in the degree that he felt his own European inclinations to be so largely emotional. Even his intellectual reasons, such as they were at the time, savored of perversity. A Thoreau might withdraw to Walden Pond and provoke no more than a few smiles from his neighbors. For Thoreau, seeking to simplify life, was after all in the tradition of the saints, the philosophers, and certain of the American pioneers. To retire from the common scene in the hope of *complicating* life, of adding to its artifices and rituals, as James thought of doing, was odd; and the fate, at least as popularly conceived, of those few individuals who had already fled to Florence or Rome or Paris with their brushes or their fortunes made an ominous precedent. But there was in the air something larger than all this; there was the celebrated promise of America itself, which the elder James had expressed as well as anyone when, in his Independence Day oration, he declared that in the United States "man himself unqualified by convention, the man to whom all these conventional men have been simply introductory, the man who—let me say it—for the first time in human history finding himself in his own right erect under God's sky, and feeling himself in his own right the peer of every other man, spontaneously aspires and attains to a far freer and profounder culture of his nature than has ever yet illustrated humanity." To abandon America was inevitably to challenge such a faith, or seem to. The prevailing myth was all of the West, of the Future. A migration eastward across the Atlantic, a plunging backward into time, was almost an inversion of the astronomical order of things. And who was Henry James, Jr.—so young, so ignorant of the United States—to undertake a revolution? Naturally he hesitated, tending to pare down his reasons till they should look very personal and very sensible (as doubtless they were), however unflattering they might be to himself. "Looking about for myself," he wrote to Norton, who was still in Europe, "I conclude that the face of nature and civilization in this our country is to a certain point a very sufficient literary field. But it will yield its secrets only to a really *grasping* imagination. This I think Howells lacks. (Of course *I* don't!) To write well and worthily of American things one need even more than elsewhere to be a *master*. But unfortunately one is less!"

And he goes on to say that he has been "scribbling some little tales. . . . To write a series of good little tales I deem ample work for a life-time." Surely his feeling that he was too little of a master to write worthily of America arose from his immediate struggles to do so. We have glanced at *Watch and Ward*, which seems to have been written in the years following his return to Cambridge. Not all of his current tales on native subjects were so unrewarding. Yet to this period belong also his first truly international narratives, "A Passionate Pilgrim" and its satellites, "At Isella" and "Travelling Companions"; and a light shone over these visions of one American's return to rural England, another's descent into passionate Italy, such as had shone over nothing he had written so far. Meanwhile he was producing, mostly for *The Nation*, a number of things in what was for him a new department of writing, the travel sketch. Now if these are singularly expert and charming, they also serve to cast some light on what was absent in his literary relation to native materials. Deciding, like many others returned from abroad, to experiment with being a tourist at home, he visited or revisited such places as Saratoga, Quebec, Niagara Falls, and Newport, and sketched them in as soberly reportorial a manner as possible. Yet, given his temperament, these sketches inevitably crystallized around certain salient impressions that were very much his own. "Niagara," one of his rare efforts in purely natural description, was a small triumph of image-making; and so was the sketch of Saratoga, which he saw as a ragged spa accidentally grown up in a wilderness "all green, lonely, and vacant" and touched with the pathos of uncomfortably idle men and sadly overdressed women ("a hundred rustling beauties whose rustle was their sole occupation"). It was not the roaring Saratoga of legend, but James made it look authentic. Nevertheless the general point of view in all these sketches *was* conventional, static, a little snobbish. Scouring America for evidences of the picturesque and of civilized society, he visited just those places that offered the most literal parallels with European "sights"; and while admiring Balzac's racy pages, he could dismiss the underworld people of Saratoga as "loafers." An American writer with no sympathy for loafers? His knowledge of Hawthorne alone should have told him this was ominous. Yet he *felt* no such sympathy and he was too honest to fake it. Meanwhile the elaborate social life that did excite him was nowhere in evidence. He might love the myth of America, but the fact of it . . . What Tocqueville had observed some thirty years before still held good for James. "Nothing conceivable is so . . . anti-poetic, as the life of a man in the United States. But among the thoughts which it suggests there is always one which is full of poetry, and that is the hidden nerve which gives vigor to the frame."

When he next went to Europe, in May 1872, it was for a stay of a year and a half. He was now 29 and in fair health. Whatever his own dissatisfaction with his work, he was well enough established as a writer, in his own and the public's mind, to make the trip something of a literary enterprise. That had not been true of the earlier trip; then he wrote little or nothing abroad. This time an agreement with *The Nation* to produce a series of travel pieces helped to make the journey possible. He produced these and a great deal besides, publishing some forty-two items during the year of 1874 alone. Among other things he wrote "The Madonna of the Future" and a part of *Roderick Hudson*, the former a long tale, the latter his first really extensive novel, and both of them turning on a question, that of the American artist in Europe, which must then have been very much on his mind. He was entering on that immense productivity which was to characterize his mature career.

"Good-bye, my lovely Harry . . . Truly I am a happy and grateful father at every remembrance of you," wrote the elder James, who, like all the family, had a way of rejoicing in one's successes and opportunities without ever appearing to be surprised by them. And during the present trip Henry was to be as closely in touch as ever with his Quincy Street admirers. Indeed his sister Alice and their Aunt Katharine Walsh accompanied him to Europe and traveled with him there for several months; and William, now a Harvard instructor but still in uncertain health, joined him later in Rome, only to contract a fever so severe that Henry was obliged to nurse him for many weeks, after which William returned home. In Henry's absence the family read his stories aloud among themselves and sometimes arranged for their publication. In the case of "The Madonna of the Future" they were obliged to consent to the censorship of Howells, who, as the elder James reported, "had a decided shrinking from one episode . . . as being risky for the magazine." While "Howells *in general* is too timid," the elder James conceded, he himself and Mrs. James and Alice had all thought the passage in question rather "scary" or "musky"; and William spoke of its "somewhat cold and repulsive details." The really cutting phrase was William's; and William it was who undertook to be the family critic of his brother's work, the elder James being content to praise in a tactfully vague manner. William's high spirits had not suffered from his crisis nor from the fact that Henry was then perhaps better established than he was and had revised and arranged for the publication of his first articles, despatched from Germany in 1867. He was the older brother still, and both of them appear to have recognized his right to play the critic, even the gadfly. "If you see what I mean," he had once written, "perhaps it may put you on the track of some useful discovery about yourself, which is my excuse for talking to you thus unreservedly." But since his objections were this time pretty fundamental—there was "a want of blood in your stories," and they were inclined to be "trifling,"—it is hard to see how they could have served Henry except to make him unhappy. There is no evidence that they *did* make him unhappy. The cheerful taking, as well as the brusque giving, of criticism was an old item in the family code. And besides, William's imagery of "blood" and "warmth" and "guts" revealed his prejudices and expectations so candidly that even a very admiring younger brother would probably know how to cope with them. Then as later William looked frankly to literature to console or inspire or instruct him; and he had moods in which he confessed to Henry that "I really think my taste is rather incompetent in these matters." Still he fired away at him, as he was to do year after year for a lifetime. On the whole he praised a little and condemned a lot. Sometimes he confessed to "the great delight which all your pieces give me by their insight into the shades of being, and their exquisite diction and sense of beauty." But this, however close it was to Henry's intention, was never quite enough for William. A reluctant pragmatist, he clung to his *a priori* concerning his brother's talents and duties as a writer even when it failed again and again to produce results. Oddly enough, it is for their deadly characterization of Henry's false notes, their deadly satire on his excesses, that William's comments are most quoted today. "They give," he wrote as early as 1868 of his brother's tales, "a certain impression of the author clinging to his gentlemanliness though all else be lost, and dying happy provided it be *sans déroger*."

William's letters, by no means always so sharp, followed Henry around Europe on his trip of 1872-74. With his sister and their Aunt Kate he toured parts of England and the Continent, regularly sending off copy to *The Nation*. He was later in Paris for a while, very much alone except for Lowell, who had turned up there and with whom he now became intimate. Save for his pleasure in the French theater, he was at present rather cold to the scene of his boyhood recognitions. It was towards Italy that he yearned; and it was mostly there that he passed the second year of his stay abroad. Less the astonished tourist on this occasion, about done with the "picturesque," he was free to enjoy the society of the American colony in Rome, to which he was introduced by W. W. Story, who had settled there long ago, come to know the Brownings, and gone through the revolution of 1848 barricaded in a rented palace. In Florence James took rooms and began work on *Roderick Hudson.*

That novel signified the end of his apprenticeship, and it was also his first large treatment of the American in Europe. When, however, he returned to the United States, he was still far from having decided on permanent exile. Indeed, success and well-being had the contrary effect on him, and for some months he was possessed by an ecstasy of common-sense on the whole subject. Europe was wonderful, but it was not an American's natural home. One missed the company of one's kind. The old world feasted the senses but starved the energies of the delightful Story, whose career he was later to describe as "a sort of beautiful sacrifice to a noble mistake." Could not a person who was increasingly independent, a writer who had discovered his theme, settle for the traditional Yankee cosmopolitanism as represented by Norton and Lowell, who came and went as they pleased? To be sure, Norton, back home after his long English visit, was "taking America rather hard." To his complaints James replied, by way of a letter to Grace Norton: "What Charles says about our civilization seems to me perfectly true, but practically I don't feel as if the facts were so melancholy. The great fact for us all there is that, relish Europe as we may, we belong much more to that than to this, and stand in a much less factitious and artificial relation to it. I feel forever how Europe keeps holding one at arm's length, and condemning one to a

meagre scraping of the surface. . . . It would seem that in
our great unendowed, unfurnished, unentertained and un-
entertaining continent, where we all sit sniffing, as it were,
the very earth of our foundations, we ought to have leisure
to turn out something handsome from the very heart of
simple human nature."

His return, in the autumn of '74, was again a matter for
family discussion. William had written him in April declaring this to be "a very critical moment in your history." William's own recent stay abroad had a little dis-
composed him for life in Cambridge, just as Norton's had,
and in trying to console his brother he was perhaps trying
to convince himself. "I have a suspicion," he concluded,
"that if you come, too, and *can* get once acclimated, the
quality of what you write will be higher than it would be
in Europe." Henry accepted this advice but on the basis of
a compromise. "Tell Willy," he wrote to his mother, "I
thank him greatly for setting before me so vividly the
question of my going home or staying. I feel equally with
him the importance of the decision." But he shrank from
"Willy's apparent assumption that going now is to pledge
myself to stay forever."

The common-sense solution turned out to be an unreal
one. He had not been home many months before he felt his
mistake. In his notebooks some years later he reviewed,
very simply, his feelings and movements during that critical
year. "I recall perfectly the maturing of my little plan to
get abroad again and remain for years, during the summer
of 1875; the summer the latter part of which I spent in
Cambridge. It came to me there on my return from New
York where I had been spending a bright, cold, un-

remunerative, uninteresting winter, finishing *Roderick Hudson* and writing for *The Nation.* (It was these two tasks that kept me alive.) I had returned from Europe the year before that, the beginning of September '74, sailing for Boston with Wendell Holmes and his wife as my fellow passengers. I had come back then to 'try New York,' thinking it my duty to attempt to live at home before I should grow older, and not take for granted too much that Europe alone was possible; especially as Europe for me then meant simply Italy, where I had had some very discouraged hours, and which, lovely and desirable though it was, didn't seem as a permanent residence, to lead to anything. I wanted something more active, and I came back and sought it in New York. I came back with a certain amount of scepticism, but with very loyal intentions, and extremely eager to be 'interested.' As I say, I was interested but imperfectly, and I very soon decided what was the real issue of my experiment. It was by no means equally soon, however, that I perceived how I should be able to cross the Atlantic again. But the opportunity came to me at last—it loomed before me one summer's day, in Quincy St. The best thing I could imagine then was to go and take up my abode in Paris."

By mid-November of 1875, when he was 32, he was settled in Paris, though England was to be his final residence. Meanwhile he had parted company with his family and the United States. How serious a step for him this was at the time we already plentifully know. And he was never able to contemplate it in later years without a sense of the extreme gravity of what he had done. As he had not been aimless in his choice, so he must not be aimless in acting on it. The purposive spirit of the James family—of his father's branch at any rate—still possessed him, as he would demonstrate. "I have made my choice," he later declared in his notebooks, "and God knows that I have now no time to waste."

The Tree of Knowledge

I T WAS clear from *Roderick Hudson*, which was still coming out in the *Atlantic* when James left America, that he expected to waste no time in his exile. That novel is a kind of portrait of the artist as a young man. Roderick is a diabolically gifted young sculptor who, taken by a wealthy friend to Rome for the sake of his artistic education, proceeds instead to indulge his passions and so degenerates and dies. Lively though it was for a first performance, *Roderick Hudson* is not much more than a museum-piece to the present-day reader, possessing some very good points but being dead in the center. Unfortunately for its central interest, it is a portrait of the kind of artist James did *not* wish to become and could not have become if he had wished. The novel is only too plainly an object lesson in the danger of converting artistic genius into a mere flair for adventurous living. The danger is always present (Roderick in Rome is strangely like Scott Fitzgerald in Paris); but James himself, one feels, had not sufficiently earned the right to his moral. Between the author and his turbulent native genius of a hero the absence of identity was complete. In Roderick's gigantic sculptures, his exploits in the Colosseum, his spectacular death in the Alps, James was being romantic about romanticism. This he was never to attempt again; instead he was to concern himself subtly with the subtler forms of self-indulgence. Furthermore, Roderick's violence prevents him, as a character, from getting into a convincing relation with his patron, Rowland Mallett, the mild conscientious New Englander who is the novel's second hero. If Roderick's temper was alien to James, Rowland's was only too congenial. As Eliot has said, "He too much identifies himself with Rowland, does not see through the solemnity he has created in that character, commits the cardinal sin of failing to 'detect' one of his own characters." This sin James had committed before and was to commit again, precisely with the Rowland type; for Rowland is his old self-doubting hero, who, like Roger Lawrence, decides he is incapable of marriage and so takes on a protégée instead—*adopts* life, as it were. But up to a point Rowland is explained, as the hero of *Watch and Ward* was not. In a charming preliminary sketch his negations are made part of the natural history of puritanism in America. And it is in such things, in its social portraiture, that *Roderick Hudson* anticipated James at his best. Northampton, where the novel opens, is solid; and the Roman studio society, with its varying types of artist and its formidable *esprit de corps*, is still solider.

Roderick's refusal to submit to the discipline of the studio world is one of the signs of his ruinous self-indulgence. James himself would have enjoyed such a society; but he was never really to find it, and least of all in France. Settled in "a snug little *troisième*" near the Place Vendôme, he spent the better part of a year in Paris, turn-

ing out travel letters for the New York *Tribune* and working on *The American*. That novel was to be the winning
product of a solemn and toilsome year. If exile "took its
toll" of James, as so many American critics have maintained, it did so in a fashion peculiar to conscientious exiles.
In his effort to be justified and to avoid the usual fate of
the wild goose, he drove himself almost too hard. He was a
new and peculiar kind of American, perhaps, but he was still
possessed by the stern ambassadorial sentiment of an older
generation of his traveling countrymen. Joseph in Egypt
could not have had a graver sense of his representative
character than James assumed in Paris. Democracy, the
tribal god, was still on trial before the world; and although
he was not pious about the god, and still less about the
tribe, he was powerfully attached to individual Americans,
those of his family above all, who continued to exemplify
for him the possibilities of the national character.

So in his exile he relaxed, if at all, into labor—the kind
of severe artistic labor to which Paris, as he felt, was so
much more favorable than Cambridge. "Your brother is
looking pretty well, but looks serious," C. S. Peirce, who
was then in Paris "swinging pendulums at the Observ-
atory," reported to William James. And although William, aware of Henry's old fondness for France, seems to
have been anxious lest it now impair his independence, he
need not have been. James himself was far from anxious,
at least on the side of himself that he showed to correspondents. He may have been somewhat less secure
within, but that can only be divined from a certain lingering tone of Brahmin touch-me-not in his letters, a habit of
trying to disinfect the incorrigibly alien, the formidably
real, by condescending to it. Of Flaubert, whom he

presently met, he wrote home that "there is something wonderfully simple, honest, kindly, and touchingly inarticulate about him"; but that "I think I easily—more than easily—see all round him intellectually." Towards everything French, in fact, his letters breathed a cool, almost a demure, reserve, much as they had done on his former visit when he had clung so exclusively to Lowell and the theater. There was a kind of eternal France, which he continued to love; and there was the France of the Third Republic, which in common with William he believed to be wallowing and foundering in its materialism. The congregated evidences of its great history and genius for enjoyment still attached him to Paris as they were always to do; and that city was never to become the scene of one of his stories without its taking on a preternatural glitter. That, however, was the Paris of his memories and desires— the ideal antithesis of his ideally uncivilized America. The actual Paris, the Paris of the gloomy Flaubert and the sceptical Renan; the Paris of swarming street crowds so vigilant of their pleasures and jealous of their interests; the Paris of which he wrote home that the passions of the Commune still worked below the surface—this Paris vexed and grieved a James to whom history considered as clash and change was ever a nightmare.

He was by no means solitary in his exile; he was rarely to be solitary. A passion for society, which almost overcame him later on in London, already showed itself in Paris. With some exceptions the Americans there, of whom he knew a good many, did not much appeal to him. They were too full of the exilic emptiness, as he was to show in the touching or amusing or sometimes terrible portraits of them in his novels. At the other extreme were the writers

who surrounded Flaubert, to whom he was introduced
shortly after his arrival. The Americans were excessively
gregarious; the Flaubert circle were too much shut up in
the mordant French mind. Great talkers and devoted pro-
fessionals though they were, the range of their interests
and sympathies was, he felt, fearfully narrow. George Eliot
they seemed never even to have heard of, not to mention
the other Anglo-Saxon writers and artists, dreams, and
causes which naturally meant so much to him. "I don't like
their wares, and they don't like any others," he at last
wrote to Howells. Yet, bitter though this sounded, he actually saw a good deal of Flaubert, Maupassant, the Gon-
courts, Zola; and became a close personal friend of Daudet
and later of Bourget. The legend that he was badly treated
by Flaubert's circle has been shown to have had no real basis
in fact; it probably came about as a result of the rather superior tone James himself was always to take towards *them*,
for literary and moral reasons. What they thought of him
at the time is not on record. A young and unknown American, he was still notably shy. He seems, however, to have
developed a habit of brilliant listening, interspersed with wry
comment, which made him a pleasant companion; and his
French was more than good, it was phenomenal. On the
whole he cannot have made much of an impression in
Paris; yet he attended several of Flaubert's weekly gatherings and once spent a long afternoon in solitary conversation with Flaubert, who talked of French verse and read him
a poem of Gautier's. Flaubert he always insisted that he
enjoyed personally ("a powerful, serious, melancholy,
manly, deeply corrupted yet not corrupting nature. There
was something I greatly liked in him, and he was very kind
to me"). But such sentiments were confined to his letters,

notebooks, and conversations. In reviewing Flaubert's published correspondence in 1893 he did not hesitate to affirm
that the author of *Madame Bovary* was "narrow and noisy,
and had not personally and morally, as it were, the great
dignity of his literary ideal." Had Flaubert been only half
the figure he was, this would still have been a gross failure
of understanding, as was the related charge that he had
never achieved "serenity." Among the inalienable rights
of man never quite recognized by the James family is the
right to be unhappy.

He had been introduced to Flaubert by Turgenev. And
his acquaintance with the Russian novelist was the great
human event of James's Paris year; even though, as we have
seen, he had also felt some concern over Turgenev's pessimism, distinguishing in an essay between his "spontaneous
melancholy" and his "wanton melancholy." This essay he
had sent to Turgenev, who, self-exiled in Paris like himself, received him kindly, made him known to his circle of
Russian émigrés, and confided freely his views and experiences as the representative of another as yet half-literate
race. Cosmopolitan and patriot, a gentleman as well as an
artist, Turgenev was far more congenial to James than were
the French writers of Flaubert's circle. But this was only
half the story. That Turgenev could relish their vehemence
and bohemianism where James could not, rather recommended him than otherwise. His charm was that he relished
almost everything, was serene with no apparent effort, and
decent in a way that involved surprisingly few repudiations.
It was "both strange and sweet," James wrote home, to see
him playing charades at the Sunday night parties of his
friend, Mme. Viardot, "dressed out in old shawls and
masks, going on all fours, etc. . . . . Fancy Longfellow, or

Lowell, or Charles Norton doing the like, and every Sunday evening." Having read *Roderick Hudson*, he observed that it was written *"de main de maître";* but although the two continued to meet after James had removed to London, James doubted that Turgenev ever really liked his work. "I do not think my stories quite struck him as meat for men." And after Turgenev's death James was to commemorate their acquaintance in one of his warmest essays. "He felt and understood the opposite sides of life; he was imaginative, speculative, anything but literal. He had not in his mind a grain of prejudice as large as the point of needle. . . . Our Anglo-Saxon, Protestant, moralistic, conventional standards were far away from him, and he judged things with a freedom and spontaneity in which I found a perpetual refreshment."

James's residence in France came to an end late in 1876 when, encouraged by William, he removed to England, there to make his home for the rest of his life. But although he had quitted Paris, he had not finished with the French mind, which, because it does our dirty work for us and does it so artfully, remains a problem to any foreigner who has conscientiously exposed himself to it. James exposed himself to it to the limit of his conscience—as freely as any considerable American had done since the days of Jefferson. This he did, however, more through his reading than by his actual residence there; and his sense of French life, his wariness in Paris, very likely reflected his judgment of contemporary French letters, about which his mind seems to have been made up before he ever left the United States. He had, as we know, already written extensively on the subject; and he had written as one who in this fashion was helping to define his own literary position. He seems, in short, to have struck a kind of bargain with himself whereby he should be allowed certain advantages of French culture in return for making certain rejections.

In the way of urbanity, detachment, and documented seriousness, the prevailing French realism had much to offer him. It was substantial and, in Flaubert at best, it was also beautiful. But James found the older forms of it more to his purpose. An entire chapter of French life owed its literary immortality to the all-mastering Balzac; whereas the present generation, whose doctrine of Naturalism was still the scandal of Europe, were as yet an embattled coterie. Thus James's ambition, which was never small, would conceivably have worked against his acceptance of the doctrine even if it had not been antipathetic on other grounds. But the grim art of the necessary—the beautifully grim art as it was to seem to later generations of Americans —was calculated to offend him philosophically as well as personally. His temperamental dislike of its sensual and plebeian aspects are what is usually stressed by his critics; and these are not to be denied. Hawthorne's disgust with the nude sculptures of Italy, a disgust which James thought provincial, lived on in his own distaste for a literature of poverty, prostitutes, and adventurers. The strange poetry of it, and its importance as criticism, were largely lost on him. He could be amused, especially when he was writing home to the less initiated Howells: "As editor of the austere *Atlantic* it would startle you to hear some of their projected subjects. The other day Edmond de Goncourt (the best of them) said he had been working very well on his novel—he had got upon an episode that greatly interested him, and into which he was going very far. *Flaubert:*

'What is it?' E. de G.: 'A whorehouse *de province.*' "
But his distaste generally prevailed over his amusement; and
even his later essays on the French school, written when
he had acquired his mature critical tolerance and wonderful powers of statement, were compromised by a surviving
reserve. In this respect he was to fail to *"ériger en lois ses
impressions personnelles,"* as Remy de Gourmont declared
that a critic should; and the failure left him a somewhat unreliable judge of Continental realism. On this subject he was sometimes to mistake deliberate satire for
mere ill-nature; to venture such hearty Howellsian as-
sertions as that "when all is said and done, art is most in
character when it most shows itself amiable"; and to
violate his own cherished critical principle that a writer
must be granted his premises.

James's own novels were to express very much better
his differences with the French mind, as well as all that he
had learned from it. He could there erect his personal impressions, not into laws, but into images—and notably into
human images, for it was his peculiar greatness, as Van
Wyck Brooks has observed, that he was "able to conceive
personalities of transcendent value." As an essayist, and
especially on French subjects, he was touched by that
academic humanism and ready-made classicism of the cultivated American who expects literature to be at all times
in the full-dress of its courtly prime. A much livelier
humanism entered into *The American* as into all the best
fiction of James's first great creative phase. This phase we
may now stop to consider as a whole, since it developed independently of his movements at the time. Important
though England was to his present comfort and future

career, his residence there did not greatly affect his work till this first period was concluded.

This was the period of the "international subject," as James himself seems to have been the first to call it. Generally speaking, it was inaugurated, as we have seen, by "A Passionate Pilgrim" (1871) and exhausted—for the time being—by *The Portrait of a Lady* (1880), though it continued to yield small occasional results throughout the '80's and the '90's. The American in contact with Europeans was his fine unique theme; and he rode it hard, treating it now briefly, now at length, now lightly, now seriously—acting, in short, the experimentalist that his family training and present independence of mind prescribed.

Roderick Hudson was a brave plunge; *The American* (1876) was a success—the most exuberant of the international stories. It too was "romantic," though in a fashion that was closer to James's mature mind—which is to say that it was occasionally arbitrary in its incidents and idealizations. Neither Christopher Newman, the so scrupulous California promoter, nor the blackguardly Bellegardes, his opponents of the Faubourg Saint-Germain, will withstand the gaze of the stricter realist; they did not—especially the Bellegardes—withstand the scrutiny of the later James. Yet *The American* differed from his more mature work only in the degree, not in the kind, of its commitment to romance. That rich self-made Americans were capable of the most delicate conduct was to remain one of his premises: he was anti-Naturalist, an apostle of the gratuitous, before André Gide. And if the Bellegardes are no more than cleverly executed pawns, Newman himself is very persuasive within his convention. Constance Rourke was probably right in observing that James was in debt to American popular humor for his long, lean, shrewd, and indomitably innocent hero; but the humor of *The American* is also the product of an extreme refinement of language and control of tone.

> He had a relish for luxury and splendor, but it was satisfied by rather gross contrivances. He scarcely knew a hard chair from a soft one, and he possessed a talent for stretching his legs which quite dispensed with adventitious facilities. His idea of comfort was to inhabit very large rooms, have a great many of them, and be conscious of their possessing a number of patented mechanical devices—half of which he should never have occasion to use. The apartments should be light and brilliant and lofty; he had once said that he liked rooms in which you wanted to keep your hat on. For the rest, he was satisfied with the assurance of any respectable person that everything was "handsome." Tristram accordingly secured for him an apartment to which this epithet might be lavishly applied. It was situated on the Boulevard Haussmann, on a first floor, and consisted of a series of rooms, gilded from floor to ceiling a foot thick, draped in various light shades of satin, and chiefly furnished with mirrors and clocks. Newman thought them magnificent, thanked Tristram heartily, immediately took possession, and had one of his trunks standing for three months in his drawing-room.

In *Roderick Hudson*, as Eliot has noted, James had been "consciously humorizing" in imitation of Hawthorne. *The American* is really funny, with James's characteristic comedy of social observation. And there are in it several further signs of a newly born confidence and mastery. For one thing, the story has much more the air of telling itself; we get the circumstances of it as they are experienced by the characters; the facts are less to be distinguished from their appearances. James is far from his later experiments in extreme subjectivity; he has merely discovered the art of narration. And with this his language becomes more concrete and the metaphors begin to flow. For another thing, the Rowland type is in abeyance in *The American*. If he is present at all, he has shrunk to the proportions of a Mr. Babcock, the querulous Yankee clergyman whom Newman encounters on his travels; and the withering away, or the "detection," of this type—of the anxious auctorial ego, in other words—is nearly always to be a sign of well-being on James's part. Christopher Newman, robustly simple as he appears, really owes his vividness as a character to his being a rich composite of various Jamesian strains. Possessed of the high principles of Rowland along with the animal spirits of Roderick, he unites two psychological types which James was elsewhere apt to set in opposition. And in his capacity as a mythic American, Newman, with his symbolic name, combines two opposing aspects under which James tended to see his fellow-countrymen. He is the American considered as *novus homo*, social upstart; and he is the new humanity produced by American democracy, "man himself unqualified by convention," to quote the elder James's Newport oration.

"You're the great Western Barbarian," Mrs. Tristram tells him, "stepping forth in his innocence and might, gazing a while at this poor corrupt old world and then swooping down on it." But what does this amiable Tamburlaine require of the old world? Not "experience" in the usual Jamesian sense. Newman has no misgivings on this score; he believes his life to have been so remarkable as to deserve some splendid sequel. It is the heroic side of the native complacency that James has caught in Newman, so perfectly self-satisfied that he can afford to be open-minded. His long legs, a little alarming to others, are a great comfort to himself; and his drily figurative idiom accommodates him like a much-used saddle. Nor is he in pursuit of culture like certain of James's Americans. A diffident if hard-working tourist, he remains as quaintly inaccessible to the arts as he was on his arrival in Paris, when, richer than a prince of the Renaissance but less happy in his taste, he was discovered ordering from a wretched girl-painter copies of the six biggest paintings in the Louvre.

> "We've one more to choose. Shouldn't you like one of those great Rubenses—the Marriage of Marie de Médicis? Just look at it and see how handsome it is."
> "Oh yes; I should like that," he allowed. "Finish off with that."
> "Finish off with that—good!" she laughed.

What Newman really wants of Europe, as he confides to Mrs. Tristram, is the perfect wife, some supreme product of old world civilization; and Mrs. Tristram is glad to introduce him to Claire de Cintré of the grand but nearly impoverished Bellegarde family. Yet although Mme. de Cintré is exactly what Newman has had in mind, and they come to love one another, he does not win her. Rather than defy her mother, who objects to her marriage with this "commercial person" (James later noted that in reality the Bellegardes "would positively have jumped at . . . my rich and easy American"), she becomes a nun, claimed by the old world institution of the Convent as her adventurous brother Valentin, who had dreamed of making his fortune in America with Newman's aid, is claimed by that of the Duel. Left to himself, Newman makes a delicate choice which marks him as something more than the natural he has been so far. He has come into possession of an incriminating document with which he might easily disgrace the Bellegardes and so avenge the loss of Claire. But he burns the paper; he waives revenge. This he does in no spirit of forgiveness, which, as James was to explain in the preface, "would have, in the case, no application." Newman, he went on to remark, "would simply turn, at the supreme moment, away, the bitterness of his personal loss yielding to the very force of his aversion. All he would have at the end would be therefore just the moral convenience, indeed the moral necessity, of his practical, but quite unappreciated, magnanimity." There are difficulties in life, he further said, from which the only issue is by "forfeiture."

As *The American* defied conventional realism in certain respects, so it disappointed the expectation of the happy ending. That expectation was more insistent in James's day than in our own; and by failing to gratify it he earned a good many reproaches. Even the friendly Howells, who had published the novel in the *Atlantic*, wrote to protest; and James, while firmly defending himself, promised the *Atlantic* another story which should better satisfy its readers. That story, as it turned out, was *The Europeans: A Sketch* (1878), which varied the usual scheme of these stories by bringing foreign characters to America, and which concluded with no fewer than *three* happy marriages. Even then James failed to please his countrymen. To Higginson, as we have seen, the novel was weak or false in its local realism; and it says a good deal about William's tastes that he found it insignificant. James's reaction to his brother's criticism was curious. "I was much depressed on reading your letter by your painful reflections on *The*

Europeans; but now, an hour having elapsed, I am beginning to hold up my head a little; the more so as I think I myself estimate the book very justly and am aware of its extreme slightness. I think you take these things too rigidly and unimaginatively—too much as if an artistic experiment were a piece of conduct, to which one's life were somehow committed; but I think also that you're quite right in pronouncing the book 'thin' and empty. I don't at all despair, yet, of doing something fat." Surely he conceded too much. *The Europeans* was so successful an "experiment" that the word scarcely applies; and if it was "slight," then so was, say, Jane Austen, whose stories it somewhat resembles. At the very least it had something of which Poe alone among the American minds of the century could fully have appreciated the value: it was *clever*. It was clever, for example, in its use of local realism, Higginson notwithstanding. An unseasonable snowstorm, a muddy road, a stony pasture, a parlor full of steel engravings hung very high on the walls, a volume of Emerson lying beside the chair of an invalid woman—such small details serve as important witnesses. And in one respect James is skilled as Poe was not: in a refinement of the language and a stylization of the dialogue which render them still triumphantly fresh today. *The Europeans* goes beyond *The American* in all this and also in making the people vivid in their relations to one another. Newman overshadows everyone in his entourage; but in the later novel it is the group that matters.

The Europeans is the story of a New England family, the Wentworths, into whose charmed pastoral circle, established some miles from Boston, there intrude two European cousins seeking their fortunes. Reaching Boston amid a spring snowstorm, the Baroness Münster and her brother Felix Young are nearly destitute and extremely determined. They are welcomed by the Wentworths but they do not succeed in shattering the Wentworth solidarity, which thrives on an innocence as foursquare as their white Colonial house, as green and open as the surrounding meadows and orchards. They succeed only in confirming its modest power. Felix, more susceptible than his sister, succumbs to the Wentworth spell; and by marrying, as he does at last, the vaguely restless and unhappy Gertrude Wentworth and thus gratifying her desire for a life of travel and art and mild bohemianism, he actually rescues the family from possible disruption by this somewhat threatening daughter. On the other hand, the Baroness, who remains a schemer, however charming, is at last quietly expelled—or rather, thoroughly disgruntled, she expels herself—from this circle in which she can do herself no good and others no harm. The Wentworths, in short, are not only invincibly innocent; it is the delicately conveyed but essential irony of the novel that they are innocent in a fashion which quite excludes them from real experience; they are refined beyond the point of good and evil.

But there is in *The Europeans* another strain of irony, of which not the innocent but the more or less worldly are the objects: The Baroness herself and Robert Acton, a well-to-do bachelor of the Wentworth connection at whom she has set her cap. The Baroness is the stock figure of the adventuress which was always to fascinate James and which he would refurbish brilliantly in such characters as Mme. Merle of *The Portrait of a Lady* and Charlotte Stant of *The Golden Bowl*. The Baroness is refurbished in a different way from those imposing women. Although shown as really witty and fascinating, she is also adjusted to the spirit of *The Europeans* by being made ever so faintly comic. She is adjusted to the spirit of the story but not to the size of the Wentworths' world, and that is where the humor comes in. The Baroness is too big for the picture; her complicated nature, her grand manner, her passion for intrigue are incongruous with the New England simplicities. Above all she is betrayed into the mistake of fishing for Robert Acton, who is likewise insidiously comic, although in a different way. The wise older shepherd of this rural group, he has seen the world; he has stocked with the spoils of his travels the house which he shares with his invalid mother, who represents "a presence refined to such delicacy that it almost resolved itself, with him, simply into the subjective emotion of gratitude." Now Acton is naturally respected by the Wentworths; but the reader is little by little brought to feel that he is not all he seems, that he is something of a *pretender* to worldly experience, the sum of whose wisdom consists in an enlarged capacity for being suspicious. Like Winterbourne in *Daisy Miller* and Vanderbank in *The Awkward Age*, he is worried that the woman in question is not respectable. "She is not honest, she is not honest," he keeps murmuring to himself. "She is a woman who will lie." And he is perfectly right in this, as far as it goes. The Baroness is given to lying; it is as much a part of her brilliant "manner" as the blunt candor of the Wentworths is part of their spare civility. She indulges the habit even in the sacred presence of Acton's mother, whom she wishes to flatter. "The Baroness turned her smile toward him, and she instantly felt that she had been observed to be fibbing. She had struck a false note. But who were these people to whom such fibbing was not pleasing?" Well, they are truthful people; and their instinct of honesty is none the less engaging for being an expression of their simple lives. Insofar as Acton abhors the Baroness's fibs he is being true to the New England sincerity; insofar as he makes it the issue in his rejection of her he is seeking excuses for avoiding an entanglement which his egoism, his prudence, and his attachment to his mother render embarrassing in any case. Walking beside her down the road, " 'By Jove, how *comme il faut* she is!' he said, as he observed her sidewise." He has never observed her any way but sidewise, and it is no wonder that on her departure from America he feels a rueful impulse "to offer a handsome present to the Baroness."

The gentle Wentworths did not establish James's reputation; it took the more spectacular Daisy Miller to do that. Meanwhile *The Europeans* was published in England as well as America; and James, extremely busy as nearly always, was continuing to write criticism. His acquaintance among writers and artists—American, French, English —was already large; and although he was directly influenced by very few authors past or present, he did have an abundance of vivid literary relations. These he was in the habit of munificently commemorating in his essays. He had his occasions and he rose to them; and the warmth of his commitments redeems even his poorer performances, like those on the French realists. Besides, he was coming to be the imaginative writer in his essays, as he was the social critic in his novels. The writing itself, the flow of witty remark, the power of definition, is notable. Even

Eliot, who allows James no importance as a formal critic,* finds him full of "charming talk."

But Hawthorne gave him the best occasion of all and he rose to it appropriately. The small book James wrote about him for the English Men of Letters Series (1879) is perfect of its sort and its sort is rare. A kind of hail and farewell to Hawthorne and his New England age, it is both tender and urbane. Its scholarship was weak even for its time (all frankly taken from Lathrop's biography, including the plot of *Fanshawe*, which James says he didn't bother to read). The estimate of Hawthorne has also been challenged many times: it is carrying urbanity rather far to assert that the author of *The Scarlet Letter* had "no general views in the least uncomfortable." Still, if James oversimplifies he does not falsify; even the chilly side glances at Emerson and Thoreau leave those writers intact; they are judged rather unfavorably but they are not unjustly defined, and so it is with Hawthorne himself. To appreciate him very much but within clearly defined limits, as James did, was better than to appreciate him, as is sometimes done, within no limits at all; and the book remains a persuasive portrait. Hawthorne, one thinks, would have recognized himself in it.

The book reads casually but was, as James wrote Howells, who objected to certain of its conclusions, "a tolerably deliberate and meditated performance, and I should be prepared to do battle for most of the convictions expressed." It represents a skilled impressionism in the service of a distinct emotion. New England is seen as

---

* Or didn't in 1918 when his excellent essays on James were published.

"little," "old," "dusky," and tending to be wintry: *Haw-thorne* is a *cold* pastoral. It is nevertheless full of charming scenes: Hawthorne skating alone on frozen Sebago, poring over a book of Flaxman's drawings in the Salem parlor of the Peabody sisters, boating with Thoreau on the Concord River. Certain clear provocations were included for the benefit of the more pious reader. A lengthy catalogue— echoing a similar list in Hawthorne's preface to *The Marble Faun*—numbers "the elements of high civilization, as it exists in other countries, which are absent from the tex-ture of American life." "No sovereign, no court, no personal loyalty, no aristocracy, no church, no clergy," James be-gins, and after running through a dozen more items, con-cludes with "no sporting class—no Epsom nor Ascot!" In the absence of all these things, James asks, what is left? And Howells, answering in all seriousness in a review, said, "Why, simply the whole of human life." But the catalogue was more than an impudent gesture. Such institutions rep-resented the pleasures and responsibilities of which Haw-thorne, as James believed, had been too much deprived. His talent had suffered as a result, and he had been in-dulged in his complacency, his "strain of generous indo-lence." Above all—and this was the main thing for James —Hawthorne's feeling for evil, although it happily distin-guished him from the Transcendentalists, expressed itself so much in fantasy and symbol as to suggest that he was excessively removed from actual experience.

The "moral," as James summed it up, "is that the flower of art blooms only where the soil is deep, that it takes a great deal of history to produce a little literature, that it needs a complex social machinery to set a writer in motion." Yet James is not engaged here in finding excuses for failure or pretexts for expatriation. *Hawthorne* is the picture of a too simple world which James knew had passed. The Civil War had abolished it and had in the process made "a great deal of history." The illusions of Hawthorne's generation "were rudely dispelled, and they saw the best of all possible republics given over to fratricidal carnage. This affair had no place in their scheme, and nothing was left for them but to hang their heads and close their eyes. The subsidence of that great convulsion has left a different tone from the tone it found, and one may say that the Civil War marks an era in the history of the American mind. It introduced into the national consciousness a certain sense of proportion and relation, of the world being a more complicated place than it had hitherto seemed, the future more treacherous, success more difficult. . . . the good American, in days to come, will be a more critical person than his complacent and confident grandfather. He has eaten of the tree of knowledge." James's historical sense was not often so explicit; but in this, too, he had his occasions.

In the summer of 1878, while *The Europeans* was failing to amuse the readers of the *Atlantic, Daisy Miller: A Study* was coming out with great success in the English *Cornhill*. It had been refused by an American publisher but was soon so famous that it was widely pirated in the United States before James could arrange for its legitimate publication. Described in the newspapers as "an outrage on American girlhood," the story was a success of scandal with the large American public; although the better critics, including Higginson, promptly recognized its justice and delicacy. In the long run the fame of *Daisy Miller* was to be a vexation to James. Reviewers were constantly to cite it as a touchstone; and none of his stories, except perhaps "The Turn of the Screw," was to equal it in popularity. Meanwhile the excitement was gratifying, especially because it spread to the English public; and henceforth James's books were to be issued more or less simultaneously in both countries. On a small scale, then, *Daisy Miller* was an international event, and it established the importance of the international subject. It also vindicated, for the moment, his methods of economy and suggestion in the telling of a story—methods which appealed so little to a public accustomed to the Victorian abundance that he took the precaution of calling *The Europeans* "a sketch" and *Daisy Miller* "a study." Today the precaution seems unnecessary. *Daisy Miller*, a mere ninety pages of finely observed incident, has become part of the American experience.

It is both a love story and a story of comparative manners. Projected through a single mind in a stricter way than James has yet attempted, it is also a story of reality and appearance. The mind is that of Frederick Winterbourne, a young American long resident in Europe, whose doubts concerning Daisy's innocence in an equivocal situation influence the reader's sense of her worth and modify her own behavior. Daisy is lightly sketched, but in one thing she is more formidable than any figure James has yet drawn. This is her effect on the reader, which, thanks to Winterbourne's mediumship, is teasingly uncertain, admitting of ironic as well as lyric overtones. The latter are the more obvious. A kind of admiration of the misguided girl comes through strongly at last; and it is all the more poignant because it has come in spite of odds, because it has been so long in coming, because it has not come fully till she is dead. Surely it is her death that puts the final seal on her charm, and quite apart from anything heroic in the manner of it. She is dead in her youth and wealth and prettiness and *nil nisi bonum. . . .* So interpreted, Daisy is a tribute to the American girl, whose radical innocence is shown to triumph over the evil-mindedness of the old world as well as over her own rash conduct and indifferent manners. She is a champion, however unconscious, of the assumptions and immunities of her kind, a forerunner of Carol Kennicott. And in this light the great question of the story is whether she is innocent in the "technical" sense, for her ways are deceptively free and flirtatious, and she runs about Rome with a dubious native in defiance of the system of curfews and chaperons which the American colony holds dear. Even Winterbourne, who is half in love with her, as she is entirely in love with him, comes at last to suppose she is really bad. But after her death Giovanelli, her shady Italian friend, resolves the mystery in her favor. She has been guilty of nothing worse than "doing what she liked." In her instinctive way she has demonstrated—almost with her life—a point of morality, vindicated the individual against the group, the spirit against the letter. She has established the doctrine, so intrinsic to native Americanism, that human nature is guiltless till proved otherwise. The Europeanized Americans of her acquaintance, as Roman as the Romans if not more so, assume the contrary theory of human nature, the more astringent one on which traditional morals and manners rest. Judging her morals by her manners, they imagine the worst and they ostracize her. They are wrong. Winterbourne most of all is wrong. "I was booked to make a mistake," he says when it is too late. "I have lived too long in foreign parts." He has not only misjudged Daisy, he has made the mistake of judging where he should have loved.

For certain readers the very setting of the major incidents gives weight to this construction of the tale. Italy, Rome, the Colosseum where Daisy, like a new martyr to the Spirit, contracts her fatal fever—such scenes had of course deadly associations for the American libertarian mind, in whose processes James was able to share at least imaginatively.* Yet within *Daisy Miller* as within *The Europeans* there are unmistakable though never insistent ironies, ironies that swim there like small gleams of welcome light to clarify, rather than annihilate, the more apparent meanings. And one of these is precisely the manner of Daisy's death, which, looked at closely, is no martyrdom. All Rome knows the Colosseum to be unwholesome by night. Daisy's death, if it proves anything, proves that not every superstition is a fraud. And Daisy herself clearly suffers as a person from the absence in her life of those very traditions for which she cares so little and of which the American colony undoubtedly makes too much. She fails to "compose," as James would say, because as a social being she is without a form and a frame. She has no sense of the inevitable—which was what traditions and taboos, conventions and manners finally signified to James when we discount his merely temperamental conservatism—and without this feeling for the limits of life she can scarcely be said to be fully alive. Her forerunner Newman is one of

* A horror of Rome as the capital of superstitious orthodoxy was strong in the elder James; and in 1873 when William and Henry were there together, they made a frightening moonlight visit to the Colosseum, which William described as "that damned blood-soaked soil," remarking of Italy in general that "the weight of the past world here is fatal."

"nature's noblemen," as someone remarks in *The American;* and he is presented as almost entirely admirable. Even his terrible taste in paintings somehow recommends him; and his manners, rough Californian though he is, conform by some magic to those of the best Parisian society. Daisy Miller is Nature construed in a more sceptical mood. Like that of the field flower she is named for, her very prettiness is more generic than individual. Extremely imprudent and somewhat callow, even on occasion rude by any standard, she has within her a strange little will, which, when it is thwarted by Winterbourne's defection, turns rather easily into a will to die. "She did what she liked!" her two lovers agree when they meet beside her grave; and the words are not all eulogy. She does what she likes because she hardly knows what else to do. Her will is at once strong and weak by reason of the very indistinctness of her general aims. Her love for Winterbourne, the one clear impulse of her nature, is itself perfectly helpless. He says ruefully at the end that "she would have appreciated one's esteem"; to which his tough-minded aunt replies: "She took an odd way to gain it!" Like her sassy and not very amusing younger brother, like her mother who has no resource in life except to be always ill, like her father who is out of the picture somewhere making more money, Daisy inhabits a human vacuum created equally by a large fortune and no commitments, much freedom and little use for it.

The story is not, then, altogether a tribute to the American girl. It is also addressed critically to the *sentiment* of the American girl, and of American "innocence" generally —the kind of sentiment which, as James was aware, frequently did duty for realism in the native mind. The legend of American innocence is not denied by the story; it is only shown to be possibly irrelevant or obsolescent from any larger point of view. As the simple probity of the Wentworths is defined by the charmed enclosure of their provincial existence; so that of Daisy is incompatible with her survival and is in fact certified only by her death.

It should be noted, however, that Daisy is a product neither of Boston nor of old New York, both of which places contributed very different types of heroine to James's work. A daughter of the provincial plutocracy—Schenectady in process of taking over New York—she is the American girl of the future. The American girl was as various as Minny Temple herself had been, and James was to follow up *Daisy Miller* with a long series of such heroines, ingeniously altering their traits and implications from tale to tale. "An International Episode," "The Pension Beaurepas," "A Bundle of Letters," "The Patagonia," *The Reverberator*— all tell of American girls whose free spirits bring them into some sort of trouble with the world of fact, which world is usually represented by Europe or Europeans. And it is natural to wonder why James, who had done the remarkable portrait of Newman, should have gone in more and more for feminine protagonists. He was, he tells us, only meagerly acquainted with the "Downtown" experience, the medium of business and industry. This is a good excuse but it is only an excuse. The deeper reason was no doubt his own exceptional identification with the feminine mind, which had probably originated in his childhood relation to his mother. If this flattered too much his notion that the Downtown world was ineffably "other," hopelessly closed to him—so that as he grew older he was to find it increasingly difficult to imagine lively masculine figures in the center of things—it also accounted for the growing subtlety and power which he concentrated in his feminine portraits. But American conditions also abetted him. With the men so much at work and the women left to care for the amenities, the United States constituted, as he once said, "a society of women in a world of men." If this is hardly the case any more, if "a world of women in a world of men with little enough society anywhere" would better describe the present situation, the rightness of James's observation for his own time is attested by countless other witnesses. And no doubt the predominance of the one sex represented a cultural weakness in the age as it did an idiosyncrasy in James's work. He overcame it to a large extent by the very intensity of his affinity with women—an intensity which Howells, for example, lacked in anything like the same degree. Except that the powers that finally distinguished him, the eloquence and energy and subtlety, belong rather to undifferentiated genius than to either sex, James might be called the great feminine novelist of a feminine age in letters. In any case he was able, without being at all doctrinaire about it, to imagine women, not as a distinct species with peculiar problems, as they had nearly always been presented by novelists, but as typical of human possibilities in general. In their relatively greater freedom from material pressures they figured for him the pleasures and responsibilities of freedom in whatever sex or condition of society. Even so robust a male figure as Newman is incomplete until he shows himself capable at last of the feminine self-denial.

If all this was untrue of the small Daisy Miller, it was the case with the more impressive heroines of James's maturer works, of whom Isabel Archer of *The Portrait of a Lady* was the first. James, it was said, conceived "personalities of transcendent value." Isabel Archer is one of these, a figure in the tradition of Rosalind and Portia, Elizabeth Bennet and Dorothea Brooke. Unsophisticated as she is at the beginning and fine as she remains throughout, her innocence, if the word is even relevant in her case, is a function of her intelligence and is capable of surviving the ordeals of actual experience.

Beginning in October, 1880, *The Portrait of a Lady* ran almost simultaneously in the *Atlantic* and *Macmillan's Magazine*, and was a considerable success in both countries from the start. Twice the length of anything James had so far attempted, the novel is well named: it is supremely devoted to portraiture. There are some ten major characters as well as many minor ones; and just as Isabel is James's American girl raised to a new power, so Osmond, the Touchetts, Lord Warburton, and the rest are familiar Jamesian types elaborated now to the last degree. His increasing command of narrative appears in his easy shifting from the epic spirit of the first half—in which Isabel invades and conquers the old world—to the dramatic mood of the second half, where she writhes in an old world that has turned into a sort of Hell. And all this is laid before the reader in a prose that is at once flexible and stately, alert equally to the lyrical and the humorous implications of what is going on—such a prose as had rarely been known before in fiction in English.

James's intimate associations, so often a source of power, seem to have been uncommonly active in him while he was writing the *Portrait*. Isabel herself, for all her kinship to the Anglo-Saxon heroine, is clearly a tribute to the memory of Minny Temple, and so thorough a one that Minny's ghost was laid for years to come. An orphan like Minny, Isabel sails serenely out of what is plainly the ancestral Albany house of the James family; and what Minny had dreamed of doing Isabel actually does: journeys to Europe, encounters experience, lives. Among the men who surround her, two could clearly have been related to James himself. Her cousin Ralph Touchett, between whom and Isabel there is more love than he in his invalid state and resigned detachment knows what to do with, was perhaps James's idea of what he had actually been to Minny Temple; while the terrible Osmond, esthete and snob, on whose too refined nerves Isabel preys in spite of herself, represented the kind of husband he fearfully fancied he might have made had he actually married Minny.

Indeed marriage as a reality figures more conspicuously in the *Portrait* than in any novel of James's so far. Much as the European scene colors and qualifies Isabel's adventures, they are strictly concerned with her finding a husband and then trying to live with him. If she is a kind of Elizabeth Bennet, she is one who operates on a world scale. In America she has already discouraged the ambitious New England manufacturer, Caspar Goodwood, who is much too possessive in his attentions to her. And it should be said of Goodwood in passing that he is the least fortunate of James's creations in the *Portrait*. Something of a Christopher Newman, only stiffer and grimmer, he is not adequately developed; and the plot, which requires that he be jockeyed in and out of Isabel's life like a wooden Indian on wheels, succeeds only in making him look superfluous. Goodwood is rich and Isabel is poor, and her refusal of him promptly qualifies her as an adventurous girl with high expectations of life. She thus earns, so to speak, her right to be whisked away to Europe, as she presently is, by her

Aunt Touchett in the guise of fairy godmother. The Touchetts, though of American origin, live in great splendor in
England, where Mr. Touchett has long been in business;
but, never entirely assimilated by English life, they are
faintly bored, so that the spirited Isabel is quite as much of
a blessing to them as they are to her. They are finely conceived both as individuals and in their relation to one
another. Mr. Touchett's immense success in England has
not impaired his native probity; but he has suffered much
through his wife and son. Mrs. Touchett, who maintains
her separate establishment in Italy, might have been one of
the Roman hostesses who forbade Daisy their drawing-
rooms. Her American rectitude has turned into an intense
observance of social distinctions and proprieties. Her own
view of herself, and she is proud of her clairvoyance, would
be that she is not a snob but a realist; and in a narrow
sense she is right. Her son, Ralph, on the other hand, who
is more devoted to his father than to her, is so imaginative, so full of his father's goodness and sentiment, but so
deficient in his father's sense of purpose (he is after all
the sole prospective heir of millions) that he is obliged to
wear the double mask of the invalid and the cynic. He is
pretty clearly in love with Isabel from the start, but as James
once said of himself, he thinks too little of life ever to contemplate marriage. As for Isabel, her intelligence is as yet a
little literal and for a long time she takes his scoffing manner
at its face value.

And anyway she is otherwise concerned. She has another
suitor, who is the perfection of the English type as Goodwood is (or is supposed to be) of the American. Lord Warburton is the master of a vast property adjoining that of

the Touchetts; every advantage of money, position, beauty, kindliness is his, and in addition he has imagination enough to be a radical in politics and to fall in love with Isabel. This fairy prince promptly makes her an offer, which she promptly and strangely refuses. "Strangely" because her reasons, which seem merely perverse to her aunt, are not very clear to herself. But they are clear to Ralph and his father, who, free spirits themselves, are also more conscious than she. They understand that marriage with Warburton would be too safe and easy for such a girl. They correctly judge her spirit, but they overestimate her shrewdness. The considerable fortune which Mr. Touchett, who now falls ill and dies, has been persuaded by Ralph to leave to Isabel in order to make her free in fact as well as in spirit, turns out to be her curse.

"The idea of the whole thing," James wrote in his notebook, "is that the poor girl, who has dreamed of freedom and nobleness, who has done, as she believes, a generous, natural, clear-sighted thing [in refusing Warburton], finds herself in reality ground in the very mill of the conventional." By way of a Mme. Merle, her aunt's ancient friend, she passes from the amiable security of the Touchett-Warburton circle into the company of adventurers. She at first thinks them merely *adventurous*, and this is what recommends them to her. Mme. Merle, whom Ralph sees as a too accomplished parasite, is admired by Isabel as an instance of the fine art of living, as a true woman of the world. And Isabel is even more terribly mistaken in Gilbert Osmond, to whom Mme. Merle introduces her, and whom she marries. With Osmond it is *Pride and Prejudice* in reverse: Isabel begins with a predilection in his *favor*, and only in time discovers that he is a monster, infinitely more cynical than Ralph, infinitely more conventional than Warburton.

"They were strangely married, at all events, and it was a horrible life." So Isabel reflects when she has been Osmond's wife for only a few years. At his wish they have gone to live in Rome, in an enormous gilded palace where they entertain a great deal, Osmond seeing to it that only the best society is received. And lingering one night "in the soundless saloon after the fire had gone out," Isabel reviews her life with Osmond—her past disenchantments, her anxiety for the future—in a prolonged reverie which is one of the fine things in James:

> She could live it over again, the incredulous terror with which she had taken the measure of her dwelling. Between those four walls she had lived ever since; they were to surround her for the rest of her life. It was the house of darkness, the house of dumbness, the house of suffocation. Osmond's beautiful mind gave it neither light nor air; Osmond's beautiful mind indeed seemed to peep down from a small high window and mock at her. Of course it had not been physical suffering; for physical suffering there might have been a remedy. She could come and go; she had her liberty; her husband was perfectly polite. He took himself so seriously; it was something appalling. Under all his culture, his cleverness, his amenity, under his good-nature, his facility, his knowledge of life, his egotism lay hidden like a serpent in a bank of flowers.

Gilbert Osmond was James's first notable study in modern perversity. So far as his role in the plot of the *Portrait* goes, Osmond, as we presently learn, is still the stock conspirator of melodrama, although in the circumstances his conspiracy is not too implausible. He has however an independent richness of being which shows, among other things, how far James has been able to go beyond Hawthorne in this respect. Osmond—who inevitably makes the Judge Pyncheons and Chillingworths of Hawthorne look somewhat waxy—was the reward of a searching knowledge of latter-day predicaments, including the author's own. He is also a good instance of how James used his international experience for wider ends. Osmond suffers even more than Winterbourne from having lived too long in foreign parts. A moral half-caste, he is determined to deny his American origins, while his very individuality makes it impossible for him to become a genuine Continental. There are "no conservatives like American conservatives," as Warburton justly remarks; and, like those renegade Yankees in *The American* who sit happily in the Champs Élysées and count the royal carriages, Osmond can only ape and envy the local pomp, can only evolve for himself a caricature of European *noblesse*. But he is very much more of a person than Tom Tristram. In Osmond, James portrayed, ironically of course, a good many of the possibilities of the eternal American reactionary: his personal dandyism, his exaggerated devotion to refined pleasures, his proud connoisseurship, his social and esthetic snobbishness which cannot afford to temper itself with the European *noblesse oblige*, his ancestor-worship, his rage for the static, his luxurious joy in the possession of a general theory—pessimistic of course—of human nature. "He had an immense esteem for tradition; he had told her once that the best thing in the world was to have it, but that if one was so unfortunate as not to have it one must immediately proceed to make it." Inevitably he admires, from his connoisseur's viewpoint, the Church: " 'The Catholics are very wise after all. The convent is a great institution; we can't do without it; it corresponds to an essential need in families, in society. It's a school of good manners; it's a school of repose.' " And he has had his daughter Pansy brought up by nuns so that she shall become the perfection of the old world *jeune fille.*

To Isabel, who once rejoiced in it, Osmond's wisdom has become a torment, spoken as it is with his peculiar unction and the slow complacent shake of his small foot. "He was fond of the old, the consecrated, the transmitted; so was she, but she pretended to do what she chose with it." His conservative pose is the antithesis of the rational, the elected, thing Isabel had originally thought it to be. She likes "systems," by which she means ways of life adopted and lived for high experimental purposes. It is in this that she remains so American. But Osmond's is a system in the wrong sense, or it has become that in the course of years. For he is more than a timeless satiric picture of a social-political type. His mind is shown to have had a history and to have been subject to distortion depending on his circumstances. As his reactionary vehemence increases with his growing hatred of Isabel—an authentic free spirit is unendurable to him—so his marriage to her (as she, like the reader, gradually learns) was the culmination of a long development in him. He had begun, years before, by renouncing ordinary ambitions in favor of a connoisseur's exquisite if modest life. In this, we are to suppose, he was originally quite genuine. But in time he has come to resent more and more his self-imposed privations; his former conviction of superiority has given way by degrees to a rank but well-concealed envy of the rich and great; until it could be said of him, as Ralph Touchett says, that "under the guise of caring only for intrinsic values Osmond lived exclusively for the world." Alas, the real free spirits are not those who make a profession of it!

Isabel's fortune has at last permitted him to play the great man, and in itself this is not objectionable to her. Indeed she has married him in the fond and perhaps slightly pretentious delusion that she can assist him to a life of ease as he will assist her to one of supreme artistic enjoyment. That he married her *only* for her money Isabel has but recently come to suspect, when she sits down by the burntout fire to commune with herself. But she is to learn worse things about Osmond: that Pansy, whom Isabel supposes to be his child by a former marriage, is really the child of an ancient affair between Osmond and Mme. Merle; that Mme. Merle deliberately contrived Isabel's marriage to Osmond in the hope of improving Pansy's situation. These terrible truths are revealed to her in the course of the action which occupies the second and tenser half of the *Portrait.* The question here is also of a marriage; but this time it is Pansy's choice of a husband which is in doubt, for the Osmonds are at odds as to whether she shall make a "great marriage" or accept the insignificant man she happens to love. Thus James supplied Isabel and her husband with a definite field of action on which to develop their deadly moral differences, and thus he kept the marriage theme alive throughout the novel.

Marriage, then, is the axis on which the *Portrait* turns. Everyone in it is involved in some significant union or exhibits some meaningful attitude towards the institution, whether it is the confirmed bachelor Ralph Touchett or the seemingly confirmed feminist Henrietta Stackpole, Isabel's

American friend. Marriage, however, figures in the *Portrait* not as a specific social institution—as it does in, say, *A Doll's House*—but as a condition of existence—of Isabel's existence in particular.

In her energy and meaning, it must be admitted, Isabel is far from easy to reconstruct. One thing is certain: a kind of felicity attaches to her whatever she does. This James feels strongly and he makes us feel it. It consists partly in her delicate conviction of selfhood, a conviction which stops just short of self-importance. It is hers to begin with, but it matures considerably as she goes on. Indeed like the other Americans in the *Portrait* she is a *self*-seeker (Osmond and Mme. Merle are that in the usual sense as well); and it is what distinguishes the Americans, even the Europeanized Americans, from such a European *pur sang* as Warburton, whose identity is so largely defined by his inherited functions as head of the family, landlord, and member of the House of Lords. Warburton is enveloped by the serene charm of a man whose individual responsibility is necessarily qualified by his place in an established social order; he is congenitally unable to break into the American circle although he tries first with Isabel and later on with Pansy. Osmond and Mme. Merle are individuals become egoists, the corruption of the best; but they are real to Isabel as Warburton never is. And as Isabel is a true individual, so her friend Henrietta Stackpole is an individualist. The comic—and at last somewhat tiresomely comic —Henrietta is a journalist; in her view the free woman advertises her status by having a career. Nothing of the sort occurs to Isabel, fond as she is of improving herself through travel and reading. In fact she is enough of an individual to give expression to all the impulses in herself which are at odds with the theoretical New Woman. In her juvenile daydreams she had imagined herself, sometimes as the heroine in a rebel cause, more often as a martyred loyalist; and, as she playfully confesses to Ralph Touchett shortly after her arrival in England, she longs to behold the ghost which she feels certain must haunt even so pleasant a country seat as theirs. Despite her inexperience at this stage, amid all her expansive motions as a free American, she has, in other words, a premonition of the fact of evil and suffering, of the quantity of defeat that is involved in any success, of the necessary limitations of life. With all this Isabel is not unwilling to become more familiar, for she acknowledges it to be the substance of experience. Her career in Europe is thus a long process of escape from the native innocence, the innocence of imagining that you can do what you like, the innocence of inexperience.

If it is pursued honestly such a career threatens to end in a kind of tragedy, and Isabel's career does end in a kind of tragedy. She has saved Pansy from one unhappy union, but she has by no means assured the girl's marriage to the man she likes; and Osmond, thwarted and exposed, is now more Isabel's enemy than ever. She has further defied him by going to England to tend Ralph in his last illness; and there Goodwood appears and urges her to leave Osmond for him. "We can do absolutely as we please," he says in his liberal American way; "the world's all before us—and the world's very big." And seizing Isabel he forces a kiss on her— the only kiss in the novel. She feels the force of his passion: it occurs to her that she has never been loved before; yet she rejects his love as she does his argument. She is not Daisy Miller; and it is no longer her idea of life to do absolutely as she pleases. "The world's very small," she replies, and returns to Osmond. It is an austere decision but inescapable in the light of her character and quest. Not only is she still in a position to help Pansy, but the very suffering involved in her marriage has given it a kind of sanctity. It has been the means by which she has seen the ghost.

Pointing to some noisy girls in Venice, a friend once observed to James that those were the *real* Daisy Millers. It was a reproach: he had "idealized" his heroine. And he recorded the remark in his preface, in order to allow for the reproach but not to apologize. Newman, Mr. Touchett, and Isabel are idealized even more, in their moral intelligence, which is shown to withstand all provocation, as well as to be consistent with great wealth, much ambition, and in Newman's case a rather rowdy past as a Western promoter. All this certainly represents an extreme refinement of life; and it is a wonder that James can persuade us that his people live and suffer, they who have so little body, so few nerves, with which to register their experience, who never seem to "forfeit" anything of their inward composure, and whose heads are not only unbowed but unbloody. They have, to be sure, as many ways of being moral as they have of being American. The conscience of a Rowland Mallet is anxious, didactic, given to judgment of self and others. But in all the more luminous figures, it is a form of sensibility, a state of mind to which judgment is alien and goodness for goodness' sake immaterial. Intelligent without being intellectual, moral but not ethical, these men and women reflect hardly at all on conduct itself. The moral sense is for them a kind of chivalry. It belongs to them by virtue of their assumption of membership in a natural aristocracy, which in

Newman's case refers to his being an American but which in Isabel's is more nearly gratuitous. Nor do they, as we have said, acquire it in the usual school of suffering. In this respect their adversities are more symbolic than experiential. They are possessed of what Edmund Burke would have called "the unbought grace of life."

"They are only winged busts," says André Gide; "all the weight of the flesh is absent, all the shaggy, tangled undergrowth, all the wild darkness." And James himself seems to acknowledge the limitation, when, at the peril of retroactively compromising his portrait of Isabel, he shows her fleeing from Goodwood's kiss. With all his wider experience, James is more Puritan—if not simply less human—than Hawthorne, for whom, in *The Scarlet Letter*, the color of adultery is also the color of life-blood and of roses. In *The Bostonians* and a dozen other stories, he is presently to give us acid accounts of too highminded people; and sexual passion is to figure more and more prominently in his plots. But it will generally be associated with cruelty and corruption; it will nearly always constitute the extreme situation, a destructive element in which only the bad people immerse. In an age of insistent naturalism like ours, we tend thus to localize James's limitation in his suspicion of sex. Almost any age would be likely to see the same problem, although in terms less specific. Presumably Gide's "wild darkness" is itself a more inclusive description, embracing all the passions. With so little knowledge of these, we may say, James's heroes are but imperfectly tempted. Their moral intelligence, for which he makes such claims in his prefaces, is something taken for granted.

Yet the wild darkness is notoriously the source of a false profundity in many writers. And in this respect as in others

James knew how to make his limitations serve him. When things are absent from his work they are not furtively but conspicuously absent. It means something that they are not there. And Gide is surely mistaken when he goes on to say of the characters that "they are desperately mundane" because "they never live except in relation to each other." It is just in their relations that they live so bravely and are so little mundane. That is their peculiar strength, their vital dimension. Isabel's energy, if it is not that of sex, is that of sympathy, and it is immense. But the interdependence of the characters is also part of James's economy of structure. Eliot's account of this is classic. "Done in a clean, flat drawing, each [character] is extracted out of a reality of its own, substantial enough; everything given is true for that individual; but what is given is chosen with great art for its place in a general scheme. The general scheme is not one character, nor a group of characters in a plot or merely in a crowd. The focus is a situation, a relation, an atmosphere, to which the characters pay tribute, but being allowed to give only what the writer wants. The real hero, in any of James' stories, is a social entity of which men and women are constituents."

Apart from his family, there was no such social entity in James's own experience. It existed hardly more in modern Europe, as he discovered, than in America, although the former was at least full of the ghosts of it. He had therefore to invent his own social atmosphere. It is none the less persuasive; and if, in his early work, he encourages his people to discover their limits, that is his tribute to sociability rather than to any metaphysic of the human condition. In his pioneering biography, *The Pilgrimage of Henry James*, Van Wyck Brooks summed up the early work as presenting "the struggle for the rights of personality—the central theme of all modern American fiction." Such a view of James was natural to a man writing in the prime of Sinclair Lewis and Sherwood Anderson, to a man intent on praising the early as against the later work in support of his contention that James's prolonged exile impaired his force. On one of his sides James *was* such a critic of modern life as Lewis and Anderson have been; and this is as important a side as any other. The pursuit of larger existences is a regular ritual with his characters. He is one of the chief novelists of the present-day mobility, the intrinsic restlessness. The oppression of dull years, the dread of missed chances and lost identities, the horror of insignificance—these emotions are common to all the international stories; they are especially powerful in some of the lesser ones which have gone unmentioned here. There are people in them who dream and dream of Europe and never get there; the poor schoolteacher of "Four Meetings" gets no farther than Le Havre, where, cheated of her travel money, she is obliged to take ship back to America. The personal past, the past of family and home town, is nearly always conceived by James as deadly, a kind of ache; and any rupture with it is a good thing regardless of the consequences. That Roderick Hudson had better return to Northampton is suggested only by his unhappy and limited mother. Nor do Isabel's troubles or her conservatism ever turn her thoughts towards Albany and the ancestral house with the strange passageways and the papered-up doorlights where she was first discovered by her aunt, whiling away a rainy afternoon over a history of German thought. Between herself and Albany stands the greatness of Gardencourt, the Touchetts' English estate, with its myriad rooms

and illimitable lawns and vistas, the scene of her first entry
into a larger world. For if the stories are full of the stress of
penury and constraint, they are far richer in the related
imagery of abundance: the summer season, the garden, the
holiday, the party, the museum, the great house. James,
moreover, was beforehand in the use of the transplantation
plot, that device of modern novelists for unsettling the mind
of a character—"transvaluing" his values—by removing
him to an exotic place. *Daisy Miller* might easily have been
called *Passage to Italy* or *Death in Rome*.

He was a "hater of tyranny," said Ezra Pound in 1918;
and surely Pound, like Brooks, was right, even though both
spoke too exclusively in the spirit of their generation. James
anticipated that generation in many ways; and its spokes-
men were sensitive to things in him which we, more en-
amored of his later work, and seeking in all fiction a similar
mythic resonance, have allowed to become obscured. They
recalled his contention that the novel as he practiced it was
equally the child of myth (he would have said romance)
and of history; they were more familiar with his claim to
have been an historian of manners. What they (including
Eliot as well) admired in him was the vivid economy of his
American portraits, his devoted rendering of native speech.
And Pound, praising his skill in the vignette, liked to quote
such lines as the following, descriptive of an ambitious girl's
attentions to her superseded parents: "These little offices
were usually performed deftly, rapidly, with a minimum of
words, and when their daughter drew near them, Mr. and
Mrs. Day closed their eyes after the fashion of a pair of
household dogs who expect to be scratched." His image-
making was a large part of James's interest for the two
poets in particular; and, in their determination to make

poetry as well written as prose and as real as the novel, they paid him the compliment of being influenced by him. But he was also, as they maintained, a cultural historian of more than native importance. There was, as Pound expressed it, "the whole great assaying and weighing, the research for the significance of nationality, French, English, American." And Pound observed that "his art was great art as opposed to over-elaborate or over-refined art by virtue of the major conflicts which he portrays."

Yet the critics of that age, Pound and Brooks in particular, ignored a whole side of James; or if they did not ignore it they dismissed it as inconsequential "fuss" or relegated it to the years of his supposed decline. This was his profound *scepticism* concerning "the rights of personality," his doubt whether anything so abstract might be said to be interesting, his entire dialectic of freedom. In reality that scepticism is as firmly present in such a novel as *The Europeans* as it is in any performance of his later maturity. If a Daisy Miller or a Gertrude Wentworth seems to assert the rights of personality, this is not to say that the author himself does so. And that he does not may be seen from the more or less affectionate irony with which he normally envelops such figures. ("You are quite right to hate Gertrude, whom I also personally dislike," he wrote to a friend.) He is sceptical of rights and even more of personality, a word he could never use without enclosing it in quotation marks. Personality is what Gertrude admires so much in the Baroness, and Isabel at first in Osmond and Mme. Merle. Henrietta Stackpole and the Countess Gemini have it, but not Warburton, whose attraction is of another sort. As distinguished from the individuality of a Newman, an Isabel, or a Ralph Touchett, personality is aggressive, self-seeking in the cruder sense; it is perverse in Mme. Merle, touching in the Countess Gemini, funny in Henrietta. It is the too easy resource of those suffering from the dread of insignificance.

Freedom and individuality were such immense things to James that he was at pains to distinguish between the appearance and the fact of them. So too with another quality much prized by his Americans, the quality of innocence. There are various degrees and kinds of it among the early characters. The natural probity of the Wentworths is winning if narrow; that of Daisy Miller is winning but fatal. Only in the more heroic Americans are innocence, freedom, and individuality fully and positively present. In them the native zest for life is qualified by a feeling for life's limitations, a feeling James associates with the European mind. And what he seems to be saying is that one's consciousness of belonging to a given race or political group, or of contributing to some utopian future, is insufficient reason for one's asserting a primal innocence and freedom. These, James would maintain, are qualities of the individual, to be earned and enjoyed by him in that capacity.

In the Great Grey Babylon

THE idealistic formula of James's early fiction presently proved less workable, partly because he had worked it so much. But it sustained him through *The Portrait of a Lady*, holding its own against the sheer magnitude of the work, the considerable realism of the settings and portraits, the attractions that lay *du côté de chez Warburton*. He thoroughly knew those attractions himself when he wrote the novel. *Daisy Miller* had made him something of a celebrity: his acquaintance now ranged from Tennyson to Fanny Kemble, from George Moore to Lord Rosebery, and in a single London winter he dined out 107 times. Recalling the anxious years in America, he wrote in his notebook: "Now that life has brought something, brought a measurable part of what I dreamed of then, it is touching enough to look back. I knew at least what I wanted then—to see something of the world. I have seen a good deal of it, and I look at the past in the light of this knowledge. What strikes me is the definiteness, the unerringness of those longings. I wanted to do very much what I have done, and success, if I may say so, now stretches back a tender hand to its younger brother, desire.''

A success of happiness, a success on his own high terms. It was as the poet—the ironic poet, to be sure—of American innocence that he was making his way in worldly old England. He was a "lion," however modest, on the strength of a tale about a Schenectady girl who would not herself have been invited anywhere. In this pleasant paradox many things were vindicated: his European residence, his love of the world, the persuasiveness of his art.

It is true that James's "perturbed spirit," as he called it, was always with him. Americans did not sufficiently appreciate his tribute; and the Cambridge circle remained, or he seems to have thought it remained, keenly vigilant of his activities. We shall return to that in a moment. Meanwhile, as his letters and even more his notebook testify, he was expanding like someone who had broken through the major confinements of his youth.

In 1881 he confided to his notebook a rapid summary of his English life so far. The passage, unique in James, is in a fluid easy prose, its keynote being a kind of breathless joy—with compunctious undertones—in his enchanted mobility: it looks forward to the pleasure-sad prose of Hemingway and Fitzgerald. Although settled in London, he continues to travel in Britain as well as on the Continent. He has begun his practice of confining his journeys to France, Italy, and Germany—expansion must stop somewhere. Yet a friend "gave me the nostalgia of the sun, of the south, of colour, of freedom, of being one's own master, and doing absolutely what one pleases. He used to say, 'I know such a sunny corner, under the south wall of old Toledo. There's a wild fig tree growing there; I have lain on the grass, with my guitar.'" But this friend—surely an American!—goes to places "simply for their own sake, and without making any use of it—that, with him, is a passion," James notes with some astonishment. He must put this delightful vagabond in a book, he concludes, as if to remind himself of his responsibilities.

"Prolonged idleness exasperates and depresses me," he wrote. And he was constantly at work on something, often turning his travels into copy for American periodicals, the manuscript of the *Portrait* accompanying him from country-house to country-house and hotel to hotel through England, Scotland, France, Italy. With the increased demand for his fiction, writing became ever more of a strenuous routine; it also remained an intimate rite, a form of daily self-communion and spiritual exercise. The vogue of the "serial" was still in force. Beginning with the *Portrait*, James produced a succession of lengthy novels (together with many shorter things) which came out in installments in the *Atlantic* or the *Cornhill*, *Scribner's* or the *Century*. Many times the initial chapters appeared before the novel was half finished. This was nerve-racking for him, but it had distinguished precedents in the profession to which he was now assimilating himself. He was, as he said of Daudet, "not an occasional or desultory poet" but "a soldier in the great army of constant producers," the army of Balzac and Dickens. The serial was a stupid convention, he insisted; yet it was sociable; and he must have been gratified to feel that readers were saying, as one of his characters says of *Daniel Deronda*, "I should have liked it to continue indefinitely, to keep coming out always, to be one of the regular things of life."

It was his way to define his limits in proportion as he

extended them: a letting out, a pulling in. Settled in England, a success and on his own, he began to evolve a vast inner structure of habit and scruple which rendered him firm, even hard, wherever he might be touched. It could give way surprisingly at times but it was always there: the sea-wall against a fearful fluidity within. If he felt the nostalgia "of doing absolutely what one pleases," he could also write apropos of a story he was planning: "the question, as a matter of ethics, seems to me to have but one answer; if he had offered marriage to Miss Rosslyn (or whatever her name) by that offer he should abide." And his heroes will usually abide by their contracts and do the correct thing, however special their reasons. So too with their manners. The invalid soldier of his early story who felt that a man could not "go a-wooing in his dressing-gown and slippers" was the forefather of all those Jamesian gentlemen who will make a perpetual fuss about rising or smoking in the presence of ladies; and Isabel's book is unmistakably the portrait of a *lady*—an *Il Cortegiano* for the new American aristocracy. This flagrant decorum, as the elder James might have called it, was carried to excess and tended towards self-parody. At its best it was a necessary part of the chivalrous atmosphere of the novels; and it had its dramatic uses, as when Isabel, seeing Osmond seated while Mme. Merle is standing, divines their guilty intimacy. In all this there is again an element of simple self-gratification on James's part. If free spirits *ought* to behave decorously in an age corrupted by romantic ethics and Bohemian manners, the practice nevertheless reflects the author's own fiercely conservative instincts. "I doubt whether there was ever a provincial man of quality so punctilious in breeding as he is," wrote Tocqueville of the

American in Europe. "He is full of scruples and at the same time of pretensions." And James presently found himself holding the line against the democratization of manners among Englishmen themselves, of whom Browning impressed him as coarse, Tennyson as inept and preoccupied. Dubious as this was, he held to it with a passion. He was unique among novelists in his feeling for the conventional, his power to associate it with the good and the beautiful. Literary traditionalism, which on philosophic grounds has since gone far beyond James, has not followed him in this. Prufrock's dandyism is a sign of Prufrock's desperation. "Do I dare to eat a peach?"

James's personal legend was still in the making in the '70's and '80's and he was not yet so freakishly ceremonial in appearance as he afterwards became. But he had a shadowy look in the eyes which made someone liken him to an Elizabethan and add that he ought to wear earrings. His beard and close-cropped hair were a Paris fashion. Gosse, who first met him in 1882, says that "his manner was grave, extremely courteous, but a little formal and frightened, which seemed strange in a man living in constant communication with the world." Yet "his talk, which flowed best with one of us alone, was enchanting."

After the reserves of his Paris year, he opened up considerably to the English. There was the bond of language and morality, and there was the conservative English genius and power. France was "clever" but England was "great"; in fact, "the English are the only people who can do great things without being clever." He said this repeatedly in various ways, playing the nations off against one another, and himself off against both. But chiefly England was strong, and London was a sign of it: "the great grey Babylon" of the modern world, deficient in style but wearing "proudly and publicly the stamp of her imperial history." He first took rooms within hearing of Piccadilly traffic; although in time convenience forced his removal, first to Kensington, at last to the country town of Rye. These lodgings were the centers of his dual existence as an immense worker in literature and a perpetual guest at dinner parties and week-end gatherings in the country. London society, as pictured in his novels, lies open to easy conquest by anyone who can in the least amuse it. And so it appears to have been with him. "I can hardly say how it was," he observes in the notebooks, "but little by little I came to know people, to dine out, etc. I did, I was able to do, nothing at all to bring this state of things about; it came rather of itself. I had very few letters—I was afraid of letters. Three or four from Henry Adams, three or four from Mrs. Wister, of which I only, as I think, presented one." Before he had been three months in London he had breakfasted at Lord Houghton's with John Morley and others; and dined there with Tennyson, Schliemann, and Gladstone; and "behold me after dinner conversing affably with Mr. Gladstone—not by my seeking but by the almost importunate affection of Lord H." Another time he found himself "being conversed with in low, but harmonious tones by George Eliot," who showed, as he must have expected, "a tendency to *aborder* only the highest themes." James's social life was never so exceptional as it inevitably appears to native Americans. Hardy and Meredith, for example, were seen in the same Pall Mall clubs and many of the same drawing-rooms. Indeed his passage into aristocratic circles was sped by the respect that literature still commanded in Victorian society, although he was soon to complain that this was not suffi-

ciently the case. A duke could be trusted to broach rather
low themes; and some daughter of an ancient family, the
flower of her race, seated with you in a room aromatic of
Queen Anne, would break silence now and then to inquire
what pack you hunted with or whether you went in much
for tennis. The company might be dull but the circumstances implied better things past or to come, especially
the ancestral houses, those symbols of "shared experience"
on a magnificent scale—"Montacute, the admirable; Bar-
rington, that superb Ford Abbey. . . . These delicious
old houses, in the long August days, in the south of England
air, on the soil over which so much has passed and out of
which so much has come, rose before me like a series of
visions." This is from the notebooks; the whole passage
is wonderful—quintessential James. And to adjust the
vision to the fact became his great purpose as an artist, although it meant that he had also to become a *kind*
of English citizen—not till just before his death did he
embrace legal citizenship.

No doubt his standard of good conversation was romantically high; so at times was his faith in his own clairvoyance. "I find people in general very vulgar-minded and
superficial—and it is only by a pious fiction, to keep myself going, and keep on the social harness, that I succeed
in postulating them as anything else or better." That to his
mother in 1879; and the following, also addressed to her,
in 1880, from Mentmore, the home of Lord Rosebery:

> They are at afternoon tea downstairs in a vast,
> gorgeous hall, where an upper gallery looks down like
> the colonnade in Paul Veronese's pictures, and the
> chairs are all golden thrones, belonging to ancient
> Doges of Venice. I have retired from the glittering

scene, to meditate by my bedroom fire on the fleeting character of earthly possessions, and to commune with my mammy, until a supreme being in the shape of a dumb footman arrives, to ventilate my shirt and turn my stockings inside out (the beautiful red ones imparted by Alice—which he must admire so much, though he doesn't venture to show it,) preparatory to my dressing for dinner. Tomorrow I return to London and to my personal occupation, always doubly valued after 48 hours passed among *ces gens-ci,* whose chief effect upon me is to sharpen my desire to distinguish myself by personal achievement, of however limited a character. It is the only answer one can make to their atrocious good fortune. Lord Rosebery, however, with youth, cleverness, a delightful face, a happy character, a Rothschild wife of numberless millions to distinguish and demoralize him, wears them with such tact and bonhomie that you almost forgive him. He is extremely nice with Bright, draws him out, defers to him etc., with a delicacy rare in an Englishman. But, after all, there is much to say—more than can be said in a letter—about one's relations with these people. You may be interested, by the way, to know that Lord R. said this morning at lunch that his ideal of the happy life was that of Cambridge, Mass., "living like Longfellow."

This was written while he was at work on the *Portrait.* The letter, like the novel, suggests that he was still the triumphant American in England, his claim to detachment uncompromised, his "point of view" intact. The attitude was admirable, it had promoted his success so far, but it could not last short of his remaining in a state of continuous initiation. Those who argue that he might have kept it up, either by returning to America or by going into a noble seclusion abroad, are saying in effect that he should have remained a perpetual youth or been some other person. James himself did the wiser thing. He ceased to argue with life, so far as he could; he took the conditions of his genius for granted, so far as he could. His intimate associations with America made any prolonged stay there unthinkable, as he was always to find on his rare transatlantic visits. To be ruled by ghosts was irresponsible; but he could act upon a deeper responsibility, which was finally to embrace some possible form of life and take his chances on his point of view. This was what he did—again to the limit of his capacity; and the point of view certainly underwent a blurring; the clairvoyance gave way to a search, sometimes patient and sometimes frantic, for enlightenment in a denser medium—a search that was to put a salutary strain on the classical equanimity of his youthful mind, add to his thought the categories of the ambiguous and the inexpressible, and turn him from a fine writer into a great one. In the United States of the Gilded Age, it might be argued, he would have been under strain as well. But are there not, as Melville and others showed, strains so great or of so peculiar a kind as to be fatal rather than salutary? James's course revealed an inspired prudence. He played the game he had a chance of winning. Meanwhile the English medium, the society of his choice, was dense not because it was English— English ways were more accessible to him than American ones—but because it was life, and he had accepted it, and because he could not pretend to find life easily scrutable.

To be sure, he overdid the sociability, made too many engagements. Complaints of the resultant fatigue and boredom and interruption of work fill his letters and notebooks. Yet he does not judge his life by its excesses and for twenty years he continues in harness, abusing the privilege of society in order to be assured that it is still his. Serenity, in other words, he rarely knew except in hours of work. While his enjoyment of the surface of life was franker, his compunctions turned inward and deepened. For it is not suggested that his old conviction of estrangement had vanished, but only that he had found a basis on which use could be made of it and his further development as an artist made possible. He claimed to be an outsider still, and there is no reason to dispute him. His English friendships were gratifying. Those with Gosse, Stevenson, Du Maurier, and other writers and artists appeased some of his early desire for intellectual companionship; and there was another kind of pleasure in the gaily maternal company of voluble *femmes du monde* like Fanny Kemble and Mrs. Greville.

Seldom did such associations reach into the depths where the passions were formed—at any rate, not yet, although the author of *The Awkward Age* (1898) would at last feel the poetry of the London hostess as deeply as ever he did that of Minny Temple. What did penetrate at once was a sense of the society as a whole: its human types, manners, routines, houses, charms, horrors. This worldly image or imaged world he embraced with an intensity to which his confirmed nostalgia doubtless contributed—no insider like a reformed outsider. And he became the extremely critical champion of luxury and privilege. "Can you imagine anything so vulgar as the gold?" his sister Alice was to demand, referring to the gifts at a wedding where it was reported that the bride even carried a silver prayer-book. "Surely," James replied, "a lady who can eat off gold ought to be able to afford to pray out of silver!" This was a joke; but when he announced, although not to his sister, "I can stand a great deal of gold," it was not only a confession and a boast but a challenge. If gold was "vulgar," there was something hardly less so, which was the failure to appreciate it; the refusal, on whatever doctrinaire grounds, to admit its sheer weight in the realm of the actual, its capacity to benefit and to harm. To benefit or harm individuals, that is, for his great sense of the importance of human being was as ever. The aristocratic society was the men and women who made it up; its quality appeared in the quality of their minds and relations. He was forever observing people—a friend, a fellow-guest, a man on a park bench; and so the unpleasanter facts of the existing *beau monde* by no means escaped him. Indeed his identification with it was advertised by his habit of taking it more seriously than it took itself; and he knew the discomfort of playing the self-appointed scourge to people who were beyond caring. But although he became occupied to the point of obsession with the actual abuses of money and leisure, he never questioned the aristocratic ideal itself. He did not even think of the existing leisure class as a class among others. All the crowded and laborious life beyond it was for him so much Limbo, inert except for the straining here and there of some ambitious soul bent on breaking loose. The working classes were the barbarians; "in England," he wrote Norton, "the Huns and Vandals will have to come *up*—from the black depths of the (in the people) enormous misery." He was to write a few stories and one long novel about men and women of the servant or the working class; and in most cases their yearning towards the superior world makes up their very substance. Unlike Flaubert of *Un Cœur Simple,* he could see nothing but pathos and unreality in states of penury and servitude. Ignorant and stifling as this was, it was nevertheless his impassioned point of view, and the very narrowness of it made him strangely eloquent on the subject. The appurtenances of poverty were "the merciless signs of mere mean stale feelings." Poverty was the total failure of the human.

He felt all this very strongly himself, as strongly as if he also had once been poor and Cambridge had been a slum. The words "vulgar" and "provincial" were compulsive with him. His snobbishness, like his prudishness, was real—even though that was not the whole story. Any deeper sympathies first told on his nerves; and whatever else his stories of plebeian life may mean, they denote an extraordinary fastidiousness on their author's part. He came in time to avow this more openly and to treat his friends to humorously arrogant displays of it. What perhaps signified to him a certain complicated wholeness of mind on his own part could be trusted to strike them as merely arbitrary and so shock or amuse them. "Economy of means—economy of effect," he could say of an evening's entertainment on which his hosts had skimped. "I was amazed . . . ," writes Desmond MacCarthy, "by . . . his remark on our leaving what appeared to me a thoroughly well-appointed, prosperous house, 'Poor S., poor S.—the stamp of unmistakable poverty upon everything, '. . . His dislike of squalor was so great that surroundings to be tolerable to him had positively to proclaim its utter impossibility." His shrinking from the squalid was the reflex of his striving towards the gold—power, beauty, freedom. And in his dream of an aristocracy of talents *and* money were reconciled two opposing American ideals of long standing, not to mention those of his own family.

Right for him though he knew his English life to be, he was so far from serenity that he began the '80's with a small crisis and ended them with a major one. The first seems to have been bound up with his search for a subject to replace the nearly exhausted "international" one, but it also coincided with a visit to the United States which began in the fall of 1881. "I needed to see again *les miens*," he wrote, "to revive my relations with them, and my sense of the consequences that these relations entail." Scarcely had he arrived when he wrote in his notebook, "Heaven forgive me! I feel as if my time were terribly wasted here." But after spending Christmas in Quincy Street, he set out to collect impressions of the country, visiting New York and Washington. In the latter city he stayed with the Henry Adamses, formerly of the Boston circle, whom he presently put in a story ("Pandora") as a couple famous for their exclusive parties, making the husband say, "Let us be vulgar and have some fun—let us invite the President."

His stay in America was given a painful turn and greatly protracted by the sudden death of his parents. Mrs. James died in January 1882 of a heart attack following a brief illness. In her immense gentle patience she had endured a great deal, her son wrote, and been very weary. He presently went back to England, only to be recalled in a few months by word of his father's approaching death. To William, himself in Europe at the time, he wrote that the elder James's death was "as full of beauty as it was void of suffering. . . . He had no visible malady—strange as it may seem. The 'softening of the brain' was simply a gradual refusal of food, because he *wished* to die. There was no dementia except a sort of exaltation of his belief that he had entered into 'the spiritual life.' " He wished to die because his wife was dead; but death was no occasion for solemnity. When Alice asked him what the minister should say at his funeral, he cried: "Tell him to say only this: 'Here lies a man, who has thought all his life that the ceremonies attending birth, marriage, and death were all damned nonsense.'" One of his last remarks was, "Oh, I have such good boys—*such* good boys." Shortly after his death Henry wrote to his brother that "I went out yesterday (Sunday) to the Cambridge cemetery. . . . I stood beside his grave a long time and read him your letter of farewell—which I am sure he heard somewhere out of the depths of the still bright winter air." The letter had reached Cambridge too late. "Good-night, my sacred old Father! If I don't see you again—Farewell! a blessed farewell!" it concluded. "Thank God we haven't another parent to lose," Henry wrote to William.

To William it fell to edit *The Literary Remains of the Late Henry James*, to which he appended a painstaking study of his father's thought. This, the elder James's last book, was William's first. As scientist, teacher, and family man, he was now very much in possession of himself. He would presently buy in the New Hampshire mountains a summer house "with 14 doors, all of them opening outward"; and in 1890, after years of exhausting labor, he would publish his chief work, *The Principles of Psychology*. With Henry his relations had reached an equilibrium. They exchanged many letters and William was an occasional and extremely impatient visitor in London. Affectionately and anxiously paternal as ever, he read and commented on Henry's important writings as they appeared; while Henry, although greeting his brother's various achievements with cheers, was rather vague about them and seems to have acted on the feeling that their continued affection for each other need not depend on any close intellectual sympathy. It was from London, in 1889, that William wrote their sister Alice: "Harry is as nice and simple and amiable as he can be. He has covered himself, like some marine crustacean, with all sorts of material growths, rich sea-weeds and rigid barnacles and things, and lives hidden in the midst of his strange heavy alien manners and customs; but these are all but 'protective resemblances,' under which the same dear old, good, innocent and at bottom very powerless-feeling Harry remains, caring for little but his writing, and full of dutifulness and affection for all gentle things." Their brother Wilky died in 1883. Their invalid sister Alice, to whom Henry had turned over his share of the elder James's estate, presently followed him to England, where she lived in seclusion under a friend's care till she too died in 1892. She and Henry had loved each other extravagantly, although no two members of the family were more unlike. She was then lost to him, and the waste and agony of her life were complete. No talk of her fortitude, no appeal to the family principle of conversion, was of much help. Her wit and her political intelligence had been acute, it was true, although both had been constricted by her long illness; and she had left a journal of her last years, a work of somewhat acid brilliance. "Try not to be ill . . . for in that there is a failure," James once advised Grace Norton.

Meanwhile, sitting in a Boston hotel room in 1881, he wrote the breathless review of his English life from which so much was quoted above. His pleasure in the recent past was somewhat compromised by anxiety over his literary future. For some months he had been almost idle, and "prolonged idleness exasperates and depresses me." He was to continue relatively unproductive for many months more while his disquiet mounted. "If I can only *concentrate* myself: this is the great lesson of life." He had "hours of unspeakable reaction against my smallness of production; my wretched habits of work—or of un-work; my levity, my vagueness of mind, my perpetual failure to focus my attention, to absorb myself, to look things in the face, to invent, to produce, in a word." He would soon be 40 years old, "it's a horrible fact!", and "I shall have been a failure unless I do something *great*." And he dramatized *Daisy Miller*, trying without success to get it produced in New York. His turning to the theater for a quick and conspicuous success was now, as later in his life, a distress signal.

Yet, back in England, he was soon immensely productive once more; and the "international" theme and state of mind were supplanted by a different state of mind and other themes.

Is Mrs. Headway, "the well-known Texan belle," respectable? Her English acquaintances are trying to find out; and Littlemore, the only one who knows—knows she is *not* respectable—refuses to help. His refusal is occasioned by no very chivalrous feelings for Mrs. Headway, although she amuses him. He is merely disgusted with London society for taking up adventurers like herself. She is respectable enough for *it*. Such is the main situation of "The Siege of London," which James published in 1883. It is typical of his work in the '80's in that it is a story not of moral initiations, like the *Portrait*, but simply of social climbing. And in another novelette of the period, "The Aspern Papers," whose scene is modern Venice, the Americans present are again merely cosmopolitans. That representative character, that sense of having a mission in life, which distinguished a Newman and an Isabel Archer, are lacking in them; and without a mission James's Americans are like the popular conception of unfrocked priests. They are either quite ruthless, as the narrator is up to a point, or sadly astray like Miss Tina, who pathetically recalls that she once rejoiced in the superior society of "the Cavaliere Bombicci and the Contessa Altemura as well as certain English people, the Churtons and the Goldies and Mrs. Stock-Stock."

But "The Aspern Papers" (1888) is cosmopolitan in time as well as space. The story was suggested by an anecdote told James of Clare Claremont, Byron's long-surviving mistress, her spinster niece, and an American collector who became their lodger with the design of getting hold of Miss Claremont's papers but who was embarrassed to discover that the unfortunate niece wanted to marry him. James elaborated this anecdote into one of his best performances, a great reverberating story on the themes of art, time, and passion. "The Aspern Papers" has been widely read and praised, but usually as an example of only a superior kind of facility, as if anything that went down so easily could not be really first-rate. It is first-rate at all points, and so thoroughly realized that it rather defies definition. We may simply mention a few of its notable elements. One of these is certainly the oppressive magnificence of the physical setting: the decaying and oversized palace, with its spot of garden, rare in watery Venice, where the Misses Bordereau are living out their days. Scarcely less important is the fact that the American collector tells the story in the first person, thus implicating the reader in his plot to violate the past, his lust to get hold of the papers. It is at us as well as at the collector that Miss Bordereau hisses her climactic reproach, "Ah you publishing scoundrel!" But the genius of the story is chiefly in the conception of Miss Bordereau herself, who is no wistful survivor of the past but a diabolical incarnation of it, greedy of its power to bargain with the present, and wearing over her eyes, celebrated in Aspern's verse, a green eyeshade like a gambler's.

The '80's were years of great virtuosity for James. He was proud of his skill and eager to demonstrate it in a variety of forms and moods. In such performances as "The Aspern Papers" and "The Siege of London," he could sound the note of disenchantment; but he could also, in "Lady Barbarina," *The Reverberator,* etc., continue to make admirable footnotes to the international theme, because this theme was popular with readers and editors. No doubt his Balzacian alter ego was then very much in the saddle. He was determined to "do something great!", to "prove that I *can* write an American novel," to demonstrate the importance of the will in literary endeavor. This attitude was presently to get him in trouble, not because it induced him to write inferior books, but because his work failed to pay off in popular recognition and he was greatly disappointed. An *unread* Balzac?

The great attempt and the great unsuccess were meanwhile concentrated in the three extremely long and ambitious novels which he produced at immense speed between (roughly) 1885 and 1889. *The Bostonians, The Princess Casamassima,* and *The Tragic Muse* are very different in tone and in the degree of their interest, but several important qualities are common to them. They are all attempts to reclaim large areas of modern social experience for James's sensibility; to convert such topical problems as feminism,

anarchism, aestheticism into the materials of the imagination. Moreover all three, but the first two most obviously,
were written out of a mood similar to that of "The Aspern
Papers," a mood that may be described as an inverted idealism since it was so far from being a settled despair or even
a reasoned scepticism. Types of human perversity now almost fill the picture, the chief sign of the prevalent evil
being the corruption of the feminine principle. Odious
women are everywhere, as if the Mmes. de Bellegarde and
Mmes. Merle had crept from their corners into the center
of things. This is one development which the three novels
have in common, and it is one of their great strengths. Olive
Chancellor, the Princess Casamassima, and in a different
way Lady Dormer and Julia Dallow, are all wonderful studies of women in whom the will to power has supplanted
the wisdom, as James conceived it, of suffering and understanding.

"I wished," he noted of *The Bostonians* (1885), "to
write a very *American* tale, a tale very characteristic of our
social conditions, and I asked myself what was the most
salient and peculiar point in our social life. The answer was:
the situation of women, the decline of the sentiment of sex,
the agitation in their behalf." He once said of George Sand
that a woman could become a man but never a gentleman;
and on the surface of the novel feminism is treated in something of this farcical spirit, while deeper down it is treated
strangely and subtly. The plot, of which there is a good deal,
turns on a struggle for possession of the beautiful Verena
Tarrant. She has a curious talent which is meant, one supposes, to represent the feminine virtue of passive receptiv-
ity: by a laying-on of hands her father can inspire her to
improvise affecting speeches on the woman question. The

implacably sunny Verena with her queer gift, the wonder of Boston, is a wraith out of Hawthorne (with some assistance from Daudet's *L'Évangeliste*) and not interesting. The two principal contestants for her are very interesting. They are the arch-feminist Olive Chancellor who proposes to save Verena for the cause of women's rights, and Basil Ransom who wants her for his wife. Ransom's fight for Verena supplies the novel with a heavily inscribed line of action and suspense; but the girl herself is so nearly blank that their relations lack internal complication. Ransom, however, is an admirable portrait: a Southerner who remembers the War, a traditionalist, proud yet easy-going, a little indolent, fatalistic, humorous, given to fits of magniloquence, fond of beer and variety actresses. As opposed to the Bostonians he is not so much worldly as old worldly; but he is trying to make his way in New York, and it is his sophisticated New York acquaintances who provide the counterfoil to New England highmindedness. Yet their value in the picture, and even Ransom's, is overshadowed by the grotesque comedy of the Boston reformers with Olive Chancellor at their head. Save for Olive's prim parlors, Boston is seen as uniformly drab and seedy:

> The western windows of Olive's drawing-room, looking over the water, took in the red sunsets of winter; the long, low bridge that crawled, on its staggering posts, across the Charles; the casual patches of ice and snow; the desolate suburban horizons, peeled and made bald by the rigour of the season; the general hard, cold void of the prospect; the extrusion, at Charlestown, at Cambridge, of a few chimneys and steeples, straight, sordid tubes of factories and engine-shops, or spare, heavenward finger of the New England meeting house. There was something inexorable

in the poverty of the scene, shameful in the meanness of its details, which gave a collective impression of boards and tin and frozen earth, sheds and rotting piles, railway-lines striding flat across a thoroughfare of puddles, and tracks of the humbler, the universal horse-car, traversing obliquely this path of danger; loose fences, vacant lots, mounds of refuse, yards bestrewn with iron pipes, telegraph poles, and bare wooden backs of places.

The people themselves are a kind of emanation from this rubbishy and insubstantial landscape. One recalls Van Wyck Brooks's phrase for the reformers of the '40's: "a queer miasmatical group of lunar phenomena"; yet James is not dealing with the original group of abolitionists and Brook Farmers, his father's generation, but with the epigoni of the '70's. A survivor of the heyday, the musty, indistinct Miss Birdseye, busy forever in an infinity of causes, is as representative as she is amusing. "The whole moral history of Boston was reflected in her displaced spectacles" —that and more: Miss Birdseye is the bookshop reformer done for all time. And she is not the less devastating because James had a tenderness for her and distinguished her from her latter-day companions. She is really disinterested, the real thing; but as for the rest, the postwar disenchantment, the shadow of Barnum, are upon them; and they crudely exploit a taste for causes and curiosities which has now become public property. Verena Tarrant has "queer bad lecture-blood in her veins," her parents being old troupers of the lyceum and the free-love colony. While his wife slyly aspires to gentility, Selah Tarrant practices mesmeric healing. He is remarkable for a mere mild unction in face of the mysteries and the realities. "Don't all the troubles of humanity come from our being pressed back?" he inquires; or laying his pallid hands on Verena's shoulders in order to launch her on one of her séances, "Want to try a little inspiration?" he asks. If we must track him down, Selah Tarrant is "a moralist without moral sense"; and so in her more complex, refined, and terrible way is Olive Chancellor.

We read in the notebook that "the relation between the two girls should be a study of one of those friendships between women which are so common in New England." But on Olive's part it is more than a friendship; she is pretty distinctly a case of perverse sexuality; and whether or not James knew what he was doing, he had certainly observed curiously some real instance of Olive's derangement. To William he apologized for including in the novel so much "descriptive psychology"; and Olive is a rare case in James of a character transfixed in its symptoms. It should be added that a candid naturalism broods over the entire narrative, which is strewn with pointed physical detail: gestures, mannerisms, the shape of hands, the color of hair, the look of garments. Olive's New York sister Mrs. Luna (the *female*, as distinguished from Olive the feminist and Verena the feminine) is openly on the make—there is no other way to put it—for Ransom. And Olive herself, with her dark hair and sharp pale face and white hands, her shaky composure and blurted speech, her habit of broadcasting tremors of suffering as a stove does waves of heat, her sympathy with the strange and exotic—"It was the usual things of life that filled her with silent rage"—is the proud Puritan spirit turned into wretched body. She stares at the gold buttons on Verena's bodice. She seizes the girl and wraps her "in the fold of a cloak that hung ample upon her own meagre person," while an irreverent intruder remarks, "You ladies better look out, or you'll freeze together." Strange though she is, poor Olive (we pity her all the more because James pities her so little) has her place in the Jamesian genealogy. A lineal descendant of Roger Lawrence and Rowland Mallett, she too "adopts" life in the form of a protégée, who in this case is Verena.

The taste of *The Bostonians* is sharp and dry; an atmosphere of littleness and remoteness hangs over it, though visibility remains high. The style is consciously bare, epigrammatic rather than allusive. The novel is the most considerable product of the social historian in James. It has the defect of not quite filling out its panoramic dimensions; it is intense only in spots, but these are unforgettable. If it had not been so badly received in America, *The Bostonians* might have become one of a series of *scènes de la vie de province*. As it was, James followed it promptly with *The Princess Casamassima* (1885), his ambitious study in the *vie de Londres*. In preparation for this novel, unprecedented in his work, he haunted London's shabby districts; got up on the anarchist movement; and read the papers with their news of strikes, riots, and assassinations on the one hand, and of high intrigues, scandalous divorces, and governmental crises on the other—all of it adding up to the picture of a social order assailed from without and corrupted from within. The *Princess* thus boldly invades the world of affairs, the macrocosm. The characters are many and miscellaneous, representing rich and poor; but London, the scene of most of the action, wraps them all—bookbinders, princesses, shopgirls, anarchists, police-spies—in a vast uniform gloom pierced by the cheerless glow of small candle-lit or gas-lit interiors. Indeed the intricate abundance of the *Princess* is thoroughly, perhaps excessively, subdued to the poetry of a point of view and the unfailing richness of a prodigious prose. For all his Balzacian ambitions James still believed the artist's prime experience to be a kind of vision. In "The Art of Fiction," written in these years, he reaffirmed his faith—which any Transcendentalist would have applauded—in the artist's "power to guess the unseen from the seen, to trace the implication of things, to judge the whole piece by the pattern." Of all his novels *The Princess Casamassima* was his largest attempt to judge the whole piece by the pattern, the whole piece being in this case the entire structure of civil society. And among his novels it is the most palpably "modern," even in its defects. It is addressed to the fate of the superior individual in a situation where things fall apart and the center cannot hold.

Hyacinth Robinson is the illegitimate child of a plebeian Frenchwoman who murdered his father, an English lord, and presently died in prison. Brought up in poverty by a kindly but limited foster-mother, Hyacinth soon learns of his terrible origins. As he grows older he feels a natural enough resentment of society; and while he becomes a skilled bookbinder he also joins a group of anarchist conspirators who are preparing to "destroy society." Among the anarchists he pledges himself to perform an act of violence when called upon to do so, an act that will almost certainly mean his death. Meanwhile he has met the Princess Casamassima, and this encounter is to be infinitely more fruitful to him than his association with the conspirators. The Princess is a lovely woman (of American birth: she is Christina Light revived from *Roderick Hudson*), who has left her Italian husband and is trying to penetrate revolutionary circles, apparently out of sheer idealism. As she uses Hyacinth for her purposes, so, by association with her, Hyacinth has a taste of the delights of aristocratic living. A change of heart begins to come over him; and this is confirmed when, his foster-mother dying, he comes into a small legacy that permits him to travel briefly on the Continent. The legacy, though soon exhausted, has symbolized his passing over morally into the leisure class. Among the splendors of France and Italy he has concluded that civilization and art necessarily rest on privilege and that his anarchist friends are motivated by a destructive envy in wanting to overturn society. He returns to London and his trade, but he is now doomed and he knows it, for he has no footing anywhere. To the Princess he is of course a renegade; and his relations with her, strangely innocent and inconclusive from the first, begin to decline. Disappointed in Hyacinth she turns to Paul Muniment, his powerful friend and fellow-conspirator, who is the strong man she has really been seeking all the time. Hyacinth has been supplanted; and he soon discovers that Millicent Henning, a handsome lower-class girl he has known in a companionable way since childhood and to whom he has finally turned in revulsion from the unreal Princess and the treacherous Muniment, is also faithless. His pledge to the conspirators, which he has not repudiated despite his change of heart, presently falls due. He is to assassinate a certain high dignitary and he receives the pistol. Now utterly alone, he wanders about London registering his final impressions of its ineffable power and glory. Then he turns the pistol on himself.

It was suggested above that the *Princess* is modern even in its defects, meaning its intrinsic defects. Other short-comings, such as the "misplaced middle" which James himself complained of, in this as in other of his long novels, and which means that the preparations for the action are over-developed, might have been remedied if he had taken more time. It was one thing to make light, as he did, of Flaubert's laborious methods of composition; another thing to draft a novel of the magnitude of the *Princess* in what seems to have been little more than a year! On August 10, 1885 he confessed in his notebook apropos of the *Princess*: "I have never yet become engaged in a novel in which, after I had begun to write and send off my MS. [to the *Atlantic*, in whose September issue it began to appear], the details had remained so vague." But the really serious flaw in the novel is made by the hero, who, although not at all like Joyce's hero in other respects, has something of the deadening effect on the *Princess* that Stephen Dedalus occasionally has on *Ulysses*. Considered as minds, simply, both characters function very well, and Stephen better than Hyacinth because Joyce was more intellectual than James. But their personalities fail to form images, or form images very much less affecting than was intended. There is something compensatory about them; they hint at a reservation on the author's part, a holding back in return for all the giving out. Hyacinth Robinson is James's sensibility cast for a time among thieves but instructed to come home at last, immaculate as ever although with a bullet through its head.*

He is supposed to be a type of moral intelligence like Newman and Isabel, James tells us in the preface—a document of great interest in which he also goes on to call

---

* Lionel Trilling's brilliant essay on the *Princess* makes out a far better case for Hyacinth than the present writer has been able to do.

the roll of his other intelligent protagonists, to name Lear
and Hamlet as if they were analogous types, and to distinguish solemnly between "fools" and "heroes." These juxta-
positions are unfortunate. They only tend to make clear
how little the Jamesian chivalry has in common with the
humanism of Shakespeare, whose protagonists are not less
human for sometimes behaving like beasts, or less heroic for
being on occasion fools. Of all his important characters, Hyacinth perhaps suffers most from being so stuffed with the
chivalry. But it is not really the characteristic Jamesian chivalry—it is a kind of gentility that Hyacinth assumes, with his
sad feckless composure, his anxious good manners, his mysterious sexual refusals in the face of such temptations as
those represented by the Princess and Millicent. All this
is not only at odds with his plebeian specifications; it is uninteresting in itself. What does it signify in terms of his
meaning and that of the novel? Unlike Isabel and Newman,
whose superior gallantry is vivid, positive, and intelligible,
Hyacinth seems a case merely of unrequited sensibility,
of the man who is too good for this world. No doubt
James's mind was in this instance *too* inviolable to ideas;
he could have done with a few. Surely Hyacinth travels
far to learn what he could have read any day in the *Times:*
that radicals are envious. Perhaps, as the early associations
that galvanized Newman and Isabel began to fail him,
James stood in need of some system of ideas to sustain and
generalize his faith in intelligence. This unfilled need is to
be more apparent in his work as time goes on. Hyacinth
Robinson is the first important example of a type which is to
become more common in James and which he is to call his
"poor sensitive gentleman," noting his embarrassment at

its prevalence. Edmund Wilson has said that Hyacinth "died of the class struggle"; but really he died of a poverty of ideas.

He *did* die, however; James did not hold back from the drastic conclusion. Such, according to the darkest of his novels, is the fate of sensibility in the present world. And whatever may be the case with Hyacinth, his surroundings are substantial, presented as they are in terms of the eloquent ambiguity and pantomime that are soon to become James's chief narrative method. Perversity has never been something taken for granted by him; it is always as if he had stumbled on a crime unawares. In the *Princess* this sense of evil is the very stuff of things; and a new province is discovered for literature, the province of the latent.

The people in the *Princess* have mostly broken loose from their various stations in society and are milling around in a waste place where betrayal is the general law. Hyacinth's foster-mother and his childhood protector, Mr. Vetch, are exceptions. By embracing their penurious status they achieve a small dignity—a *very* small one, for poverty here is a night in which all cats are gray. The inner body of anarchists with its hideous but effective *esprit de corps* of destruction is an exception of another kind. James does it this much honor; and although he is not interested in the revolutionary temperament as Dostoevsky was interested in it in *The Possessed*, he was able to make some shrewd genre studies in the type. Among the anarchists it is Paul Muniment who, half an outsider and a potential betrayer, is more to James's purposes in the *Princess*; and Muniment is a resonant figure, the plebeian on the make, the future labor politician. For the rest, even the well-meaning Hyacinth cannot help disappointing his foster-mother and Mr.

Vetch, who want him to settle in his trade; and of course from the point of view of the Princess, he lets the conspirators down as well. But the logic of treachery is most delicately shown in a character who is technically no more than a *ficelle*. Divided between her affection for the Princess and her obligations to the Prince, Mme. Grandoni, the Princess's companion, is a touching case of mental suffering and the most tragic figure in the book. At the other extreme is the amusingly lurid Captain Sholto, a police spy (apparently) who also preys on pretty women and for whom betrayal is a business.

The most elaborate portrait, and one that likewise strains towards comedy, is that of the Princess herself. Like all first-rate characters in fiction she is constructed, with whatever richness and subtlety, from a formula; and in this case the formula includes the various ways in which such a woman might appear to us, depending on how well we knew her. First seen in the vague light of a theater box with diamonds in her hair, she is all grace and loveliness; even her solemn insistence on discussing with Hyacinth "the social question," as she calls it, argues a noble condescension. Great ladies are necessarily a little humorless. Our appreciative sense of her survives several glimpses, including the scenes at Medley, the country house which strikes Hyacinth as so appropriate to her but which we gradually learn to be in a rather bad state of repair and to have been leased by her for a song from its needy owners, the rental including the servants and the carriage. At Medley, however, her habit of secluding herself, her rather histrionic performances at the piano, seem to be in excess of her role as a great lady; and when she is finally reduced to making almost a prisoner of Hyacinth, with his scanty wardrobe and his need to get back to work in London, her humorlessness begins to look like a function of her habit of getting herself into false positions. As we learn that she continues to take money from her abandoned husband, as we see her false positions reflected in the moral distress of Mme. Grandoni, the Princess becomes increasingly sinister. If her relations with Hyacinth have been sexually innocent, with Muniment they are not innocent; and the scene in which Hyacinth and the wretched Prince watch from a street corner late at night while the Princess and Muniment, returned from some protracted meeting of the conspirators, reveal their intimacy by entering her house together, is fine as all such scenes of exclusion and betrayal are fine in James. But the Princess goes through a final phase. Muniment, who is himself under suspicion by the anarchists, soon lets her down, telling her in a blunt scene that only her money is useful to the cause and that she had better return to her husband. "Ah, Paul Muniment," she says "you *are* a first-rate man!", and she bursts into tears. And we see her at last as a rather futile woman whose surrender of her feminine and aristocratic status has left her with nothing but an insatiable appetite for adventure and for men. It was not James's purpose to suggest that she *ought* to have retained her status. The novel is so far from didactic that it presents the Prince as himself pathetically unequal to his noble and Catholic heritage. Nor does either Mme. Grandoni, who is good but helpless, or the socialist-minded Lady Aurora, who is good but dreary, imply any future for the class. The best lack all conviction, while the worst are full of passionate intensity.

The Princess Casamassima, like *The Bostonians*, was a failure with the public. Only a few devoted followers of James, such as Howells, admired the two novels. The macabre satire of *The Bostonians* shocked those Americans whom it did not simply leave cold. William James himself surrendered to local prejudice to the extent of scolding his brother for presumably having based Miss Birdseye on the celebrated Boston reformer Elizabeth Peabody, Hawthorne's sister-in-law; although, presently relenting, he found things to praise in the novel. William was working more and more completely into the national life at the same time that Henry was growing away from it, seeing his reputation at home fall to pieces, and his name become almost a byword for queerness. William's fraternal affection never failed, but his literary patience was greatly taxed. Mark Twain declared that he would rather be consigned to the puritan heaven than have to read *The Bostonians*; and it was Mark Twain's America. Alas, that one remarkable humorist should so fail to appreciate another! In England too, although his prestige was always higher there, he was under attack by another generation; he wrote fiction as if it were "a painful duty," observed Oscar Wilde; and Hardy said that he had "a ponderously warm manner of saying nothing in infinite sentences." There was little truth in Wilde's remark, and none in Hardy's; and the obvious defects of his recent novels—their too great length, their failures of concentration—were not really responsible for the public indifference. He had leapt ahead of his time. With his dark view of things—less palatable than Hardy's pessimism, perhaps, because less reducible to doctrine and in any case not relieved, as Hardy's was, by a traditional poetry of the countryside—his growing taste for the anomalous and the grotesque, the increasing density of his verbal textures, and the more and more austere organization of his narratives, he was so far in advance of his age that the interposition of a later school of writers—who made explicit many of his aims and methods, carried them farther, and created a sizable audience for that kind of story—was required before he came into full recognition. In the '80's James himself evidently failed to preceive how widely he had departed from 19th-century Anglo-Saxon standards, although he was to perceive it soon. Far from defying popular taste, he had sought to captivate it with two timely novels full of arresting incidents and characters. When they failed, he wrote to Howells in January 1888: "I have entered upon evil days. . . . I am still staggering a good deal under the mysterious and (to me) inexplicable injury wrought—apparently—upon my situation by my two last novels . . . from which I expected so much and derived so little. They have reduced the desire, and the demand, for my productions to zero."

"However, I don't despair," he added; and the following year saw the appearance of *The Tragic Muse*. This lengthy book was his last prodigious attempt at topical realism along more or less standard lines. There is scarcely an ominous note in the rational, four-square, patiently documented, daylight world of *The Tragic Muse*, in which the theme of art versus politics is explored with almost the consistency of a formal debate. The effort called forth an astonishing virtuosity; what remain in the mind are brilliant fragments, such as the French theater scenes, the coldly external but still effective portrait of the actress Miriam Rooth in her immense egotistical vitality, and the sketches of Miriam's amusing mother, of Mr. Carteret the retired politician, and of the political matriarch Lady Dormer. It is the two young Englishmen, twin heroes of *The Tragic Muse*, who devastate the novel by failing to supply it with an engrossing center. Hyacinth had at least the advantage of being a plebeian on whom James could lavish the fruits of his own experience as an initiate. Nick Dormer and Peter Sherringham are the sort of cultivated upper-class Englishmen whom he has never been able to imagine except as futile. Supposed to be links between politics and art, society and Bohemia, they are too dryly reticent to get into relation with much of anything, and least of all with Miriam Rooth; for James refuses to allow what the situation obviously calls for, which is for them to have affairs with her. Each in his way renounces her; and although they are not of course the first or the last of James's characters to make such refusals, they do so here within a social atmosphere so broadly and conventionally realistic as to render the whole procedure unintelligible. And *The Tragic Muse*, after its remarkable if bumpy flight, begins slowly to buckle and fall, with a depressing sound as of escaping energies.

No wonder James's labors on the book left him exhausted and sad. The reviewers were unusually kind to it; but it had no sale and he soon wrote it off as another failure. To William, who praised it highly, James wrote in a bitter-cheerful mood: "I shall never make my fortune—nor anything like it, but—I know what I shall do and it won't be bad." This was a curious thing to say, for he was even at the moment intent on making his fortune in the theater and what he was to do there was pretty bad.

The Awkward Period

SOMETHING of a crisis overtook James as a result of the public indifference to his large novels of the '80's. As his expectations of them had been high, so his response to their failure was profound. Yet he was by no means without emotional resources and literary plans, dubious though some of these might be. He would write no more lengthy novels, he announced while still engaged on *The Tragic Muse;* and till 1895 he kept to this resolve. Short stories, including some of his finest, continued to pour from him; but for some five years his main effort went into the writing of plays and the wooing of actors and producers. The theater had supplanted the Balzacian novel as the image of power.

On the surface, at least, as Leon Edel's admirable studies in the period have shown, James's turning to the stage was far from arbitrary. It was not at all the usual case of the literary man essaying the theater casually and perhaps a little contemptuously. The stage, for which his respect was at all times unbounded, had long tempted him. We hear of his intentions to write for it as early as 1882, when, during his American visit, he turned *Daisy Miller* into a play

and collided with the greed and vulgarity of the managers
of the Madison Square Theater in New York. Although
Daisy Miller, A Comedy was never produced, James
emerged from the encounter undiscouraged. The theater
was still a passion with him. Illusionistic, professional, social,
it remained, after fiction, his art of arts; and as a novelist
he was constantly profiting by its vividnesses and econ-
omies. All his life he remembered the melodramas of his
New York childhood. He knew and loved the *Théâtre
Français*; he knew and mostly despised the contemporary English stage, often scandalizing his friends by
loudly voicing his distaste for some play in clumsy progress before their eyes. And Ibsen, "provincial of provincials"
though he was to James, found in the novelist one of his
most discerning English admirers, even though James's own
plays were to owe all too little to his influence. Nor, once
James had decided to try the theater in earnest, was he
satisfied to rest on his scholar's and spectator's knowledge.
If his predictions of success were shrill, he was actually a
patient apprentice. Not only did he visit Paris in order to
discuss his plans with authorities there, but, as he told William, "I have worked like a horse—far harder than any one
will ever know—over the whole stiff mystery of 'technique.'" He can hardly have been unaware, moreover, that
a dramatic revival was then in the English wind, bringing
Wilde and other literary men into the theater.

For James himself, however, it was anything but the psychological moment for such a venture. The young and relatively self-confident author of *Daisy Miller* and *The Europeans* might conceivably have turned playwright with
success, though it is significant that he was not very serious
about it then. Had the stage meanwhile come to mean al-

most too much to him, both as a source of literary inspiration and as a possible way to glory? The dramatic
structure and immediacy he had already mastered in his
fiction. To pursue the embodied drama rather than the
dramatic effect represented a considerable risk on the part
of a writer whose perception of things was so much a matter of effects and essences. And in any case he had post-
poned the attempt too long. He had put it off to a moment
when, because he could least afford to fail, he was likely to
know both rashness and panic. Even the attempt of 1882,
like a third and final one in his old age, had been a storm
signal advertising a mood of exhaustion and uncertainty
following a productive period of novel-writing. In 1890 the
mood was upon him with a vengeance. The whole complicated experiment of his life seemed to lie open to question: his celibate dedication to art, his European residence,
his ambitious idea of the novel, his pursuit of a career in
letters.

It is true that he was rather consistently possessed by
a radical sense of powerlessness and estrangement. But
at his best moments the ambitious designs we have just
named served rather as deliberately accepted challenges
than as furtive "compensations" for supposed weakness.
Only at times of apparent failure did the question of compensation really come up for him; and the early '90's was
one of those times, indeed the chief of them. "It was wholly
for money I ventured," he told William and others in explanation of his play-writing. This was in large part swagger,
protective cynicism. What he craved, as Edel suggests, was
recognition; and the more this was denied him the greater
became his need, till what he wanted was simple gross
success. Whatever the theater had once meant to him,

it had now become mainly an agent of power and rejuvenation and reunion with the tribe. The cheerful obfuscation of his letters of the time leaves no doubt. The stage was action, bustle, the gratifying hardships of the rehearsal and the road, the fellowship of actors, the right to talk a sacred professional jargon, the dream of applause and curtain calls. To be sure, his humor, which never abated for a moment, was constantly exercised by his misadventures; and his natural kindness and love of people expressed itself in repeated generosities. Never before, as an actor in one of his plays remarked on one occasion, had a playwright gone to the trouble of having his servants bring to rehearsal a hamper of sandwiches in order to feed a hungry and exhausted cast. Yet James was as full of visions of a calculated triumph as if he had taken to roulette or the stock-market. Not only had he worked hard over the mystery of technique; but, as he added to William, "I have run it to earth . . . I have made it absolutely my own, put it into my pocket." And this blithe assurance survived his theatrical misfortunes of the '90's. The suspicion that he had possessed the right "system" and lacked only a favorable opportunity remained with him to the end.

It was with his system, rather than his sensibility, that he wrote his plays. Perhaps he was rash in attempting the theater at all; almost certainly he was unduly cautious in his estimate of its uses. This was not a matter of the *kind* of play he was trying to write. To build as he did on the example of Sardou and Augier, to assume a tradition where none existed, was not in itself fatal; although the good modern drama, from Ibsen to Chekhov to Shaw and beyond, does seem to have been an affair of single engagements fought by a series of brilliant irregulars. Nor were his conventions, such as the aside and the soliloquy, objectionable in themselves, merely because they were inconsistent with a maximum of realism. Furthermore, he was able to turn out in play after play admirable stretches of dialogue, one speech wittily provoking another. Often, too, entire scenes are neatly accomplished; and only a kind of ultimate emptiness prevents one of his plays, "The Reprobate," from being good as a whole. But there is a deficiency of emotion in them; and in the absence of this, all the skill is so much chatter and contrivance. The play written "merely to entertain" has its own variety of emotion. James, who could not encompass this, proceeded instead to draw off the complexity from his own mind. He learned everything about play-writing except how to evoke character and atmosphere. And so, although his plays constantly echo the themes of his fiction, they do so in a strangely dehumanized and unresonant medium. This naturally appears most sharply in the stage versions of his stories, *Daisy Miller* and *The American*, to which he attached happy endings, taking in general greater liberties with the originals than the authors of *The Heiress* took with *Washington Square*. Christopher Newman, whose tenuous blend of refinement and bravado is the peculiar triumph of *The American* in its fictional form, is in the play reduced to a cartoon-Yankee:

> *Claire.* (Closing her eyes an instant.) You'll make me dizzy!
> *Newman.* You can be as dizzy as you like, with *my* arm round you!

James's reviewers at the time had no trouble in agreeing on one point. Literary men, one newspaper critic remarked, are more than welcome in the theater "provided they bring their literature with them." And William Archer: "Mr. James has never taken up a natural and unconstrained attitude towards the stage. . . . If he will only clear his mind of critical cant . . . and write solely for the ideal audience within his own breast, he will certainly produce works of art, and not improbably successful plays."

Of the several dramas James wrote in the early '90's only two then reached the stage. Certain of the others were published in a pair of volumes called *Theatricals* or eventually turned into novels, among which *The Other House* is alone noteworthy. The dramatized *American*, with its farcical Newman dressed in a gaudy coat, amused provincial audiences; in London it closed after 70 performances, but not until the Prince of Wales had seen and enjoyed it. The fate of *The American* was, in short, equivocal; its success, while not great, was sufficient to lead the author on. This was in 1891. The next four years were for him given over to ironies and frustrations not unlike those that torment the obsessed men and women in his tales. But the climax—a personal humiliation combined with the treachery of his producer and rumors of a hostile cabal in the audience —was more in Dostoevsky's vein: Stepan Trofimovitch at the *fête*.

Guy Domville, the cause of James's misfortune, was a "costume play" in two senses: not only was it laid in the eighteenth century, which was evoked on the stage with an elaborate flummery of rich garments and old furniture; but its theme, the world *versus* the monastery, was anything but topical. And the circumstances of the production were in themselves ominous. In his eagerness James had made a deal with the actor-producer George Alexander, a popular player who, accustomed to easy successes, saw little of *Guy Domville*'s doubtful character and prepared neither himself nor James for possible difficulties with the less literate public, who, but for Alexander's participation, would doubtless have stayed away in any case. *Guy Domville* opened at the St. James Theatre in London on the evening of January 5, 1895. Naturally anxious, James wisely decided to be absent from the performance, and spent the evening at Wilde's *The Ideal Husband*, which was playing to delighted audiences at a nearby theater. The Wilde play ended, he walked, full of misgivings, to the St. James, where he had the bad luck to arrive just before the final curtain. Many friends were in the brilliant audience as well as a number of expectant reviewers: Shaw, Bennett, A. B. Walkley, William Archer. The stalls had been mildly gratified by *Guy Domville* despite a boring second act and a rather absurd drinking scene; but there had been unrest in the gallery. Someone had greeted the oversized bonnet worn by one of the actresses with "Where did you get that hat?"; and when the hero, played by Alexander, declared himself "the last of the Domvilles," someone else had sung out "good news" or words to that effect. James, arrived late and standing in the wings, was unaware that the final curtain had fallen on a thoroughly unnerved Alexander. Disaster was too much for the actor, says H. G. Wells, who was in the audience. "A spasm of hate for the writer of those fatal lines must surely have seized him. With incredible cruelty he led the doomed James, still not understanding clearly how things were with him, to the middle of the stage, and there the pit and gallery had him."

"There followed," James wrote William, "an abominable quarter of an hour during which all the forces of civilization in the house waged a battle of the most gallant, prolonged and sustained applause with the hoots and jeers and cat-calls of the roughs, whose *roars* (like those of a cage of beasts at some infernal 'zoo') were only exacerbated (as it were) by the conflict. It was a cheering scene, as you may imagine, for a nervous, sensitive, exhausted author to face." It was probably the worst moment of his mature life. His inward sufferings, his nightmare pursuers, were temporarily objectified in this scandalous scene—the kind of scene from which he had always sought to spare not only himself but his characters; for, courageous though he was in so many respects, a humiliation of this kind was for him the un-speakable. While the tumult went on he raised a hand as if about to speak, hesitated, then rushed for the wings, so shaken that the actors, who had grown fond of him during rehearsals, and his friends, who hastened backstage, were seriously alarmed. But if they expected him to collapse he did not; and Gosse, who went to see him next day, found him grimly in possession of himself.

It was rumored that an actress with a grudge against Alexander had somehow been responsible for the disturb-ance. James himself appears not to have taken much stock in this story nor to have tried to console himself with it. He was vehement about English audiences; but for the pres-ent he was more or less resigned to his failure as a play-wright, even though *Guy Domville*, after various revisions, had a respectable run of four weeks in London. Nor was he beguiled by the kindness of many of the reviewers, among them Shaw, who praised *Guy Domville* for raising serious issues and compared its style to Mozart's music. The praise, however sincere, clearly owed much to irrelevant considerations: disgust with the hecklers, respect for James's name, a widespread campaign in favor of the man of letters in the theatre. *Guy Domville*, as James evidently saw, was a failure *d'estime*. And if he did not conclude with Flaubert that the theater was "*l'école de démoralisation*" for literary men, he at least said of himself that "you can't make a sow's ear out of a silk purse." His play-writing ambitions did not die out but they went underground. Yet his disappointment was great; once more he observed to Howells that he had "fallen upon evil days—every sign or symbol of one's being in the least *wanted*, anywhere or by anyone, having so utterly failed." No doubt his feeling of isolation was in excess of the actual circumstances, but it was his feeling that mattered. A merely honorary position in letters failed to assuage his old sense of powerlessness; nor was it ever to do so. Although he grew calmer later on, it was not altogether, as sometimes maintained, because he had resigned himself to a near oblivion. Rather it was because, on the strength of his later work, he acquired, if never a large public, at least a fervent and indeed very estimable body of devotees and disciples. With the growing commercialization of letters, his measure of a career had turned out to be no longer feasible. When he emerged from the crisis of those years, his measure of a career had changed; he had ceased to expect the old kind of recognition. He had lived through the stresses of his own *fin de siècle*, the unquiet passage from one literary age to another. The Victorian idea of the writer as elder brother—energetic, conscientious, respected, rewarded—was passing with the Victorian society.

Shaw was to conclude years later that James had failed as a playwright because his language, however distinguished, was too literary for the stage and because his "19th century fatalism and pessimism" were outmoded. Yet Chekhov's "pessimism" had not prevented him from making a great contribution to the theater; and if James had written his plays with his sensibility he would probably have been closer to Chekhov than to Sardou. Certainly his tales of those same years show him to have been increasingly preoccupied with the queer, the futile, the terrible. The stories, we may confidently say, engaged vastly more of him than did the plays. They kept his sensibility alive through the evil days. They were a token of his eventual recovery from crisis.

In the body of his work the shorter narrative led at all times something of a life of its own. Although necessarily a simpler affair, the Jamesian story like the Jamesian novel rested on a firm core of anecdote, "a little organic and effective Action." To the history of the short story he contributed little or nothing except in taking the form seriously and writing well in it. He had no part in the limbering-up of the form which was to give rise to such tales as Chekhov's "The Kiss" or Joyce's "Araby." These works would probably have impressed him as inconclusive and hence inartistic, not because they are deficient in "action," which they are not, but because the action serves to reveal the quality of a life rather than to change the life. However much James in his later work anticipated modern writers in his images of futility, his concern with the vagaries of consciousness, the importance he allowed to moments of fantasy and revelation, he nevertheless remained traditional in his sense of the relation of mind to character and character to action. Like his novels, his stories normally present some intrigue whose working out leaves people decisively altered in their being as well as in their circumstances.

To accomplish so much effectively, he required a certain amplitude even of the tale. His few attempts at the very short narrative have mostly the effect of seeming too busy. It was in the story of from fifteen to sixty thousand words, the "blest *nouvelle*," that he excelled as a tale-teller, even achieving in it a kind of ultimate perfection which can be claimed for but few of his long novels. The latter he seems to have thought of as properly the vehicle for broadly representative situations and for characters of a considerable complexity and stature. To shorter treatment he assigned what he would have called the "special cases": exercises in sheer technical facility, fables of the artist, ventures in the supernatural, studies in extreme obsessions and other anomalies. These are not all the types of subject to be found among James's stories, nor do the stories themselves necessarily adhere strictly to type. There is in most of them a kind of cross-reference, illuminating to a reader acquainted with the categories. For example, "The Liar," while primarily concerned with obsession, glances obliquely at the artist fable; and "The Turn of the Screw" is notoriously a tale of which it is hard to say whether the pathological or the supernatural predominates in it.

The early '90's witnessed the flourishing of the artist tale among other types. If James then seemed intent on escaping his fate as a serious novelist by way of the theater, he was nevertheless all the time reflecting on that fate in his stories of artists. These were very numerous and some were little more than anecdotes. His knowledge of the predicaments of the dedicated artist in an increasingly commercial world conditions all of them, even such a tale as "The Coxon Fund," which is based on the Coleridge legend. *Embarrassments*, the ironically frivolous title of one collection of them, indicates something of their tone. If he still sees art and life as unalterably opposed, as he did in his youthful cycle of narratives on the same subject, he is now less inclined to preach the importance of the disjunction than to smile bitterly over its consequences for artist and public alike. The essential melodrama of the conflict persists in the later stories, where, however, it is translated into contemporary idiom. "Life" is no longer represented by some *femme fatale* like Roderick's Christina but by one's wife, who wants to be able to keep a carriage and send one's sons to Sandhurst. Not America with her poverty of culture, but the universal public, is the present enemy. And James's artist-heroes have now a more distinct professional existence. They are usually writers, often novelists, beset by modern problems of craft and the market, encircled by a noisy London of dinner parties and week ends, yellow journalism, lionizing hostesses, pre-Raphaelite girls, and aesthetic young men. In one way or another the ordeals of the artist-hero, who is pretty much the same person in most of the tales, are often close to James's own. In "The Next Time" this hero tries, for the sake of popularity, to write a bad book and produces only another esoteric masterpiece; in "The Figure in the Carpet" he complains that criticism has failed to discover the inner meaning of his work; in "The Death of the Lion" he is killed by the equivocal kindness of hostesses; in "The Lesson of the Master" his work, as a result of certain compromises on his part, has acquired "inequalities, superficialities. For one who looks at it from the artistic point of view it contains a bottomless ambiguity." One thing is common to many of these performances: they turn not only on the trials of creation but on the rigors of appreciation. Isolated though he may be from the public, the artist-hero is apt to enjoy the devotion of one or two impassioned students of his art. And certain of the young men of *The Yellow Book* seem to have been James's own devotees in those years, forming the nucleus of what was presently to swell into a considerable following. The editors of *The Yellow Book*, at whose affinities with Wilde and Beardsley James looked askance, proudly published two of his artist tales, including the one that is probably his most memorable effort in the genre. Long starved for recognition, Neil Paraday of "The Death of the Lion" (1894) is at last surfeited and crushed by the attentions of people who exploit his prestige without bothering to read his books. They even nonchalantly mislay the manuscript of a work in progress; and when he insists on dying, they transfer their flatteries to a lady-novelist known to the public as Guy Walsingham and a gentleman-novelist whose pen-name is Dora Forbes. "The Death of the Lion" is frankly an extravaganza and it is full of vivid incident. There is place in it for both cleverness and pathos, two qualities which are common to most of these artist tales and which in many of them are felt to be at odds.

"The Middle Years" (1893), another good story in this cycle, perhaps spoke more of James's mind at the moment than did any of the rest. This time the question of public recognition is united with the question of a writer's acceptance of himself. Dencombe, conscious of imperfections in his work so far, dreams of redeeming them "in a certain splendid 'last manner.'" But he will have no final phase; he is fatally ill; and the young doctor who attends him and is also an admirer of his genius helps him to die moderately content with himself. "A second chance—*that's* the delusion," Dencombe concludes. "There never was to be but one. We work in the dark—we do what we can—we give what we have. Our doubt is our passion and our passion is our task. The rest is the madness of art."

What he has accomplished so far *is* his work; *he* is what he has so far *done*. This hard truth Dencombe comes at last to embrace with a rueful ecstasy. And thus "The Middle Years," an unusually brief tale to which James brought a concentrated richness of image and phrase that looked forward to his own splendid last manner, carries us beyond the artist fables to another class of stories which also flourished in the '90's and to which he made distinguished contributions as long as he remained productive. These are the stories of "What Might Have Been," as the editors of James's notebooks aptly describe them. They are about estranged and solitary men, each in some measure possessed by what James, referring to the hero of "The Jolly Corner," called "an 'unnatural' anxiety, a malaise . . . incongruous and discordant." Sadly familiar with the streets, even when they have comfortable places of their own, they are to be observed, like the tutor and his doomed charge of "The Pupil," "wandering idly through the Jardin des Plantes as if they had nowhere to go, sitting on the winter days in the galleries of the Louvre, so splendidly ironical to the homeless, as if for the advantage of the *calorifère*." In a cold and vulgar world they cherish their idealism and their self-esteem, often carrying their passion to the point of mania. And whether the obsession consists in their habitually telling picturesque falsehoods, or their maintaining private altars to their dead friends, or their being haunted by ghosts

and alter-egos, they live in the shadow of a common fear—
they dread lest they be defrauded, not simply of recognition, like the artists, but of life itself, of significant experience. "My attested predilection for poor sensitive gentlemen almost embarrasses me as I march," wrote James
on reviewing these stories for The New York Edition.

About even the boy-hero of "The Pupil" there is something rather elderly and gentlemanly; he is hustled and
humiliated by his shady parents, life fails to materialize
for him at all, he dies on the verge of it. On the other
hand, George Dane, of "The Great Good Place," has known
only too much of robust experience in the way of success
and honor; for him living has come to be synonymous with
a surfeit of mail and engagements; what he craves, and
finds, is a quiet place where the spirit may re-awaken; for
"it was the inner life, for people of his generation, victims of
the modern madness, mere maniacal extension and motion,
that was returning health." A rich man and a public
official, Stransom, of "The Altar of the Dead," is again in
the thick of things; but the death years ago of his beloved
fiancée has paralyzed a part of his nature, which he has
dedicated to her memory and, with the passage of time, to
the memory of his ever-lengthening list of departed friends,
so quickly forgotten by everyone else in busy London, till at
last he hits on the idea of maintaining in a Catholic church
a private altar to his dead, a candle for each of them, even
finally consenting to revere the memory of the man who,
when he was alive, had most injured him. There is a great
deal of the later James, his increasing piety and withdrawal,
in "The Altar of the Dead." But as a story it is overwrought; there are failures of proportion and of humor
in it, and the "social entity" (in Eliot's phrase) has shrunk to

almost nothing. Except for a shadowy woman confidante and fellow-worshiper, Stransom is nearly alone with his anguish, which seems insufficiently earned in terms of circumstance. In this respect "The Birthplace," though less celebrated than "The Altar of the Dead," is a far better tale. There is more of a detached ingenious humor in it; and there is more of the world, the world of bluff official persons and cynical professional routines, to justify the pathos of the hero, who is the caretaker of a literary shrine operated by an awful invisible Body for the tourist trade. "The Birthplace," like "The Pupil," is one of the world's great tales.

But the story of What Might Have Been culminated, as did a whole strain of James's work, in "The Beast in the Jungle." This he was to write in 1901, immediately after completing *The Ambassadors*, which he considered his most perfect novel. And although its *donnée* dated back, "The Beast in the Jungle" may have owed its peculiar lucidity to the happy moment of its execution. Then in the heyday of his recovered powers as a novelist, James was conceivably in a position to be lucid, even apocalyptic, about his themes; and in Strether of *The Ambassadors* he had just drawn the densest and ripest of all his sympathetic portraits of the poor sensitive gentleman. Even so, the triumph of celibate spirit over passionate matter is still, in *The Ambassadors*, a tenuous one; it still tempts us to turn the tables on the poor gentleman, to see him as the victim of his own self-love. This James had done in the confident days of the international novel with such types of superior sensitiveness as Acton, Winterbourne, and Osmond; and the wry portrait of the ineffable Vanderbank in *The Awkward Age* (1898) is one of the numerous signs by which that novel proclaims James's returning serenity. In John Marcher of "The Beast in the Jungle" the poor gentleman attains a disastrous apotheosis.

In their discussion of the story, the editors of the notebooks suggest that its antecedents are not only in James's earlier work but in Hawthorne as well. As Hawthorne had his generous portrayals of the superior man, his Fanshawes and Coverdales, so he had his wretched Ethan Brands. But Marcher is an Ethan Brand who has, so to speak, read Pater, if not James himself; and for him the Unpardonable Sin consists in his refusing life under the impression that he is being reserved for "something rare and strange," some fate that will involve his having "felt and vibrated . . . more than any one else." As the years pass and nothing happens, his expectations turn to dread; he waits and waits, not so much for his dream to come true as for "the hidden beast to spring." And it does so at last in the form of a revelation: Marcher, he learns, was destined to be "the man to whom nothing on earth was to have happened"; he was to have had no experience beyond the searing knowledge of his inexperience. If a pathos not altogether earned is sometimes the fault of James's poor-gentleman stories, it is here richly justified by Marcher's ultimate recognition; and everything in the tale falls into place. The very abstractness of it, the absence of reinforcing and qualifying circumstances, the vague airless unfurnished unpeopled medium in which the action, consisting mostly of low-toned conversations between Marcher and a woman friend, takes place, is all in the spirit of the subject. And the woman, so often merely a confidante in these stories, is here brought squarely into the picture. Weary of waiting for Marcher to perceive the truth, which she has long since discovered just as she has long been in love with him, May Bartram at last dies. So tenuous, so secret, has their intimacy been that he is not even asked to her funeral. This episode, one of James's great images of exclusion, is swiftly followed by as impassioned a scene as any he ever wrote. Marcher can at least visit May Bartram's grave; which he does; and it is in the cemetery that light finally comes to him. She was not merely his confidante but his lover, whom he has sacrificed to his delusion.

In all the poor gentlemen so far there has been an implicit desire of being loved. A kind of fraternal-homosexual affection unites boy and tutor in "The Pupil"; the aging author of "The Middle Years" is tended by his doctor-admirer as by a devoted son; Stransom's confidante in "The Altar of the Dead" assumes at last the maternal posture: "He let himself go, resting on her; he dropped upon the bench and she fell on her knees beside him, his own arm round her shoulder." In "The Beast in the Jungle" the implicit is made overt in the case of passion as of so much else. The failure of love is Marcher's own failure *to* love, his forcing of May Bartram into the attitude of a mother.

Between people haunted by What Might Have Been and people who live with veritable ghosts, the difference is not great; and in the '90's, as for some years after, James produced a number of tales of the supernatural. "The Jolly Corner," which he wrote following a visit to the United States in 1904-1905, was close to home in every sense. The setting is New York; the hero a returned exile who, by routing the phantom of the brutal man of business he might have become if he had passed his life in America, relieves his mind of apprehensions and frees his heart to love. Unlike Marcher's revelation, Brydon's act of courage comes in time to save him as well as the woman who loves him. Thus in "The Jolly Corner" the poor gentleman's trials have a happy outcome at last, if only through the magic of exorcism. The ghost in this story is the hero's spectral alter-ego; and in general James's ghosts are not gratuitous as they are apt to be in the average terror tale. Like those of Shakespeare, they appear only to people whom distress has first qualified for the adventure.

But is this true of the most celebrated of all James's ghost stories, "The Turn of the Screw" (1898), with its seemingly conscientious governess, its two apparently charming children, and its pair of infamous phantoms—if that is what they are—who evidently want to "get hold" of the children? Those who maintain that the ghosts in "The Turn of the Screw" are hallucinations of the sexually repressed governess have done the great service of showing that there is something problematical in the story and that the governess is full of erotic fancies. But this interpretation points to only one of the large possibilities of a story that seems by intention to deal in possibilities rather than facts. Like "The Aspern Papers," it is a first-person narrative; the effect is again that of deeply implicating the reader; but in this case he is never sure in what he is being implicated. The ghosts are often felt to be there; the governess is sometimes felt to be a misguided hysteric. Terror is the one constant. To this James remains faithful throughout even though he gradually shifts the ground of it from animal fear to metaphysical and moral doubt. Uncertainty, the reader's uncertainty, as to what is real and who is innocent is perhaps the final source of apprehension. And the apprehension is poignant beyond that in the usual mystery story because it plays upon scenes and situations, people and problems, which are themselves vividly human: the pleasant old house and grounds of Bly, so irresistibly English and Victorian; the solid kindly housekeeper Mrs. Grose; the radiant children with their large fund of natural playfulness, affection, and malice; the governess, fresh from her "small smothered life" in a Hampshire vicarage, faced suddenly with an improbable dilemma, loving in excess perhaps but nevertheless loving, and capable of a fearful honesty: "for if he *were* innocent what then on earth was I?"

Because he pretends even more than other artists to know what is real and to deal in it, the novelist, if he is sensitive to the problem, is apt to play the game of illusion and reality with special zeal. This James does in "The Turn of the Screw," to a degree of which he himself appears to have been unaware, for he wrote and said many conflicting things about the story. A tale, as we might say, of total irony, it is saved from being a mere exercise in mystification by its great charm and pathos. It was, moreover, close to James's mind at the time. Concerned with the difficulty of *making sense*, of piercing the moral and metaphysical mysteries, the story was an incident in the strenuous work of reconstruction to which he addressed himself in the five years following the theater crisis.

This work was carried on most conspicuously in his fulllength novels of the time. So far as public success was concerned, the longer form had proved a treacherous medium for him. It remained a tempting one, if only because it could be more readily serialized; and a few days after the *Guy Domville* disaster James solemnly rededicated himself to it. "I take up my *own* old pen again—the pen of all my old unforgettable efforts and sacred struggles," he wrote in his notebook. Confidence was once more strong in him; he had only to "face my problems," to "produce, produce," and all would be well. And he did produce. Between 1896 and 1901 there appeared *The Other House, The Spoils of Poynton, What Maisie Knew, The Awkward Age,* and *The Sacred Fount,* together with the two considerable novelettes, "The Turn of the Screw" and "In the Cage."

Some of these are among James's best books; others represent him at his most exasperating; and of all his various "periods," that of the years 1896-1900 is the least readily summarized and appraised. The reason for this unevenness is fairly clear. Having ceased to expect a wide acclaim, he was frankly trying his hand; "difficulty" alone interested him now, as he was later to observe to Howells. Yet the difficulty he courted was not, as often supposed, merely that of a writer endeavoring to tell stories in perversely complicated ways. The imposition of a stricter form on fiction was certainly one of his aims; and it was the one about which his notebooks and letters were most eloquent. Indeed, to *"face* my problems" signified, in the first instance, to find some means by which to "convert"— the word still did service—his play-writing experience to his uses as a novelist so that the exertions and sufferings of those years should not be wasted. Yet the novels themselves show him to have been engaged simultaneously on another difficult enterprise. This was the task of making sense, of wresting a meaning from modern life.

This is not to say that he was reflecting systematically or even consciously. If he was, we have no way of knowing it. His notebooks, seldom very discursive, were in the '90's as reticent as ever on the subject of his general views. Probably he had none, time having made no change in him in this respect. And this is singular, considering all that he had been through. The implications of Hyacinth Robinson's suicide, the critical years that ensued for the author himself, might easily have induced another man to seek light and support in church or party, science or myth. They seem to have left James's mind as inviolable to doctrine as ever; and even his continued adherence to a native self-reliance and empiricism may well have been instinctive. Stransom tending his private altar in a Catholic church is an emblem of James's mind, late as well as early. He had, to be sure, his old pieties, his fundamental idealism; and these were strongly to the fore in the novels of the '90's. His particular moral ideas arose, however, from his pursuit of literary form; or so it would appear from his notebooks, whose detailed entries on *The Spoils of Poynton* are a case in point. Here we learn that the conception of Fleda Vetch, the heroine whom he was later to describe as a "free spirit" and on whose gratuitous renunciations the plot turns, came to him as a result of his search for a structural "center" and a telling "dénouement."

However casual her origin, Fleda Vetch is central to *The Spoils of Poynton* and, in what she represents, to the novels that follow. She embodies what another character describes as "the moral sense"; and the fate of the moral sense in a corrupt or obtuse world is the common subject of the *Spoils, What Maisie Knew,* "The Turn of the Screw," and—with a difference—*The Awkward Age* and *The Sacred Fount.* The Jamesian chivalry is for the moment in abeyance; his concern is now with the conscience naked and unqualified. This appears in the reduced proportions of the novels themselves, which are no longer social panoramas like the *Princess* and *The Tragic Muse* but miniatures.

And as the novels are stripped, so to speak, for actions of conscience, so are the characters—especially, as might be expected, those who represent the conscience itself. If they are not, like Mr. Longdon of *The Awkward Age*, rendered angular and charmless and unbeautiful through the effects of age and long rustication, they are made so by being unwanted children or solitary governesses or impoverished dependents. Strictly outsiders, they are capable of great love, although it is just their fate as embattled souls that they rarely inspire it in others and that they are sometimes absurd in their shy hankering after unobtainable persons. Their tempestuous virtue cuts them off; they have scarcely any relation to life beyond their wish to "save" others; they are very limited people. Mrs. Wix, the blunt aging unlovely governess of *What Maisie Knew*, with her eternal brown dress and absurd passion for the scapegrace Sir Claude, who can be hired cheaply because she is so incompetent in everything except goodness, is the extreme type. And it follows that they are never, like Isabel and Hyacinth, passionate pilgrims of experience; if they have any such feelings they quickly subordinate them to duty. James now went as far as it was in him to go to mute the magical overtones of his work, to confine the imagination of his people to the imagination of good and evil. As there are few Americans in these novels, so the English scene is simply the world rather than the old world. London, as it appears in *What Maisie Knew* or *The Awkward Age*, is merely the modern metropolis where the weather is rainy or fair and cabs are hard to find; and the beauty of Bly, the old country place in "The Turn of the Screw," is no more than an ironic value in the story. If James had wished to symbolize his relinquishment—temporary, to be sure—

of "the inward romantic principle," he could not have done so more vividly than by the fire that at last consumes splendid Poynton with all its disputed spoils (the novel was first titled, less subtly, *The Old Things*). Was James engaged in disciplining his sensibility? Had he heard too much of that faculty in the age of Marius the Epicurean, Dorian Gray, and—Hyacinth Robinson? For a James who felt himself isolated and at sea there was possibly also an intimate motive in the moral affirmation, as if he were thus returning to his origins, renewing his energies, confirming his identity. This is a guess; but one thing is clear. His faith in the Good Woman is now reviving. Reborn in the shape of a small girl, a governess, a little telegraph operator, she once more takes the field.

Yet the asceticism of these years remained a point of view rather than a fundamental commitment. The need of reversing the medal still possessed James; and read in sequence, the novels of the '90's are discovered to be a series of statements and counterstatements on the subject of the moral sense. If *The Spoils of Poynton* and *What Maisie Knew* strenuously affirm it, the stories that follow present rather the dilemmas to which it may lead when pursued to extremes in given situations. In "The Turn of the Screw" there is doubtless a calculated ambiguity on this point; *The Sacred Fount*, evidently a self-satire that misfired, seems pretty clearly to associate the unrestrained moral sense with mere snooping and malice on the part of its author-hero, who is given to discovering far-fetched perversities among his friends. Meanwhile there was *The Awkward Age*, the masterpiece of this period, in which the world scores what looks like a distinct victory over innocence become stiff-necked and grotesque.

The Spoils of Poynton (1896) achieves a balance between its moral austerities and its attractions as a comedy of manners; Fleda brings her crusading spirit into a finely modulated human atmosphere. This is dominated by Mrs. Gereth, the mistress of Poynton, a country house which she has discreetly stocked with treasures of art and handicraft. Mrs. Gereth is a high-handed woman of much charm and force, a familiar type, inevitably a widow, fairly wealthy, and full of robust combativeness. Her love of fine things and fine manners is richly genuine; her frank happy humorous habit of self-interest, the pleasure she takes in the contemplation of her own mind, the unexpected generosities and flexibilities of which she is capable—all these traits make her a persuasive example of enlightened egotism. And it is no wonder that Fleda, a poor imaginative girl whom she takes to live with her, is enchanted by her patroness. But Fleda also likes Mrs. Gereth's son Owen, who, kindly, insensitive, a little stupid, is his mother's opposite. Owen foreshadows those characters of E. M. Forster's of whom Lionel Trilling, quoting Forster himself, says that they represent "the undeveloped heart." And Owen is what he is because his mother is what she is. In reaction to her large presence and brooding cleverness he has become a figure of mere amorphous good-nature, pleasant but helpless. He is especially vulnerable to the militant philistinism of Mona Brigstock, the girl he proposes to marry and who will in that case, by the English law, become mistress of Poynton, which she dreams of "modernizing" along the lines of Waterbath, her parents' cozy chintz-and-stucco villa. Mrs. Gereth, to meet the threat of Waterbath, conceives a plan: it is that Fleda shall develop Owen's heart. And on the surface the plan looks promising. Fleda will thus secure a husband, one whom she is thoroughly prepared to love; and Poynton will be saved from the awful Mona. Owen also stands to profit, or so it seems, for he proves to be susceptible to Fleda once he is exposed to her. But this is just the point on which Mrs. Gereth's scheme comes to grief. Much as Fleda would like to oblige her friend and possess both Poynton and Owen, she will coöperate only if assured that Owen's heart is really matured, that he is acting on his own. Abruptly to abandon Mona for Fleda is to argue a certain levity on his part, as well as to put Fleda in the position of having intrigued to get him. No sooner, therefore, has he discovered his love for Fleda than she sends him back to Mona, reminding him of his duty to his affianced. If this seems perverse, it is none the less the chief nuance of the novel. The average heroine in such a situation would put it to Owen, or at least to herself, that she was "testing" him. But this in itself would be subtly to assert prior rights and thus to influence his behavior and predetermine her own attitude. For Fleda, testing him fairly means not testing him at all but simply dissociating herself from the entire business as inconspicuously as possible. This she does, and the rightness, the fatal rightness, of her decision is confirmed in the sequel; for Owen, removed from Fleda's presence, promptly returns to Mona and marries her. If his heart has at last developed, it has done so in a fashion fatal to his mother's plan.

The burden of *The Spoils of Poynton* is thus perfectly clear. To exercise the moral sense, as Fleda insists on doing, is frankly to risk natural happiness, which is shown to depend on just the kind of compromises she refuses to make. The end of the novel leaves us, protesting its astringency perhaps, but nevertheless with a feeling of issues sharply drawn and vividly presented. Owen is carried off by Mona, Fleda returns to her poverty, Mrs. Gereth is left in her lonely and dispossessed state, and Poynton burns to the ground. The fire with which the novel concludes destroys but it also purifies.

What Maisie Knew (1897) carries much farther the ethical and structural complexities of *The Spoils of Poynton.* It carries them so far as to give rise to a doubt whether the novel, witty and remorseless as it certainly is, is not more of a torment than a pleasure for the reader, however broadly "pleasure" may be defined. The disparity between exercising the moral sense and enjoying animal happiness is again the subject, and this time the ordeal of choice is visited upon a mere child. Fleda Vetch had at least the comfort of her young maturity and developed conscience; Maisie Farange is obliged to acquire a conscience at an age and under circumstances which make existence itself difficult. She lives a wandering life among hard pleasure-loving people of the West End, dependent first on her divorced parents and then, when they more or less abandon her, on an odd couple of whom one is her mother's second husband, the other her father's second wife, and who have made her the pretext of a shady romance. Thus the cruelty perpetrated on Maisie is of a different order from that done Oliver Twist and the other small victims in Victorian novels, who are so often sacrificed to poverty or snobbishness. Her life is poor chiefly in affection and serenity; it is poor in candor, in transparency. Except with her governess Mrs. Wix she never knows where she stands with her elders. The rare embraces of her begemmed mother, a famous society beauty and billiards-player, are so convulsive that Maisie feels she is being "pulled violently through a jeweler's window"; and her father's insistent affability is even more deceptive. Maisie's world is opaque, but she finally comes to see the truth of things, as a result of her own anxious curiosity as well as of the promptings of the almost diabolically righteous Mrs. Wix. What Maisie knows at last is that she is being used by her elders for their own disreputable ends; that she is in fact an instrument of badness among them and a not unwilling one so long as she goes along with them in her desire for support and affection. Her only escape is to renounce them altogether, which she does in the end, going off to live with Mrs. Wix in the back streets of London.

It is not unusual in James for the overtones of one novel to become the themes of the next. And *What Maisie Knew* is peculiarly, perhaps excessively, dense in overtones. The most relentlessly experimental of the books of this period, it bore to the later work the relation of a forcing-bed to a garden. With "The Turn of Screw" its affinities are especially close and interesting. If Mrs. Wix is "almost diabolical" in her furious missionary moralism, the governess of the later tale seems to have been imagined with diabolism as one of her definite possibilities. It is as if James, in carrying to extremes one of his old concerns, the beauty of being good, had collided with another, the ugliness of imposing on helpless people. But *What Maisie Knew* anticipates the later work in other respects as well. Not the least of the hardships visited upon Maisie is that her small mind is made the sole register of the intricate events of the novel. She has to make things out for herself; and while in this case the things she makes out—the depravity of her elders, the goodness of Mrs. Wix—are objectively present for the reader as well, in "The Turn of the Screw" and *The Sacred*

Fount the reader has no such assurance. He has left the realm of morals for that of epistemology. He is in a strange medium of exasperated curiosity, and one which has for its object the unknowable sexual relations of people. Sex, which figures hardly at all in *The Spoils of Poynton*, is conspicuous in *What Maisie Knew*, with its incessant coupling and uncoupling on the part of Maisie's elders, and really lurid in "The Turn of the Screw," where it is a question whether the children have not been corrupted by the dead servants in ways that are left to our imagination. And the sexual theme will be present in all of James's important later work.

His prose is likewise changing in these years, and changing considerably, although the process is gradual. In his effort to make the story self-sufficient, his sentences have always carried an abundance of suggestive detail; they now simply carry more. The urbane and relatively impersonal rhythms of his earlier style become more nervously responsive to the currents of feeling. There are bizarre shifts of pace, unexpected brevities. "Her little world was phantasmagoric—strange shadows dancing on a sheet." At the same time, as the entire medium becomes denser and tauter, it risks parallelisms of sound and cadence which would formerly have been rejected as too poetic. "There was a general shade in all the lower reaches—a fine clear dusk in garden and grove." Increasingly the language rejoices in sudden colloquialism, raffish jargon, and a habit of turning abruptly and alarmingly concrete. "Mrs. Wix gave the jerk of a sleeper awakened or the start even of one who hears a bullet whiz at the flag of truce." Above all, the medium begins to put forth remarkable metaphors without fear of violating its prose character. The following, from *The Portrait of a Lady*, is an easily predictable image, formally introduced and logically developed. "It had lately occurred to her that her mind was a good deal of a vagabond, and she had spent much ingenuity in training it to a military step and teaching it to advance, to halt, to retreat, to perform even more complicated manoeuvres, at the word of command." Compare this with the following from *The Sacred Fount*: "The last calls of birds sounded extraordinarily loud; they were like the timed, serious splashes, in wide, still water, of divers not expecting to rise again." These self-doomed divers, like Mrs. Wix's whizzing bullet, are entirely original and perfectly irrelevant to the surface facts of the story. Rather, it is by such eruptions, as Stephen Spender has said, that "there arise, as from the depths, the dream images of the unconscious." They also connect James's refined-appearing world with the realm of the physical and the elemental, of latent horror, of "the thing hideously *behind*."

There was danger that the verbal abundance of the later style might become an end in itself, overwhelming the story and the characters. This James at his best averted, partly by making the characters themselves more articulate. They have always been eloquent about their concerns; they now talk, besides, about the language itself, evidencing its richness in nuance at the same time that they are furthering the action. The internal structure of dialogue, as well as its relation to the enveloping narrative, undergoes an intense stylization. The theater's influence is felt in monolithic scenes and resounding curtains. Patches of talk are set off from the rest like parks from their adjacent streets, except that the business of the story is mainly done in them. Of business, moreover, there is a definite sum to be accomplished in each area of dialogue, some item of revelation or decision to be added to the whole account. And although the talkers are as a rule vividly individual, they eagerly subordinate themselves to this larger enterprise like the participants in a relay race or a morris dance. However much at variance in other respects, they all "pull together," as James would say, in the interests of a common task, a common intensity, a common style. Extremely sociable, they pause in mid-sentence to allow a friend the pleasure of finishing it; or they offer him an irresistible come-on in the form of an equivocation or a floating pronoun.

> Mrs. Beale furthermore only gave her more to think about in saying that their disappointment was the result of his having got into his head a kind of idea.
> "What kind of idea?"
> "Oh goodness knows!" She spoke with an approach to asperity. "He's so awfully delicate."
> "Delicate?"—that was ambiguous.
> "About what he does, don't you know?" said Mrs. Beale. She fumbled. "Well, about what *we* do."
> Maisie wondered. "You and me?"
> "Me and *him*, silly!" cried Mrs. Beale with, this time, a real giggle.

This habit of leading with a doubtful pronoun certainly grew on James's later characters, and like other of his devices for securing internal unity it became customary, part of a large body of conventional usage which, of course, is felt as a strength or an infirmity of his style depending on whether the emotion is itself forceful or weak in the given case. On the whole, for richness, for subtlety, for attention to concords of sense and sound, James's later style was the most remarkable style in English since the 17th century. With all its artifices, there is something elemental about it. Unlike the virtuoso styles, admirable though they are, of a Stevenson or a Swinburne, that of James refers us back, not to the eloquence of the author, but to the resources of the language.

The Awkward Age, which began to appear in *Harper's Weekly* in October 1898, is the most elaborate expression of James's preoccupations in the '90's. It is also one of his masterpieces, and clearly the chief work of its period. This, to be sure, is not the received opinion. Even among his admirers *The Awkward Age* has long figured as a companion piece to *The Sacred Fount*, the two books being widely regarded as products of a misguided virtuosity. The fact, moreover, that it was followed shortly by *The Ambassadors* and *The Wings of the Dove*, in which the author returned triumphantly to the international theme, has also cast a shadow over it. *The Awkward Age* is assumed to have represented a last vain assault on a subject—English life proper—for which James was not really equipped and which he thereafter wisely abandoned. Nor is the novel, in some of its aspects, very characteristic of his mind. The usual elements are there, in particular the innocent-child-and-worldly-parent situation of the '90's; and the familiar crusader type is embodied in Mr. Longdon. But all these pieces are subtly reassorted to produce the picture of a quite different moral atmosphere.

Once the charm of this atmosphere is felt, the objections mostly fall away. In form, it is true, the novel is an experiment, and one that would seem to lead nowhere so far as the art of narrative is concerned. As James explained in the preface, he had tried once more to achieve the self-sufficiency of drama. He had wanted to banish all "going behind," all of the usual novelistic commentary. So *The Awkward Age* reads as much as possible like an extended play. It is largely dialogue; and this is arranged conspicuously in scenes, with much attention given to pointed climaxes, forceful curtains, the grouping and movement of the characters, their entrances and exits. Now these are the mere mechanics of the stage, and no more lovely in themselves than the mechanics of the novel. Solemnly transferred to fiction they only appear the more banal; and in such books as *The Other House*, which originated as a play, the synthetic method does considerable harm. It is better naturalized in *The Awkward Age* and there are even incidental benefits. The commentary, not so much banned as reduced to a minimum, is admirably cogent and witty. And, what is almost unique in James, there is no central observer.

Whether as cause or effect, the absence of this familiar figure seems to be connected with a certain relaxation of the moral, or at least the magisterial, impulse in *The Awkward Age*. James is on notably easy terms with the life described, neither outside it nor above it nor beneath it. In all his best stories, it is true, there are moments when the usual enchanted perception of things gives way to a sense of the simple wear and tear of existence. *The Awkward Age* hums with this note throughout. If the old outsider in James is still latent here, his presence is felt only in the luxury of a general surrender to the way of the world. The social entity is more literally the hero than in any of the novels. Superficially the book is satire at the expense of fashionable London: the matchmaking and fortune-hunting, the insincerities, the false positions, the abuse of innocence, the violation of family pieties. Beyond the West End follies, however, is society itself; and at a deeper level in *The Awkward Age* this presence, so vital to James and his work, is celebrated, transfigured. For all its vices, it is shown to be the human medium; the source of amiability, proportion, beauty, wit. The novel is thus a kind of *Misanthrope* and its heroine, Mrs. Brookenham, a kind of Célimène, while Vanderbank and Mr. Longdon divide Alceste between them.

"I think Mrs. Brook the best thing I've ever done," James told a correspondent. He had certainly done nothing like her. She belongs with the charming rogues of literature, those characters whose energy redeems their badness and who, consequently, have no place in his regular scheme. It is she, the genius of conversation, who presides over the social entity in *The Awkward Age* and gives the novel its gravely festal air of having been written by someone on a dignified moral spree. Like Falstaff she is not only witty but the cause that others are so. Like all the better rogues she has a *kind* of conscience, if this may be said without the impertinence of seeming to try to whitewash her. Her conscience is her exacting sense of social fitness, her awareness of others, her heroic respect for delicacy, imagination, humor, composure, and candor. Her badness consists in her willingness to sacrifice other people—notably her daughter, Nanda—to her own system; and, apart from her wish to provide for her own in a practical way, she has no family sentiment. But she is not naturally perverse, as is her kinswoman, the Duchess, who, though also brilliant, is both self-righteous and a hypocrite. Circumstances work heavily against Mrs. Brook. She and her husband have too small an income to keep them socially afloat without great labors of tact and contrivance on her part. Nanda, moreover, on whom she counts to make a profitable marriage, is too romantic to coöperate. The girl is foolish enough—from her mother's point of view—to be in love with Vanderbank, a bachelor of 34, handsome, impeccable, and poor. Mrs. Brook exerts herself to discourage this senseless attachment, not merely because Vanderbank is without funds but because she knows—alas, she has been in love with him herself—that he is constitutionally indecisive. " 'He'll never, never,' Mrs. Brookenham resolutely quavered—'He'll never come to the scratch.' " And Nanda will be strung along until it is too late for her to find anyone else. Mrs. Brook's main effort, then, goes into hastening Vanderbank's withdrawal by putting him on the spot in various ways, all subtle and excruciating. Meanwhile, having failed to interest Nanda in the jolly Mitchett—very rich and in love with the girl besides—she decides to get her adopted by Mr. Longdon. With this wealthy old gentleman from the country Nanda has, indeed, a curious bond. He was once vainly in love with her grandmother; and both the old man and the young girl hark back to an unfashionable romanticism of high virtue and unrequited love. After great endeavors, Mrs. Brook finally succeeds with Mr. Longdon. In a scandalous scene she makes herself and her friends so odious to him that he at last takes pity on Nanda and proceeds to rescue her from their corrupting influence. But in thus settling her daughter, the mother has come close to ruining herself.

One of those irresistible creations who cannot heave a sigh without being in character, Mrs. Brookenham is made vivid primarily in her relations with her circle, from whose various members she is delicately distinguished. At first she seems worse than most of them, more cynical and heartless. By degrees it appears that she is merely more honest, with herself as well as others. Hypocrisy is foreign to her; it makes people ridiculous in her eyes; any breach of confidence is a false note. Her rhetoric, like that of her circle, is composed equally of a teasing reticence and an alarming frankness. It is part of the game that they alternately evade one another and let one another have it. But just as Mrs. Brook is more amusing than they, so her candor surpasses theirs. When her seemingly obtuse husband inquires the reason of their long intimacy with Vanderbank, "Well," she replies, "we were in love with him." And to Vanderbank himself she finally observes, "I sometimes think in effect that you're incapable of anything straightforward." Given their usual formula of genial banter, and the effect of this blunt speech is almost the same as if she had produced a gun and shot him.

Living in society necessarily involves one in false positions; its values collide with those of personal honor and family piety; it is half a splendid art, half a sordid and exhausting business. This is the tragicomic fact which Mrs. Brook alone faces fully and which she tries to make endurable by her policy of honesty among friends. No one else quite matches her in this, though all are in false positions of one kind or another. Only Mitchy seems to rival her; but Mitchy, at once rich and innocent, a fantastic creature, "the son of a shoemaker and the grandson of a grasshopper," is beyond temptation. Vanderbank is her real foil. Too good for a world of which he is nevertheless an admired ornament and an immovable fixture, he is in the most awkward position of all. Attractive though he is, much as he exercises the charm which his friends call "the sacred terror," "old Van," as Mrs. Brookenham says, is not straightforward. Though disapproving of his friends, he is nevertheless unthinkable without them. This is his dilemma, and the reason why he is so rarely at peace. A consuming disquiet appears in his small habits of shaking his foot, looking at his watch, falling silent in conversation, and laying jocularly brutal hands on the shoulders of friends. But Mrs. Brook is likewise capable of suffering. Her peculiar sincerity lays her open to reproaches which the others escape by their double dealing. In a sense she is her circle's scapegoat. Because she is relatively poor, her need of plotting and planning is great; her zest for it is also high, and so she goes farther than anyone else. In the eyes of Mr. Longdon she relentlessly compromises the entire group; they are annoyed and fall away from her: the Duchess, old Van, even Mitchy for a while. And her children also let her down; no doubt they are a judgment on her. Young Harold, possessed of her worldliness without her grace, insists on translating her delicate terms into the grossest vernacular. From her own son, in her own house, she hears the unfamiliar sound of vulgarity and insolence. "Don't we live beyond our means, mummy dear?" he inquires; and while she plays for millions, he touches her friends for five-pound notes.

In the long run, it is true, Harold succeeds in becoming a comfort of sorts to Mrs. Brook; Nanda, however, with her exasperating clairvoyance, her lovely accusing primness, is almost her mother's undoing. The final scenes are, ironically, given to the daughter. Grown up now and secure in the knowledge that she is about to take off with Mr. Longdon, Nanda queens it in the chaste privacy of her upstairs sitting-room. There she entertains her mother's former friends at tea and begs them please not to neglect the unfortunate woman downstairs. "Do stick to her," she urges Vanderbank, and, in a burst of impertinence, dreadfully reveals her mother's secret. "I suppose it *would* be immodest," she chatters, "if I were to say that I verily believe she's in love with you." If there has ever been any serious doubt, it is now clear that Nanda, as Mrs. Brook has remarked, is "as bleak as a chimney-top when the fire's out." Yet the daughter invites final judgment as little as does the mother. If she is the moral sense gone bleak by contrast with the world's radiance, she is nevertheless allowed, in this so equable novel, her own quaint sad appealing phosphorescence.

The Lion of Lamb House

THOUGH fallen on evil days, as he believed, James continued to dine out with Lady Playfair and the Archbishop of Canterbury, to mention only two of his more distinguished entertainers. He was as much as ever at the mercy of his friends' attentions and his own sociability. But at last, in 1898, he could take no more and fled London, settling at Rye, Sussex, in an 18th-century house which he presently bought for £2000. The sum was large and the house in need of repairs. He was able to convince himself of the wisdom of the purchase only after debating it by letter with William, who was not convinced. It turned out to be abundantly wise. Lamb House, as the place was called, was the perfect small residence—small by English standards. He loved it and was uncommonly happy there.

To settle in a country town did not mean to shun London altogether. He kept rooms at the Reform Club and was often in them, especially in winter when Rye was cold and lonely. His removal was, rather, a compromise highly typical of him. Instead of an abandonment of city and society, it signified a changed relation to them, the assertion of a partial independence. It was as if, having paid them in *The Awkward Age* the great tribute of taking them for granted, he was now free to keep his distance. And for some years the new arrangement proved benign. The period from 1899 to 1903, during which he did not stir out of England, was the most productive of his entire life. Then, and at Lamb House, were written in rapid succession *The Ambassadors, The Wings of the Dove,* and *The Golden Bowl,* as well as many lesser things. And the same years witnessed the crystallizing of his great legend as a talker and personage.

Rye was fairly quiet without being grimly secluded. An old seaside town, encircled by breezy downs, it was much frequented by golfers, water-colorists, and writers. James was no recluse there, says A. G. Bradley, one of his neighbors, but "fond of his fellow-creatures—after three P.M., till which hour his privacy was sacrosanct." Lamb House itself dominated a narrow thoroughfare in the upper town. The street was sometimes so full of water-colorists and local traffic that he could get out of his door, as he said, only by "taking a flying leap over the heads of Art and Industry." Near by were several ancient cottages which, threatened one time with demolition, were saved largely by vigorous exertions on his part. And there were the routine cares and crises of householding, including on one occasion a struggle with a small midnight chimney fire which he richly described in telegrams and letters to his friends. He found pleasure in being equal to such emergencies and in so representing himself to his correspondents. He was beginning to enjoy, more than hitherto, the possibilities of Henry James in various roles. Formerly so unphysical and so wary of personal humiliation, he no longer minded picturing himself, portly and short-legged as he was, in the unlikely act of "leaping" from his door. By virtue of such discreet clowning he could encompass a relation to the usual and the elemental. It was a relation of juxtaposition. There was in it, as in the increasingly violent imagery of his prose, a conscious extravagance, a new point of view. On his hall table, says H. G. Wells, another neighbor, "lay a number of caps and hats, each with its appropriate gloves and stick; a tweed cap and a stout stick for the marsh, a soft comfortable deerstalker if he were to turn aside to the golf club, a light brown felt hat and a cane for a morning walk down to the harbour, a grey felt with a black band and a gold-headed cane of greater importance if afternoon calling in the town was afoot." With his bad back, which still troubled him at times, his only sport had been walking. At Rye he continued to walk for recreation, moving rather slowly and with occasional long pauses for breath and conversation. But in these latter days he also took, somewhat boastfully, to the bicycle. Golf likewise interested him, if only as a spectator; it was such "a princely expenditure of time" and involved the wearing of picturesque plus-fours. Although he "never touched a niblick in his life" (as still another neighbor, Ford Madox Ford, remarks), he belonged to the local club and was solemnly consulted by the secretary as to new traps and bunkers. The annual cricket week was one of the social events of Rye. James attended the matches, says Reginald Blomfield, "but he always used to sit in the tent talking to the ladies and with his back to the cricket." Even this was a "relation."

He enjoyed the gossip and small rituals of life at Rye. On terms with the postman and the butcher's boy, he strolled about, as Hamlin Garland wrote after a visit, like "a curate making the rounds of his village." Apart from the writers and artists, Rye society was composed of a few families of retired army or government people together with the local professional men. With these people, says Bradley, his talk was "light and human, but always whimsical"; and Blomfield describes him as "a kindhearted and sympathetic man, full of consideration for others, modest and even diffident considering his great and well-deserved reputation, and yet conscious of what was due to him."

Lamb House itself, with its green door and brass knocker, its chimneys and angles and cascades of ivy, its walled garden, its pleasant interiors severely furnished, its succession of pet dogs, its several servants (as many as five at times), was the scene of much hospitality. This, rather than mere retirement, seems to have been what James aimed at in buying the place. Having so long been a guest, he was eager to be the entertainer—on his own terms. "Come down! Come down!" he would write to his friends. And pretty frequently they came: Gosse and A. C. Benson, Howard Sturgis and Hugh Walpole, not to mention the many pilgrims from America—the William Jameses, Howells, T. S. Perry, James T. Fields. Met with ceremonial gaiety at the railroad station, they would be escorted the short distance to Lamb House; installed in their rooms very attentively and with many small jokes about plain living and high thinking; left to themselves during his hours of work when from his study could be heard the incessant boom of his voice and click of his secretary's typewriter; conducted on afternoon tours of the village or the downs; and treated to long evenings of fireside conversation.

A bachelor domesticity is inevitably self-conscious,

especially when the guests are women. Mrs. Fields observes that James was "intent on the largest hospitality," and evidently she meant some stress on the word "intent." Edith Wharton, often at Lamb House after 1904, says that "an anxious frugality was combined with the wish that the usually solitary guest (there were never at most more than two at a time) should not suffer too greatly from the contrast between his or her supposed habits of luxury and the privations imposed by the host's conviction that he was on the brink of ruin. If anyone in a pecuniary difficulty appealed to James for help he gave it without counting; but in his daily life he was haunted by the spectre of impoverishment." Mrs. Wharton, however, may have been a special case. Rich and lavish herself, she seems to have been one of those who like entertaining better than being entertained and who, in return for lionizing a man, and even treating him to a great deal of reverent affection, require him to be a little helpless in sign of his dependence on them. No doubt James did what was expected of him, and even enjoyed playing the captive, as he more and more enjoyed playing other parts. The occasional malice and frivolity of Mrs. Wharton's account of him are easily disengaged from the better parts of it, to which we owe much charming and profound detail about the later James. If she perhaps enjoyed him most when she was the hostess, this was possible even on her visits to Lamb House, because she usually arrived in her motor car. Loving mobility, he rejoiced in touring. "Everything pleased him," wrote Mrs. Wharton, "—the easy locomotion (which often cradled him into a brief nap), the bosky softness of the landscape, the discovery of towns and villages hitherto beyond his range, the magic of ancient names, quaint or impressive, crabbed or melodious. These he would murmur over and over to himself in a low chant, finally creating characters to fit them, and sometimes whole families with their domestic complications and matrimonial alliances, such as the Dymmes of Dymchurch, one of whom married a Sparkle and was the mother of little Scintilla Dymme-Sparkle, subject of much mirth and many anecdotes. Except during his naps nothing escaped him, and I suppose no one ever felt more imaginatively, or with deeper poetic emotion, the beauty of sea and sky, the serenities of the landscape, the sober charm of villages, manor-houses and humble churches, and all the implications of that much-storied corner of England."

On one such occasion, as Mrs. Wharton goes on to recall, James musingly said: "Summer afternoon—summer afternoon; to me those have always been the two most beautiful words in the English language." No doubt she recognized the prevalence in his prose of imagery suggested by that season and time of day—"the long waning light of summer afternoons." She must likewise have understood all that was behind this imagery: that hunger for the imperturbable which was so strong in James in counterpoise to his eternal inner disquiet and which may be felt everywhere in his mind and work, from his idea of history as a humming museum or sublime tableau-vivant; to his idea of the narrative art as properly a series of distinguished scenes; to his feeling that life itself was a succession of incandescent moments frozen into images. And a serenity of sorts had finally come to James himself in his later life, although it was a serenity which, like the metaphors of repose in his novels, was full of implied threats and tensions.

As so many observers agree, a change came over him in

the later '90's, no doubt as a result of his having turned fifty
and been obliged to digest the implications of his theater ca-
lamity as well as of a lifetime that was now fairly long and
sufficiently dense with memories. Very likely he went
through some such process of self-acceptance as is ascribed
to Dencombe of "The Middle Years," except that in his
own case he was thinking of his life as well as his work.
"My life is after all my life and such as it is I might as well
be proud of it" is something that anyone in his senses finally
says to himself. James could now say it with special fervor
because, on the one hand, he had suffered so much from his
conviction of inexperience, and on the other his experience
was actually remarkable. It only required a shift of viewpoint for him to see that he had lived long, written much
and venturesomely, traveled widely, and enjoyed the respect and affection of many. Certain of his friends, too,
acquired a new perspective on him in these years. His way,
as someone said, of "inexorably displacing space" became
increasingly apparent. Mrs. Wharton knew him only in his
old age but Mrs. Humphry Ward, another literary disciple
and mothering intimate who, beside the dashing American
woman, was like the mask of tragedy, had been his friend
since the early '80's. In 1899, *The Awkward Age* just
finished, he visited her at her villa near Rome. "Never did
I see Henry James in a happier light," she wrote, in her so
un-Jamesian prose. "A new light too. For here in this Italian country, and in the Eternal City, the man whom I had
so far mainly known as a Londoner was far more at home
than I; and I realised perhaps more fully than ever before
the extraordinary range of his knowledge and sympathies.
Roman history and antiquities, Italian Art, Renaissance
sculpture, the personalities and events of the Risor-

gimento, all these solid *connaissances* and many more were to be recognised perpetually as rich elements in the general wealth of Mr. James' mind. That he had read immensely, observed immensely, talked immensely, became once more gradually and delightfully clear on this new field."

We can only divine the inner process of this change of heart from the visible evidences of it as recorded by his contemporaries. And to distinguish effects from causes is practically impossible. Was it effect or cause that he took to dictating to a secretary his books and much of his correspondence? For this practice he seems at first to have had the excuse of a lame hand, but some time during the later '90's it became standard with him. His apologies to correspondents for his "Remingtonese" were profuse; they verged on boastfulness, as if he were proud of an achieved intimacy with the alien Machine and of bringing Downtown into his study. He was always recommending dictation to others, including writers already so desperately businesslike as Arnold Bennett. Did the dictation habit contribute to the complication of his later style? Very likely not, although he was not unwilling to encourage those who claimed that it did and who pretended to trace the beginnings of the complication to such and such a chapter of *What Maisie Knew*.

It was perhaps an event of the same order as the dictating when, in 1900, he shaved the beard worn since early youth. In so doing, said Gosse, he "revealed the strong lines of mouth and chin, which responded to the majesty of the skull"—he had long been partly bald. Another acquaintance, W. G. Robertson, agreed that whereas his appearance had formerly been inconspicuous and his beard a kind of "disguise," "the special and only genuine Henry James face was not 'delivered' until he was a comparatively old man." He then became extremely noticeable, acquiring, in Gosse's words, a "radically powerful and unique outer appearance." But what *was* this genuine Henry James face? The essence of it seems to have been that it was many faces. Where it had once been content with mere disguise, it now wore a flagrant composite of masks. "Sometimes," wrote Gosse, "there could be noted—what Henry would have hated to think existing—a theatrical look which struck the eye, as though he might be some retired *jeune premier* of the Français, *jeune* no longer." But Gosse, too solemn to guess that James was not averse to a little polite play-acting, was exhaustively clever in rendering the effects of it: "I remember once seeing a canon preaching in the cathedral of Toulouse who was the picture of Henry James in his unction, his gravity and his vehemence . . . and often the prelatical expression faded into a fleeting likeness to one or other celebrated Frenchman of letters (never to any Englishman or American), somewhat of Lacordaire in the intolerable scrutiny of the eyes, somewhat of Sainte-Beuve, too, in all except the mouth, which though mobile and elastic gave the impression in rest of being small." Other observers similarly ransacked their minds for comparisons, but all agreed that James looked alien, both to his profession and his race. He was "only doubtfully Anglo-Saxon," resembled now "a successful lawyer or banker of the old school," now a Daumier, a Roman death mask, a member of the house of Rothschild, the Mad Hatter, an admiral, a merciful Caesar, a benevolent Napoleon. His eyes, it was often observed, were penetrating and sad—"age-old and world-weary, as are those of cultured Jews."

And he could now afford to be arbitrary, contradictory, even absurd without risk to his essential equilibrium. This last was sustained by his entire genius, but chiefly by his humor, in which his many aspects were resolved. He had, said Barrie, "a smile with which he was on such good terms that it was a part of him chuckling at the other parts." It flickered disarmingly, Barrie went on, "while he rummaged for the right word." And this conversational rummaging rivaled his fantastic appearance and extraordinary prose as a distinguishing trait of the later James. At the root of this much-written-up prodigy lay his insistence, as one who had long been passive, on being heard. Added to that, as A. C. Benson says, was "the natural expansiveness of a great mind and a deep emotion." Benson had James's confidence and doubtless knew his talk at its best. For it was not infallible, like Wilde's, any more than was the personality of which it was an expression. It was an intimate rather than a public manner. The collaboration and sympathy of the hearers were required. Displayed under unfavorable circumstances it could bore and exasperate. It could frighten children, antagonize drunks, and wilt under the scrutiny of impatient vitalists like G. K. Chesterton. Yet a surprising number of men and women found it fascinating, nor were they all of James's "sensitive" type or of his personal following. Certainly Arnold Bennett was of neither; yet he remarked of his first meeting with James that "although I was nearer fifty than forty I felt like a boy"; and of James's talk one evening shortly before his death Bennett observed that it was "detached, just, passionless and a little severe—as became his age." The memoirs of his contemporaries are full of attempts to describe or imitate his conversational habits. By its elaborateness and precision, Benson's account would seem to be the best. "The extreme and almost tantalizing charm of his talk lay not only in his quick transitions, his exquisite touches of humor and irony, the width and force of his sympathy, the range of his intelligence, but in the fact that the whole process of his thought, the qualifications, the resumptions, the interlineations, were laid bare. The beautiful sentences, so finished, so deliberate, shaped themselves audibly upon the air. It was like being present at the actual construction of a little palace of thought, of improvised yet perfect design. The manner was not difficult to imitate; the slow accumulation of detail, the widening sweep, the interjection of grotesque and emphatic images, the studied exaggerations; but what could not be copied was the firmness of the whole conception. He never strayed loosely, as most voluble talkers do, from subject to subject. The *motif* was precisely enunciated, revised, elongated, improved upon, enriched, but it was always, so to speak, strictly contrapuntal. He dealt with the case and nothing but the case; he completed it, dissected it, rounded it off. It was done with much deliberation and even with both repetition and hesitation. But it was not only irresistibly beautiful, it was by far the richest species of intellectual performance that I have ever been privileged to hear."

A son of the then Archbishop of Canterbury, Benson was one of the first of the younger men to attach themselves to James; and such friendships were among the great satisfactions of his later life. There were the old deprivations, too, and in 1910 he was to experience another crisis. There was the unavoidable sadness of old age; and there were the cumulative solitude and the never quite curable guilt of his lifelong celibacy. And then his position as

a writer remained anomalous, and he had only an intermittent patience with anomalies. Pride, both literary and
personal, was his in a large degree; but it must needs give
way sometimes before the fact of his eccentric reputation.
Did a correspondent request him to use his influence in
some cause or other? He was welcome to it, James would
reply, *such as it was*. And although there was no comfort
in it, he more and more saw his own fate as a writer reflected
in the general condition of civilization. He might have been
speaking of himself when he wrote to Wells in 1905: "You
set a magnificent example—of *caring*, of feeling, of seeing,
above all, and of suffering from, and with, the shockingly
sick actuality of things."

Yet few of James's acquaintances saw in him any deep
pathos, for all his ghosts, his literary failures, and his historical pessimism. Benson clearly did not, nor did Conrad
or Howells or Gosse or a dozen more. If he was not unwilling to *foster* the impression of pathos, that is another
story, and one that tells us much more about his later mind.
Introspective he had always been. With age, however,
the more comforting confessional habit came upon him.
It was a distinct development, and its salutary implications
must always be weighed against the sad things it sometimes
made him confess to. When he confided to Gosse and
again to Walpole that he had once been miserably in love;
when he told Walpole that he regretted "in my chilled
age, certain occasions and possibilities I didn't embrace";
was he sadder than formerly or simply more candid? And
what of "the starved romance of my life," a phrase that
has rung like a knell in his biographies? As with most
of his confessions, the context greatly qualifies the effect
of these words. They are found in a letter of 1900 to

A. F. de Navarro, who, with his wife, the actress Mary Anderson, were hardly the people to whom to address a *cri du cœur*: "I am a very sentient and affectionate, albeit out-of-the-way and out-of-the-fashion person. I *like* to add with my own clumsy fingers a small knot to the silken cord that, for the starved romance of my life, does, by God's blessing, happen to unite me to two or three of my really decorative contemporaries." It is all a delicate tribute to the brilliant Navarros, and such tributes became a stock in trade of his later correspondence. If they were a way of confiding real regrets, they were equally a means of transforming them into harmless "manner." Rarely had the old conversion principle served him more happily.

There was conscious caricature, moreover, in his telling Navarro that he had "two or three" such associations. As Navarro certainly knew, he had dozens; they made up, as we have said, the anything but impoverished romance of his later life; and he repaid the devotion of his friends to him by heaping them, much as he did the people of his novels, with praise of their subtlety and splendor. It was only misplaced Dowsonism that made Thomas Beer write that he was "the pet of cynical voluptuaries." On the whole his friends were a typical younger generation, with a greater freedom of wit and manners than he had known in his own youth. This he enjoyed up to a point: their jests, their sophistication, their coterie spirit. He was even to encourage Walpole in his "high jinks": "It's good healthy exercise, when it comes but in bouts and brief convulsions, and it's always a kind of thing that it's good, and considerably final, to *have* done." Yet James was interesting to his young acquaintances partly because he could be trusted not to go all the way with them but to stand out, in exceptional situations, for morality and decorum. "I deeply lament and deplore the lamentable position in which I gather you have put yourself," he once wrote Violet Hunt, whom he had known since her childhood and who was rumored to be having an affair with Ford, married though he was. "It affects me as painfully unedifying, and that compels me to regard all agreeable or unembarrassed communication between us as impossible." His reliance on such friends was considerable; but it did not preclude, it in fact necessitated, much independence on his part and even occasional shows of stern paternal admonition. This seems rarely to have been of the kind experienced by Violet Hunt, and she herself was quickly forgiven. It was more often literary and had to do with their writing, for most of them did write. In this respect he knew how to feel and to praise, sometimes extravagantly, the effect of fresh energies and intentions. He was, nevertheless, almost invariably critical as well, often severely so; and Howard Sturgis, for one, was said to have been discouraged by James's strictures from continuing to write at all. "I *am* damned critical—" he once said, "for it's the only thing to be, and all else is damned humbug."

He had once expressed his wish not for a son but for a grandson, and he was now in a kind of grandfatherly relation to many men and women. He had even two actual godchildren, offspring of London acquaintances. But his friendships are a large subject; to explore them would require a volume in itself. So too with his correspondence, to which, following a day of arduous dictation, he often addressed himself in the nocturnal seclusion of his Lamb House study, "to be sociable, by my loud-ticking clock, in this sleeping little town, at my usual more than midnight hour." Stranger or friend, everyone was treated in his letters to prodigies of tossed-off wit, kindness, and amenity. Contrary to the usual way, even *old* friends came in for their portion of his elegant spontaneity; perhaps they had it at its best. Had Grace Norton of Cambridge observed Kipling's falling off? "In his earliest time I thought he perhaps contained the seeds of an English Balzac; but I have quite given that up in proportion as he has come steadily from the less simple in subject to the more simple —from the Anglo-Indians to the natives, from the natives to the Tommies, from the Tommies to the quadrupeds, from the quadrupeds to the fish, and from the fish to the screws and engines."

James kept his native connections remarkably alive. On leaving the United States in 1883 he had written T. S. Perry of his hope that they might continue to commune "across the wide waters of time, as well as of space." They did, if only at considerable intervals; and Perry's biographer, Miss Virginia Harlow, describes him as trying hard, when James was dead and he himself was nearing 80, to persuade Van Wyck Brooks, then at work on the *Pilgrimage*, to a happier view of his subject. "He was staunch and true, his affection once given was never shaken," this oldest of James's friends wrote to Brooks in 1923. Perry's devotion, like that of Howells, Grace Norton, and others, survived the long decades, the protracted separations, the near-oblivion of James's American fame. On James's side there was clearly affection for the persons in question; there was also piety for his past; and there was finally, it appears, a dread lest the lapse of ancient associations precipitate him into a cold cosmopolitan age. He often had reason to apologize—and he did so rather too elaborately—

for delays in answering letters from America, but his replies were never perfunctory. On the contrary he assumed, if not always without effort, the point of view of his correspondent. To such as Howells and Henry Adams he said things which only a long intimacy and a common past could have evoked. But it was naturally to William, of all his American intimates, that he remained closest. Now a famous man with scientific and philosophic associates all over the world, William James was often in Europe in those years. In the late '90's he was there for two years for his health; again, in 1902, he was in Edinburgh delivering the lectures that were to compose his *The Varieties of Religious Experience*. There were new elements in their feeling for each other, or at least in Henry's feeling for William. He was less ready than he had once been to take umbrage at his brother's criticism. When William wrote slightingly of *The Golden Bowl*, he replied, with what looks like an impatience too long restrained, that "I'm always sorry when I hear of your reading anything of mine, and always hope you won't—you seem to me so constitutionally unable to 'enjoy' it, and so condemned to look at it from a point of view remotely alien to mine in writing it, and to the conditions out of which, *as* mine, it has inevitably sprung—so that all the intentions that have been its main reason for being (with *me*) appear never to have reached you at all—and you appear even to assume that the life, the elements forming its subject-matter, deviate from felicity in not having an impossible analogy with the life of Cambridge."

But this intellectual independence of William, far from compromising their affection, seems actually to have reinforced it. Their differences in the open, Henry could

love more freely because he could love more nearly as an
equal. And there was now William's large family to multiply
the affection on both sides. Henry took a great interest in
his niece Margaret, and his nephews, Henry, William, and
Alexander (a third son had died an infant). A *new* Henry
James, a third William!—another chapter was beginning in
the anxious romance of the James family. Concerning Margaret, then 13, he wrote as follows to her mother in 1900—
and the few words will show how easy he was with his
brother's wife: "I . . . want a little to warn you against the
preoccupation (too strong, at least) of the moral and the
spiritual in her training and formation! *We* (father's children) were sacrificed to that too exclusive preoccupation: &
you see in Wm and me, & above all in Bob, the *funeste* consequences! . . . . With her so definite Puritan heritage
Peggy could easily afford to be raised on almost solely *cultivated* 'social' & aesthetic lines." Another confession!—this
time with a didactic edge. For the rest, Walpole was probably right in noting that James's love for his brother's
family "had a real pathos, for although they beautifully returned it they could never be so deeply absorbed in him as
he was in them." They were, however, as deeply absorbed as
possible, especially his nephew Henry, who was to pay
visits to Lamb House in James's later years and greatly to relieve his solitude. This solitude, then, like the other unhappy
consequences of his peculiar life and art, was intermittent
rather than regular, relative instead of absolute. His brother's
family was the core, and his friends the enveloping tissue, of
a shared experience which he had finally in some sense
attained.

In this way, it appears, he made more endurable an inner
solitude which we may guess to have remained constantly

with him. And this solitude, we have said, he tended to see written large in "the shockingly sick actuality of things." It made him something other and very much more formidable than the brother of William James, the anxious host of Lamb House, or the half-wistful half-humorous aging man of the occasional confessions. When, for example, he objected to William's treatment of *The Golden Bowl,* he did so on quite different grounds from those of disappointed fraternal feeling. In the same letter he charged William with admiring "things, of the current age . . . that I would sooner descend to a dishonored grave than have written." And although some of his London circle sought to neutralize his hold over them by turning him into a "character"— the character, as Lionel Trilling says, of an "impotent divinity"—they had continually to reckon with surprising things in him. It was to A. C. Benson that he had observed in 1896: "But I have the imagination of disaster—and see life as ferocious and sinister"; and it was to Howard Sturgis, as we shall see, that he was to address a prodigious letter on the significance of the war of 1914.

And there were others, not of his following, for whom he occasionally sprang the trap of his mind. There were, above all, Bernard Shaw and H. G. Wells, the former only an acquaintance, the latter a literary friend since the mid-'90's. The encounter with Shaw was brief and hardly more than exhilarating; but with Wells the whole affair was more serious. Yet he did not become embroiled with either until his sense of them and their tendency had settled into a kind of relation. It is of this relation that we must speak first.

Shaw and Wells exemplified for him, as for everyone else, the omnivorous literary intelligence, the energy and frankness, of the new century at its best. In them had been realized the prophecy of Tocqueville when he said that in democratic societies "the imagination is not extinct; but its chief function is to devise what may be useful, and to represent what is real." James felt a strong fascination for the real and useful, together with a strong impulse to recoil from them. More than some of his intimates may have suspected, he had affinities moral and literary with the generation of Wells and Shaw. If he was not actually influenced by them, he was at least moved by certain of the same tides of feeling that moved them. Some of the zest of men who rejoiced in their powers of recovery from the sickness, real and artistic, of the '90's reached James with his own history of sickness, his own sickness of the '90's in particular, and his related pride of energy and achievement. Even his language, in his letters at least, proved to be susceptible to the new vehemence and provocation. It was Henry James, after all, who in these years wrote, "I *am* damned critical"; who assigned to Andrew Lang "the puerile imagination and the fourth-rate opinion"; who insulted the taste of the day (and doubtless any day) by describing as "fluid puddings" the novels of the most celebrated Russians. But more to the point was his sympathy, as one who still admired Balzac, who continued to write and even lectured about him, with the regenerate naturalism of the English novel. "Your spirit is huge, your fascination irresistible, your resources infinite," he early wrote to Wells; and for some years he was Wells's almost abject admirer, thinking him better in some things than Thackeray and Dickens.

But he had his reservations, as to Wells among others, and with time they mounted. As he had felt the wonder of Stevenson's abundance to be qualified by Stevenson's disposition to "romp," as he had watched Kipling's animal energy deflect him towards the fishes and screws, so in these more recent cases of the British literary power he was awake to signs of excess and unseriousness. He remained watchful and fundamentally independent; and among the rampant realists and roaring democrats of 20th-century London he was like no one so much as Don Quixote keeping his single and past-honoring vigil in the inn courtyard. Indeed he recalled Don Quixote in many particulars, as well as in his general propensity to be at once strangely limited and strangely magnificent. He had not only the knight's love of honor but the knight's imponderable community with the past—a past only half "real." If inspired madness made this possible for Don Quixote, in James it was perhaps the consequence of his being the kind of American he was—the kind whose mixed blessing, whose joint penalty and privilege, it was to be able to make the past his own precisely because there stood between himself and it so little culture that was actively his. If in the prescientific and predemocratic ages there was ever a moment when literature was taken for granted, its existence and value simply assumed, James instinctively harked back to that moment as Don Quixote to the Golden Age; and this gave him an ambiguous distinction among writers cursed or blessed with the historical sense, writers conscious of the modern need to justify their profession by calling it either perfectly utilitarian or perfectly self-sufficient. He was altogether absorbed in literature; he knew its processes and powers as the knight knew those of the art of chivalry. And what each of them knew, each knew with a single-mindedness that was exemplary and terrible. They had, moreover, a common impulse at once to exalt and to travesty the role of the imagination; and they had this in the degree that men, obedient to other notions of what is real, pretended to teach that faculty its duties and circumscribe its operations. Was there not an element of travesty in the extremer reaches of James's later style, in his cultivated ambiguities, in the liberties he sometimes took with historical fact, in his habit of revising or repudiating his early work as if it existed in some timeless void? With all this they were in the position of inevitably attracting irony, the worst effects of which they were both able to fend off. If there was irony in the fact that Henry James, an American, was England's chief conservative critic of the time, he did not allow it to stick to him. And besides irony, they both of course attracted abuse and ridicule, but this too they knew how to be proof against. In the end, it is true, James did not become the hero of the occasion to the extent that Don Quixote did—or not in his lifetime. But he had his peculiar effectiveness; and it is not too much to say that even this was in substance like Don Quixote's effectiveness. In what he wrote and how he wrote, in his talk and the way he talked, in his dress and manners and very person, he represented a distinction for which there was no known category but from which there was no easy means of escape. The man whose slow and charming conversation proliferated as he lumbered beside you across Sussex downs or sat expectantly next you in some club or drawing room of London, this man was singularity raised to a peculiar eminence, singularity become representative.

So in his age the "otherness" of James's boyhood was transfigured. And so in the written criticism of his later years he spoke more and more for the open sensibility. This taste in living writers was inconsistent: he was unfortunate enough to remark that D. H. Lawrence "hangs in the dusty rear" of Maurice Hewlett and Compton Mackenzie, but he

was enchanted by *Du côté de chez Swann*. Yet the "awareness," the "discrimination," that he was always advocating
and exemplifying as a critic had as their end the celebration
of differences and the pleasure in variety. In fiction he admired "form" because it was among the chief guarantees
against monotony of effect: by means of it a writer com-
municated that hold on his subject which made the subject
his own, that feeling for life which was properly his. Nor,
with all his sense of tradition in the arts, was James partial
to any one tradition: he was not a "traditionalist." His was
in part the tradition of the studio—transmitted skill and
transmitted dedication—in part the tradition, however much
attenuated in him, of humanism itself—diversity, complexity, imaginative synthesis. In a time of professed democrats
and scientists in literature it was he, by a curious turn, who
was most consistently and eloquently the empiric. "But I
have no view of life and literature," he was to write to
Wells after Wells had lampooned him in *Boon*, ". . . other
than that our form of the latter in especial is admirable exactly by its range and variety, its plasticity and liberality,
its fairly living on the sincere and shifting experience of the
individual practitioner." Such, in his time, was the state of
the liberal-radical mind in literature that this view made him
the conservative we have called him; and it was more to
the fore in his differences with Shaw and Wells than any
political or philosophic conservatism on his part. More than
anything else it accounted for his force as a critic. "There
was no other antagonist possible than yourself," Wells assured him after *Boon*.

But Shaw was to engage him before Wells, since one of
James's affinities with the new generation was his continuing
interest in the stage. In 1909 he submitted to a theatrical so-

ciety of which Shaw was a member a play called *The Saloon*. It was based on his story of "Owen Wingrave," whose hero, a young pacifist, achieves a moral victory over an ancestral ghost but dies in the process. The situation was typical of James; the play was bad as most of his plays were bad; and Shaw, undertaking to write to him of the society's objections to it, was himself strictly in character. Though full of respect for James he was in no fear of him; and being without fear he was free also of any impulse to patronize. He wrote with a peremptory friendliness that made light of all inequalities of age and reputation, clearing the field for exercises exclusively intellectual. "What that play wants is a third act by your father," he began, and went on to insist that James rewrite the act so as to give the young pacifist an unqualified victory over the ghost. Owen Wingrave must win and live; to have it otherwise was to "preach cowardice"—"No man who doesn't believe in ghosts ever sees one"—and to perpetuate that "fatalism which broke out so horribly in the 1860's at the word of Darwin." *The Saloon* was "very talented," Shaw allowed, "but is it any better than Turgenef?" And he concluded by declaring: "People don't want works of art from you: they want help."

The mention of Turgenev and the elder James, like much else in the letter, showed an acquaintance with James's mind and history which surprises us in Shaw and may well have surprised James—an acquaintance Shaw of course diligently exploited. James replied at once. His old relish for such occasions, and for being equal to them, was still with him in 1909; but his long—his too long—letter shows him to have been unwell at the time. (Actually he wrote two letters and Shaw two as well.) He was, as that letter further suggested, greatly charmed and no little confused by so much unsolicited attention from so conspicuous a source, as well as slightly at a loss to cope with the alarming directness of a critic who brought into the open, as Shaw effectively did, all that was self-indulgent in his habitual death-and-transfiguration scheme. But coming at last to Shaw's outrageous juxtaposing of "help" and "works of art," he rose to the provocation and answered it with all his sincerity and passion. Works of art, he declared, "are capable of saying more things to man about himself than any other 'works' whatever are capable of doing—and it's only by saying as much to him as possible, by saying, as nearly as we can, all there is, and in as many ways and on as many sides, and with a vividness of presentation that 'art,' and art alone, is adequate mistress of, that we enable him to pick and choose and compare and know, enable him to arrive at any sort of synthesis that isn't, through all its superficialities and vacancies, a base and illusive humbug."

On the subject of art and other "works," art and causes, art and ideologies, no word of course is final; and James's word is not necessarily final for us. But it was final for him; and for that reason it was perfect of its kind. In Shaw, we may observe, James was confronted with the exceptional man of the age, whether he knew it or not. Believing that art could not be made to serve other ends without great risks all around, convinced in the depths of his private judgment of the irrelevance to the best art of all causes and ideologies, he had in Shaw the artist to dispute him on both points. For certainly Shaw embraced his risks as a man of ideas and causes; and mainly, we think, he triumphed over them; his kind of didactic comedy—his "exquisite art" as James called it with evident sincerity—was itself a kind of art of taking chances with art, but one with precedents among the great comic writers. Nor was his respect for his profession any less intense than James's because he made much of its practical responsibilities and annexed art to the forum. Indeed on these grounds his sense of its dignity could be said to have exceeded James's. But if Shaw was James's ideal foil, Wells for all his enormous talent was not; and his was the kind of mind against which James's proved most effective. He was one of those men who were—and are—more distinguished for literary energy than for literary finesse or literary conscience. In him, as in others, the utilitarian aesthetic that was often so liberating in itself tended to become confused with something theoretically quite distinct from it. To call this commercialism would be too much; it would be closer to the fact as well as to James's estimate to speak of a kind of inveterate busy-ness in Wells, a drive to write too much and in too many fields and thus to diffuse and overreach himself. As we have said, James's regard for him was once high and it was never to be low, even though his early panegyrics were to give way more and more to skepticism, as when he complained to Mrs. Humphry Ward of "the co-existence [in Wells] of so much talent with so little art, so much living with (so to speak) so little life!" And in 1914, in his critical survey called "The New Novel," although he named Wells as the chief of his school, James did deplore the flood of fiction set in motion by that school. He did so, as he explained—and the reasoning was intensely his—"not in the least because prose fiction now occupies itself as never before with 'the condition of the people,' a fact quite irrelevant to the nature it has taken on, but because that nature amounts exactly to a complacent declaration of a common literary level, a repudiation the most operative even if the least reasoned of the idea of differences, the virtual law, as we may call it, of sorts and kinds, the values of individual quality and weight in the presence of undiscriminated quantity and rough-and-tumble 'output'— these attestations made, we naturally mean, in the air of composition and on the esthetic plane, if such terms have still an attenuated reference to the case before us."

It seems to have been "The New Novel" that provoked the cruel reprisal of *Boon*, the satire fantasy with a long passage on James which Wells published the following year. To begin with, *Boon* was cruel on personal grounds: their fifteen years' acquaintance, their exchanges of visits, letters, and books, above all James's eternal praise of Wells, presupposed an understanding between them which the satire now belied. *Boon* was cruel too because it lent the authority of Wells's great cleverness and fame to the old practice of pronouncing James irrelevant through parody and epigram —and at a time when he was old and neglected. But chiefly *Boon* was cruel because it was intrinsically unjust: it went beyond those "incurable differences" Wells alleged as its motive and sought, as James said, to "resolve me into . . . an unmitigated mistake." It made effective and, from Wells's point of view, legitimate sport of certain things in James. But it did not stop with this. Beyond the fine language and contrivance of the James novel, it maintained, there is a "nothingness," and James was only a "leviathan retrieving pebbles."

The effects of *Boon* were felt for a generation. Satire so amusing must be true, and many were to quote Wells instead of reading Henry James. For years to come the rampant realists and roaring democrats had their invaluable caricature of him, a James sacrificially reduced to the proportions of an ideal fatuity, a James despoiled of his relevance.

If he foresaw the harm *Boon* would do to his reputation, he did not make that the burden of his two letters of protest to Wells. Rather he made the shortcomings of *Boon* serve his own cause. Its essential flimsiness supported his old contention as to the bad state of current criticism; its vehement one-sidedness was another sign of a widespread intolerance, a general failure to discriminate, a common disposition to seek literary pleasure and enlightenment along the lines of the expected. Wells in answering regretted his failure to express their differences "with a better grace." But "writing all that stuff about you was the first escape I had from the obsession of this war," and in any case *"Boon* is just a waste-paper basket" to which he had committed some random observations. "I am bound to tell you," James replied to this, "that I don't think your letter makes out any sort of case for the bad manners of 'Boon'. . . . Your comparison of the book to a waste-basket strikes me as the reverse of felicitous, for what one throws into that receptacle is exactly what one doesn't commit to publicity and make the affirmation of one's estimate of one's contemporaries by." He went on to affirm, in words we have already quoted, the "plasticity and liberality" of art; saying that: "Of course for myself I live, live intensely and am fed by life, and my value, whatever it be, is my own kind of expression of that." Dissenting then from Wells's artistic pragmatism, he concluded: "It is art that *makes* life, makes interest, makes importance, for our consideration and application of these things, and I know of no substitute whatever for the force and beauty of its process. If I were Boon I should say that any pretence of such a substitute is helpless and hopeless humbug; but I wouldn't be Boon for the world, and am only yours faithfully, HENRY JAMES."

In these letters to Wells, written the year before James's death, there was much of his later mind: the pride, the passion, and even the humor—the latter naturally gone astringent for the occasion. There was meanwhile still more of him in the three long novels he had written during his early years at Lamb House.

The Last Novels

AS THERE were quarters in Lamb House for servants and guests, so there was space for James's many books, papers, and mementoes, and there were separate workrooms for summer and winter. His secretary, says Percy Lubbock, "would be installed at the typewriter by ten o' clock in the morning, and for three or four hours he would pace the room, pausing, hesitating, gradually massing and controlling the stream of his imagination, till at a favoring moment it rolled forward without check." A story had sometimes to be abandoned as unworkable, but unless he was seriously ill James had few unproductive days. More than ever he wrote with a speed which, considering the quality of his writing, is probably unique in literature. This was possible because his natural eloquence was so astonishing and because he was given to the prolonged gestation and planning of his books.

Much of this preliminary work can still be studied in his notebooks and other papers; and when a story of his is interesting in itself, the record of its inception and birth (and after-life, if we include his revisions and prefaces) may be highly instructive. His notes, when he is working out an idea, resemble the reflections of man warming towards some challenging new acquaintance while looking anxiously into himself as well. Thus, apropos of his plan to return to the long novel, he writes, in 1899: "Ah once more, to let myself go! The very thought of it soothes and sustains, lays a divine hand on my nerves, and lights, so beneficently, my uncertainties and obscurities. *Begin* it—and it will grow." He had kept a notebook for many years—the earliest surviving entry, devoted to *Confidence*, is dated 1878; and with the exception of two journal-like passages written during his American visits of 1881 and 1904, his notes are strictly professional, seldom opening out into the area of general ideas or free introspection.

To his notebooks he confided the "tiny air-borne particles," or anecdotes, which promised to germinate as tales or novels. These occasionally stemmed from his reading; more often they were dropped, casually or with intent, by companions at the dinner-table or the fireside. Not all of his work originated in this way. The plot of *The Princess Casamassima* seems to have sprung like its hero "from the London pavement," with the aid of the newspapers; while *The Portrait of a Lady* and *The Wings of the Dove* were both inspired by memories of Minny Temple. But the conversational anecdote accounted for a great many of his ideas, and in making notes of them he liked also to specify the person and the occasion responsible. It was not enough, for example, that he should record the suggestion for what was to become "The Birthplace," but he must begin it by saying: "The other day at Welcombe (May 30th or 31st) the Trevelyans, or rather Lady T., spoke of the odd case of the couple," etc. And we may perhaps infer on James's part the possession of an unconscious system in

respect to his inspirations. The workable fable was preferably authentic and came to him sanctified, as it were,
by its origin in a social occasion. The talk of his friends
had thus the value for him of a continuous *Golden Legend*
or *Gesta Romanorum*, rich in evidences of the representative heroes and predicaments of the society to which he
played historian. Like his plots, a surprising number of his
characters were suggested by actual persons: historical
ones, like Byron and Coleridge, or people he knew, like
Howells or Browning or Julia Ward Howe. But an anecdote was spoiled for him if it happened to be too complete in
itself: the bulk of it was apt only to show "life at its
stupid work." The total process of creation, as he practiced
it, called for a division of labor between history and inven-
tion. If his *données* belonged to the former department, the
working out of their implications, the discovery of motives,
foils, centers of interest, dénouements—in short the whole
effort of form and significance—was the office of the
imagination. And the researches of his imagination, sometimes accomplished in a flash, sometimes extending over
pages, make up the principal burden of his notebooks.

Thanks to the notebooks we may study the inception,
dating back to 1895, of *The Ambassadors*, the work in
which James returned to the long novel and the international theme and so inaugurated his great final period. It
all began in the most intimate way. In 1894, we learn,
Howells was in Paris for the first time in many years, to
visit his son who was then enrolled in the École des Beaux
Arts. Howells had worked incessantly to maintain his literary position and support his family; he was a stranger to
what James called the world; and—or so the latter liked to
suppose—he knew hardly anything about women apart

from his wife. And now in Paris he seems to have felt a little weary and rebellious for he was seized one day by a confessional impulse of the kind occasionally experienced by the later James. At a party at Whistler's he surprised a young friend by suddenly exclaiming in effect: "Oh, you are young, you are young—be glad of it: be glad of it and *live*. Live all you can: it's a mistake not to. It doesn't so much matter what you do—but live. This place makes it all come over me. I see it now. I haven't done so—and now I'm old. It's too late. It has gone past me—I've lost it. You have time. You are young. Live!"

Howells's friend, Jonathan Sturges, who was also known to James, reported the incident to him the following year; and he promptly confided it to his notebook, going on at once to outline a possible story based on "the figure of an elderly man who hasn't 'lived.' " The theme throbbed with possibilities, especially for the James of those unhappy years; it had, moreover, for purposes of objectivity, the advantage of being associated with a man who had always figured to him as a kind of alter-ego and whose sacrifices to the prevailing American gentility James clearly remarked, while hastening to add that he himself was similarly lamed. That the suggestion would eventuate in one of his great novels, *The Ambassadors*, he did not foresee: it was to be only a tale "of a tiny kind," one of a series to be published under a common title, such as *The Old Men*. Nor, despite the subject, did he see that it would entail a full-dress revival of the international theme.

Similarly with the origins of the two other important novels of his final phase, *The Wings of the Dove* and *The Golden Bowl*. The notebooks show them also to have begun in random suggestions received during the '90's;

and in neither case does any large recrudescence of James's early theme appear to have been in view. The notebooks are silent as to any deeper reasons for that remarkable event. They do, however, show the practical considerations involved, which as usual concerned editors and magazines. In 1894 Henry Harper asked for "a little international story on American snobbishness abroad." This, although James kept it in mind, appealed to him very little. "They want, ever, the smaller, the slighter, the safer, the inferior thing,"—*Daisy Miller* warmed over. In 1900, Howells really struck fire by proposing a supernatural tale with an American ghost. James, as it happened, was at work on just such a story, *The Sense of the Past*, the American hero of which is magically translated to the England of 1820. But this tale began turning into a full-length novel, and the execution of it proved difficult. James abandoned it for the present, returned to it briefly in the stress of the war of 1914, and when *The Sense of the Past* was finally published, the year after his death, it was still a fragment. Meanwhile, no sooner had he laid it aside, in the summer of 1900, than he began to project *The Ambassadors*.

Such is the natural history, as it might be called, of the process that culminated in the international revival and the three great novels; and the process should be given due weight in any attempt to account for the revival or to envisage the novels as composing, not merely a "triad" (in Percy Lubbock's phrase) but a veritable trilogy. James's *œuvre*, as we know, was not a consciously ordered one like the *œuvres* of novelists who stem from Flaubert; behind the relation of book to book and period to period there was a mixture of internal compulsion and practical necessity. This is not to say, however, that the writing of *The Ambassadors, The Wings of the Dove,* and *The Golden Bowl,* remarkable as those novels are, did not express some urgent need of James's nature, situation, and time of life. As a man who had long been absent from it, and whose absence had become a legend, he was increasingly curious about America; he felt for it more and more a kind of nostalgia. And these feelings were all the stronger because he knew the country to be greatly changed, both internally and in its relation to Europe. The America which, at the time of the Civil War—the time, also, of his own coming of age—had guaranteed its industrial unity and at the same time withstood British interference, and which meanwhile had been steadily growing in population and wealth, had finally come to figure as a world power in the imperialist intensities of the turn of the century. As usual James got at political fact through private symbolism. He gauged America's improved position in the world by the increasing number of international marriages involving American millions and European titles. And that he was right in seeing such marriages as entailing not only money but dreams of cultural power and psychic rejuvenation was to be proved once and for all, many years after his death, by the most spectacular of all such unions, that of the English king with an American woman—a union which, because it did not involve money at all, brought the whole moral aspect of these transactions into the open, and at the same time, causing as it did the King's abdication, finally destroyed the prestige of titles and so brought the cycle to an end. And in *The American Scene,* a book that explores the internal implications of American prosperity, he was to describe New York Harbor in such terms as to

make it emblematic of the whole magnificent and disquiet-
ing spectacle.

The aspect the power wears then is indescribable; it
is the power of the most extravagant of cities, rejoicing,
as with the voice of the morning, in its might, its fortune, its unsurpassable conditions, and imparting to
every object and element, to the motion and expression
of every floating, hurrying, panting thing, to the throb
of ferries and tugs, to the plash of waves and the play
of winds and the glint of lights and the shrill of whistles
and the quality and authority of breeze-borne cries—
all, practically, a diffused, wasted clamor of *detonations*—something of its sharp free accent and, above
all, of its sovereign sense of being "backed" and able
to back. The universal *applied* passion struck me as
shining unprecedentedly out of the composition; in the
bigness and bravery and insolence, especially, of everything that rushed and shrieked; in the air as of a great
intricate frenzied dance, half merry, half desperate, or
at least half defiant, performed on the huge watery
floor. This appearance of the bold lacing-together,
across the waters, of the scattered members of the
monstrous organism—lacing as by the ceaseless play
of an enormous system of steam-shuttles or electric
bobbins (I scarce know what to call them), commen-
surate in form with their infinite work—does perhaps
more than anything else to give the pitch of the vision
of energy. One has the sense that the monster grows
and grows, flinging abroad its loose limbs even as some
unmannered young giant at his "larks," and that the
binding stitches must forever fly further and faster
and draw harder; the future complexity of the web, all
under the sky and over the sea, becoming thus that of
some colossal set of clockworks, some steel-souled
machine-room of brandished arms and hammering fists
and opening and closing jaws. The immeasurable

bridges are but as the horizontal sheaths of pistons working at high pressure, day and night, and subject, one apprehends with perhaps inconsistent gloom, to certain, to fantastic, to merciless multiplication. In the light of this apprehension indeed the breezy brightness of the Bay puts on the semblance of the vast white page that awaits beyond any other perhaps the black over-scoring of science.

In his last novels, then, James revived the international subject and made it serve the present balance of power as well as his own accumulated experience as an American in Europe. Europe is still, in these novels, the school of worldly experience, and America still representative of the process by which that experience may be transmuted into moral significance. But there are unmistakable developments over the earlier cycle. Americans now mate directly with Europeans rather than, as so often in the early books, with Europeanized types of their own race. James sacrificed that nuance in his desire to show the two peoples as implicated in a common fate, whether it was the "communities of doom" of *The Wings of the Dove* or the communities of salvation of *The Golden Bowl*. Out of the stress of national differences, then, come great ultimate images of identity: Strether's final fraternization with Mme. de Vionnet, Milly Theale and Kate Croy at one in their fatal "talent for life," Maggie and the Prince reconciled in their marriage.

The Ambassadors was the first of the three novels to be written, although it was not published till 1903, a year after *The Wings of the Dove*. In spirit it recalls the urbane comedy of *The Awkward Age*, as if, having himself come to terms with the *femme du monde* in that novel, James was eager to show another elderly American accomplishing the same feat. But there were advantages in drawing on Howells for his hero. In this, the most notable of his transplantation novels, he could revive what was almost dead in his own experience—the whole rich *adventure* of the provincial in contact with the world, the outsider *vis-à-vis* the inner circle.

The ambassadors of the title are the emissaries of a certain Mrs. Newsome, the first lady of Woollett (roughly, Worcester, Massachusetts); and their mission is to restore to the home town and the family business her son who is being detained in Paris by what Woollett believes to be a sordid passion. There is the amusement of seeing a private affair treated by the author as a diplomatic venture: the instructions from the all-powerful home office, the constant reports and cables, the rewards for success and the penalties for failure, the danger of going over to the enemy (American ambassadors are notoriously susceptible). But the Americans of the novel are ambassadors in the deeper sense that they are representative types of their countrymen. And not the least of these, although she remains invisible, is Mrs. Newsome, whose ominous strength consists partly in her large fortune, partly in the moral zeal, the habit of good works, by which she tries to make up for the money's having been acquired by her late husband in the hard fashion of the old New England manufacturers. Given her money in conjunction with her will to expiate it, and she is, for poor Strether, the first of her ambassadors and the hero of the novel, a formidable figure indeed. It was part of the *donnée* that Strether should be getting on in years and be possessed by a rueful conviction that he hasn't "lived." In planning the novel, however, James was at pains to discover a suitable profession for him. A clergyman was too obvious, a lawyer *would* have lived, a novelist was too much like Howells and too special anyway. But a way was found to preserve something of Howells's literary situation without offending Howells. The situation was also James's own to a degree, and that of the native culture itself on its weaker side—the side of it which, in the absence of any flourishing professional tradition, was dispersed, dependent, propitiatory: in a state of gentle servitude to women of good will. Strether is an intermittent man of letters. After years of desultory effort he has at last settled proudly into the editorship of a highbrow Review whose readers are loyal but few. The Review, although it carries Strether's name on the cover, is one of the good works of Woollett. It is financed by Mrs. Newsome.

But James does not insist very much on Strether's identity as an artist. It is one of the subtleties of the novel that the freedom of the American writer is shown to be involved with the freedom of the American considered as an individual. Between Strether and Mrs. Newsome there is a personal intimacy which makes their relationship still more interesting and very much more precarious. His advice has long been useful to her in her various enterprises; and these have been really vital to him, starved as he is for responsibility, a place in the human community. Will he also win a place in the Newsome family? It has come to be understood, in the veiled manner of Woollett, that Strether will probably marry Mrs. Newsome. There are difficulties, however, although these too are obscured by the local idealism. The least threatening of them are the practical ones: Strether's future share in the family fortune, the still flourishing business, the affections of Mrs. Newsome's two grown children—Chad, who delays in Paris, and Sarah, who, married to Jim Pocock, the present head of the business, is very much in Woollett. The great question is whether Strether, who greatly respects but doesn't love Mrs. Newsome, and whose dependence on her is materially greater than hers on him, will find a real place in the family or merely a roost for his old age. This question, of course, gives a peculiar edge to his Paris mission, little as he recognizes it on starting out, and little as Mrs. Newsome insists. He is engaged, as he gradually realizes, in a kind of knightly quest or ordeal, with honor and the princess's hand as the rewards of success. The serving of Mrs. Newsome, the saving of Chad, are an extension of the responsibilities already granted him by the lady of Woollett; they are the responsibilities, now, of a husband and father. Thus, little by little, he comes to conceive of his mission; and it cannot be said that in so doing he exceeds his instructions. A subtle and humane woman in her fashion, Mrs. Newsome has herself seen the assignment in this light. But, in the exercise of his paternal duties, what if his appraisal of Chad's position, his very notions of good and bad, come to conflict with hers? What if the test of Strether turn into a test of Mrs. Newsome, her willingness to abide by his judgment, her capacity to be a reasonable wife?

Woollett and its questions are in the background of the novel, which opens with Strether's arrival in Europe. In their more fateful aspect they are also, to begin with, in the background of Strether's mind; and it is the first lesson of Europe, the school of reality, that whatever is unconscious or semiconscious had best be made explicit. This much is accomplished for Strether by a lively disenchanted

woman of a certain age whom he meets and takes up
with on his arrival. In her kindly inexorable way—a way
that would pass for cynical in Woollett—Maria Gostrey
hastens his sophistication by making him acknowledge the
true state of his relations with Mrs. Newsome, the true
nature of his mission. But Miss Gostrey's function in the
novel is only that of the abstract spirit of truth and voice
of comedy. Strether's further education is left to the spirit
of Paris, where, caught up in an intrigue the outcome of
which is of great moment to himself, he undergoes a rapid
dissociation of his received ideas with respect to class and
culture, sex, love, and morals. In the beginning James was
inclined to deplore the Paris setting as too banal, but he
soon saw that it was for that very reason indispensable.
Woollett entertains certain assumptions concerning the
French city, and these at first govern Strether's mind as
well as Mrs. Newsome's. Because Chad lingers in Paris he
must, they suppose, be involved with a woman, and the in-
volvement must be sordid and the woman vulgar. But by
degrees, a point at a time, all this proves to be mistaken.
An awkward boy in his Woollett days, Chad turns out to be
the charming center of an accomplished circle of artists
and aristocrats. This discovery constitutes Strether's first
shock, and from having been ignorantly evil-minded about
Chad's affairs he now rebounds in the opposite direction. As
a good American he likes nothing better than to contemplate the spectacle of a changed man, someone transfigured
by culture and experience. So, and although he has not yet
seen her, he assumes that the woman responsible for the
altered Chad must be better than he had supposed. This
impression is confirmed twice over when he meets her,
which he presently does at a garden party in the Faubourg

Saint-Germain, an occasion luminous with the summer sun of Paris, the elegance of duchesses, and the wit of famous artists. Mme. de Vionnet, as she is called, is the very expression of the scene, a countess herself, beautiful, sympathetic, and the mother of a girl in her teens. Being a generous as well as an imaginative man, Strether promptly voices his confidence in her. But he can do this only at the price of making another precarious assumption. It would seem that in the novels relished at Woollett there are only wicked liaisons or ideal love affairs—nothing in between. Romancing after this pattern, Strether now fancies Chad to be, not adulterously involved with Mme. de Vionnet but innocently in love with her daughter.

Meanwhile his fate as a man is bound up with the fate of his ideas. The garden party has marked a turning-point in the history of his soul. He has begun to feel very strongly his own deficiencies; and in the garden, *tête-à-tête* with one of Chad's friends, he has been suddenly eloquent (as Howells was) on the importance of living all one can. At his age he can live more adventurously only in his mind, but even this is dangerous. Any new life means the death of the old. In being liberated from his more ungenerous illusions, he is also being removed by degrees from Mrs. Newsome and the security of Woollett. To sympathize with Mme. de Vionnet, to treat with her at all, is to exceed "instructions"; and his reports to Mrs. Newsome have not pleased her. Clearly suspicious of his temporizing with evil, she presently ceases to temporize with him. There is an alarming lapse in communications from Woollett. If Paris is increasingly wonderful, he is nevertheless terribly alone with it. And then the extent to which his mission is judged a failure by Woollett and he himself discredited as an emissary is suddenly made clear. A second ambassador arrives, possessed of all his old zeal as well as of his forfeited portfolio. This is Mrs. Newsome's married daughter, Sarah Pocock, who is like her mother, only more so (the two of them, sighs her husband, are "as intense as they can live"), and who descends on Paris accompanied by her husband, come along for the ride, and his pretty sister Mamie, included as an enticement to Chad. Strether's position with Woollett is not yet entirely hopeless; some allowance has been made there for his susceptibility. Sarah is prepared to save him as well as Chad, on the condition that he promptly denounce Mme. de Vionnet. But this, of course, he is less and less ready to do.

The Pococks' bustling entrance is one of the fine moments in the novel, serving to deepen the intrigue and to bring Woollett incarnate on the Paris stage. The overwhelming questions of the story, Chad's and Strether's, are now rolled into a ball. Chad has intimated that he will return home when and if Strether advises him to; and Strether, still believing Chad to be interested in Mlle. de Vionnet, sensible of the young man's human debt to her mother, aware of the life-giving properties of a Paris which Mme. de Vionnet more and more embodies for him, counsels delay. This finishes him with Sarah. Apart from the knowledge of the disinterested part he has been playing, Strether has now only the comfort of his new sophistication. But this, too, proves to be partly illusory. Going alone one day to a riverside resort near Paris, he is astonished to discover Chad and Mme. de Vionnet companionably floating in a rowboat. Mlle. de Vionnet is not with them, the pair are inescapably alone, and there is every evidence that they have planned to spend the night at the riverside inn.

So Chad's affair, with all it implies, is adulterous after all! So Woollett was right all along! But Strether will not have it this way; he will no longer oversimplify. The moral sense of individuals, as distinguished from the practical simplifications forced upon actual ambassadors, is complex and tenuous, and sometimes consists in a willed suspension of judgment. If Strether judges anyone it is himself, for his failures of perception. Thus he makes Chad's affair his own in the most useful sense, possesses himself wholly of the lesson of Paris, and transmutes adventure into experience. To Mme. de Vionnet, however, he remains attached with what is a kind of love. This is no longer because she has made Chad a gentleman (a criterion savoring of Woollett), but because, as it turns out, she desperately loves Chad, and even more because Chad now gives signs of being weary of her. This, too, Strether comes to accept. It is the tragic aspect of all such liaisons, momentous as they otherwise are for French culture. It is the likely concomitant of physical passion itself as distinguished from the career of the free imagination. With Mrs. Newsome, of course, Strether's relations are at an end—*that* liaison, with its peculiar implications for *American* culture, has concluded, as it began, tacitly. And Chad, as it appears, is going home after all. Like so many repentant prodigals he has thought up a compromise between his new culture and the family business: he will go into what Chad's generation liked to call the "advertising end" of it. And so in a sense Strether has succeeded in his original assignment. By bringing Chad's tensions out into the open, by taking upon himself so much of Chad's former role of love and rebellion, he has allowed the young man to depart in comparative peace. In a priestly or scapegoat sense, he has actually played the father; and his reward, although it is not to be Mrs. Newsome's hand and fortune, is nevertheless considerable. He who formerly felt so isolated, so useless, is now confirmed in a modest sense of self-sufficiency; and he too, after taking leave of his Paris friends, departs for America although presumably not for Woollett.

James believed *The Ambassadors* to be his most perfect novel; and certainly it boasts his most perfect plot, certainly it gathers up into a powerful design all his major themes. If he drew on Howells for Strether's adventures, he drew far more on himself: his European residence, his bachelor status, his artist's relation to his audience. There is more beauty and horror in *The Wings of the Dove* and *The Golden Bowl;* but *The Ambassadors* is mainly comedy, as they are not, and its virtues are the appropriate ones of grace and clarity. Nothing is developed at the expense of anything else; the novel means many things, but those things are all consonant with one another. Even when Strether refuses at the end to consider marriage with Maria Gostrey, he is not "renouncing" in the sometimes awkward way of James's heroes; he is only conceding frankly to the actualities of his mind, heart, and time of life. Like James during his Paris stay of years ago, he has given much of himself to the world; but he has retained his original faith in the primacy of spirit; and he has done this in order that he may survive as an entity and have a self to give. True, Strether's innocence is of the kind usually reserved for the fools or dupes of comedy. In refusing to draw this conclusion, in making Strether entirely charming, James risked perpetrating a fable *for* provincials as well as about them. His fears, as expressed in his notes, that Strether might cloy were partly justified; and Mme. de Vionnet in turn, observed as she is so exclusively from without, tends to go stiff under the weight of all her representative grandeur.

These are casual defects in a book that remains an uncommonly persuasive whole. The wholeness is felt in a variety of ways. There is the sheer momentum of the novel, which, among James's large efforts in the "scenic" kind, is unique in its steady advance towards an irresistible conclusion. The capacity, moreover, of his characters to throw light on one another, to enter into meaningful (and diverting!) relationships, is here carried as far as James was ever to carry it. We begin by noting the interesting symmetry made by Mrs. Newsome, Maria Gostrey, and Mme. de Vionnet; or by Strether, Jim Pocock, and the angular old Yankee, Waymarsh. But everyone in the novel, as we soon realize, is vitally connected with everyone else and there is no end of "foils." Finally there is the supremely successful setting—successful because so thoroughly subdued to the purposes of the novel. As distinguished from bourgeois Woollett, Strether's Paris is a city exclusively of artists and members of the noblesse united in a conspiracy of pleasure, enlightenment, and artistic creation. A place of fine surfaces, Paris is nevertheless seen to contain a mystery, a something that is at first merely postulated—it lurks behind that high window observed from the street, or in those animated streets observed from a balcony. Then by degrees Strether penetrates the mystery: at the party in the secluded urban garden, over luncheon with Mme. de Vionnet in a quayside restaurant, in her drawing-room dense with suggestions of the First Empire and beyond. Indeed, this room is for him the ultimate Parisian interior, and there, during his final interview with a Mme. de Vionnet ravaged and diminished by her pas-

sion for Chad, he remembers Mme. Roland and the guillo-
tine, feels the tragic French energy behind the great French
elegance, and sees what Woollett in its idealism refuses to
see: the amount of sheer sacrifice entailed in the perpetua-
tion of any culture worth the name.

Incredible though it seems, James appears to have written *The Ambassadors* in less than a year, probably between September 1900 and June 1901. He must then have
turned promptly to *The Wings of the Dove* and composed
it with the same speed, for it was published in 1902. "It
is a great book," wrote Howells in the *North American Review* in 1903, and time has confirmed the praise. Among
those who admire the late novels, *The Wings of the Dove*
has always held a special place. It is not so perfect in form
as *The Ambassadors*. The preliminaries are overdone, and
the chief masculine figure, depressingly named Merton
Densher, is unequal to his ambitious role. But the two girls,
Milly Theale and Kate Croy, are magnificent; and at its
best the writing reaches some kind of high-water mark in
English prose. *The Wings of the Dove* is uneven but, as the
editors of the notebooks remark, it is James's "principal
tragedy." It is also, in its reticence, a modern tragedy, for
the horror grows out of the most casual circumstances, and
the full weight of it is felt in the color of a girl's dress, the
look of a room, the turn of a sentence, the impact of a
glance.

As *The Ambassadors* was inspired by the image of Howells, so *The Wings of the Dove* drew on that of Minny
Temple. Her counterpart here, Milly Theale, is one of those
characters, Achilles or Faust, who convey the essential
pathos of all mortality by being under special sentence.
She is ill and will probably die before her time, indeed in

her early twenties; and because she is very rich her desire for life is the greater and her fate the sadder. "Such is life," as Minny herself liked to say—such are its inevitable deprivations. And there is the second girl whose zest, fully equal to Milly's, is bound up with another kind of deficiency. In a world where the possession of money is postulated as essential, Kate Croy is without funds. Thus the tragedy of the book is finally in the pairing of the two girls. Meanwhile the plot, by setting them at odds and bringing out the best in one, the worst in the other, serves the lifelike end of masking communities with differences. And then there are the international variations in tone and manners, for one girl is a Londoner, the other a New Yorker.

Milly Theale, the rich and ailing New York girl, travels to Europe in the company of her excellent Boston friend, Susan Stringham. Now Mrs. Stringham has in London an old acquaintance, Mrs. Lowder, and Mrs. Lowder has a protégée, her niece Kate Croy, the girl of no means whom Mrs. Lowder, herself a wealthy and social woman, is trying to force into a "good" marriage, preferably with the eligible Lord Mark, although Kate is secretly engaged to Densher, a young journalist as poor as herself. On a recent visit to New York Densher has already met Milly and considerably attracted her. And now the fateful circle—the Americans and the English, the rich and the poor, the loved and the unloved—constitutes itself in London during the season. The girls are fond of one another; but acting on some obscure impulse of simple tact or possible gain, Kate conceals her engagement to Densher from Milly as she has done from her Aunt Maud Lowder. Milly is ignorant of Kate's secret, but Kate guesses Milly's; which is, of course, that she is very ill. And while her physician hopes that she may recover if she falls in love, Kate is evidently sceptical. In time, as the circle moves on to Venice, where Milly has rented a huge old palace on the Grand Canal, Kate's vague reserves towards her come to focus in a definite conspiracy. This she unfolds to Densher in Milly's thronged drawing-room and practically under Milly's eyes. "Since she's to die I'm to marry her?" demands Densher, understanding at last. "To marry her," Kate replies. "So that when her death has taken place I shall in the natural course have money?" Densher continues. "You'll in the natural course have money," Kate concludes steadily. "We shall in the natural course be free." Kate's plot has the moral advantage that it would seem to give Milly what she wants in her last days, which is Densher; and, knowingly or not, it is fostered by all the others—by Milly in the innocence of her love, by the doctor and Mrs. Stringham in the hope of saving Milly, by Mrs. Lowder and Lord Mark in the hope of getting rid of Densher. "I have pleased too many people," Densher remarks when the plot fails.

For it does fail, through a combination of bad intentions, bad judgment, and bad luck. Supposing Kate to be free, Lord Mark makes her a final proposal of marriage; and when he is bluntly refused he guesses the conspiracy and in revenge reveals it to Milly. For her it is the fatal shock and, alone with Mrs. Stringham in her Venetian palace, she "turns her face to the wall." Densher can only go back to London; and there, amid the dreary onset of winter and the ironic suggestions of the Christmas season, the end is played out. Kate has been pleased to liken Milly to a dove; and now, as it turns out after her death, Milly has forgiven them and left Densher money after all. "She has stretched her wings," says Kate, "and it was to *that* they reached. They cover us." But Densher, horrified at his falsity, cannot forgive Kate; and when she suggests that he has fallen in love with Milly's memory he does not deny it. He will marry Kate without the money or he will make it over to her and remain single, but he will not touch it himself. " 'I'll marry you, mind you, in an hour.' 'As we were?' But she turned to the door, and her headshake was now the end. 'We shall never be again as we were.' "

Howells was struck by the portrait of "all that terribly frank, terribly selfish, terribly shameless, terribly hard English gang." And whatever may be true of the rest of them, Mrs. Lowder is unmistakably and immovably hard. Enthroned in her large house in the midst of fashionable London she has for Kate the virtue of at least being representative. Her own room—"her counting-house, her battle field, her especial scene, in fine, of action"—is on the ground-floor, "opening from the main hall and figuring rather to our young woman on exit and entrance as a guard-house or a toll-gate." There she presides, "majestic, magnificent, high-colored, all brilliant gloss, perpetual satin, twinkling bugles and flashing gems, with a lustre of agate eyes, a sheen of raven hair, a polish of complexion that was like that of well-kept china." What is Mrs Lowder, Kate asks herself, but "Britannia of the Market Place . . . as passionate as she was practical, with a reticule for her prejudices as deep as that other pocket, the pocket full of coins stamped in her image, that the world best knew her by"? And Kate concludes that her aunt needs, to complete her emblematic character, only to be equipped with "a helmet, a shield, a trident and a ledger." Mrs. Lowder's hardness, of course, is that of the imperial society she so fixedly represents. And James succeeds in animating this portentous emblem, in bringing to bear on her all his feeling for the realness of the representative. She never appears but what she is intensely alive and herself. Her talk at the dinner table? "She called at subjects as if they were islets in an archipelago," and if interrupted quickly "resumed, with a splash of her screw, her cruise among the islands."

"Hard," however, is not at all the word for her niece, Kate Croy. Whatever she may become at the end, and however much she is meanwhile "the modern London girl" in the freedom of her ways, the ease with which she first picks Densher up at a Bohemian party and then continues to meet him, in defiance of her aunt, in the parks and streets, Kate Croy is possessed by the same tangled idealism that James usually attributes to his American girls. Indeed her original situation recalls that of Isabel in Albany. Kate too dreams of having love and glory both; and, because she does not love him, she discourages Lord Mark much as Isabel turns down Warburton. The source of her passions in the general "failure of fortune and honor" among her immediate family—her shady dandy of a father who has done something dishonorable, her sister who has married for love only to go sour and envious in her poverty—is the subject of the splendid early chapters. That poverty is an unqualified curse is the first premise of Kate's world, and indeed of the entire novel. Yet Kate, like her mother before her, like Marian her sister, is in love with a poor man of small practical promise. She is aware of these ironies and determined to surmount them; in all this lies her "talent for life," which is matched by her singular beauty. The extraordinary gestures and decisions of the novel are mostly hers. She knows how to galvanize Densher by suddenly exclaiming, "I engage myself to you forever"; more than anyone else she figures for Milly the poise and wit of London society. When Densher wonders how, caring for him, she can like lending him to Milly, she cries, "I don't like it, but I'm a person, thank goodness, who can do what I don't like." Even in crime she remains a romantic, resolved to walk as straight as the crooked road of her choice permits her. And it is her desperate honesty in so bluntly refusing Lord Mark that precipitates the tragedy.

The tragedy, insofar as it is Kate's, is one of mixed motives. Impelled to treachery by her very feeling for fortune, honor, and love, she is absorbed at last into the dreaded configuration of her unhappy father. It is part of her predicament that she must finally surrender the initiative to Densher, who, once he has agreed to the plot, must act for himself, remaining in Venice while Kate and her aunt depart in order to leave him alone with Milly. Kate instigates but Densher carries through; in doing so he develops a fatal independence; and it is his inner response to the later events of the novel that registers for us their quickly mounting horror. But he must first, before Kate leaves Venice, make clear his supremacy. Long made uneasy by her refusal either to marry him or to acknowledge their engagement or to become his mistress, he is at last in a position to demand that she sleep with him as the price of his agreeing to the conspiracy. She does, but the act is no real consummation, only part of a bargain; and after she has left Venice Densher rejoices at his conquest and cherishes the traces of her intimate presence in his room. Indeed he is so full of Kate that, on visiting Milly, he is quite unable to pretend love to her. There is a delicately painful interview, in the course of which he can speak nothing but false notes and Milly can only inquire pathetically about his comfort, his "writing," and his plans. With the impulsive *noblesse oblige* of the naïve rich girl, she asks that she and Mrs. Stringham be allowed to come to tea with him in his rooms; but he like Kate has his desperate chivalry, and this, Milly's one request, he refuses because he feels his rooms to be sacred to the other girl. Meanwhile, he has made the revealing blunder of referring too openly to Milly's illness, and she has met this violation of tact with "an exquisite pale glare." The dreadful visit ends, and Milly is left more or less prepared for what she is soon to hear from Lord Mark. And now, while the first sea-storm of the autumn chills and drenches Venice, everything goes to pieces. The holiday spirit of the little circle evaporates in silence and suspicion. Once more the Jamesian drama of exclusion is enacted, with the insider becoming the outsider. Going to visit her again, Densher finds Milly's door closed to him and is obliged to treat with her smirking major-domo. Anxiously he repairs to the storm-bound Piazza: its pavement is "greasy now with the salt spray; and the whole place, in its huge elegance, the grace of its conception and the beauty of its detail, was more than ever like a great drawing-room, the drawing-room of Europe, profaned and bewildered by some reverse of fortune." And here Densher, made clairvoyant by his own sense of guilt, quickly discovers the cause of the closed door. Behind the window of a café, reading the *Figaro*, sits Lord Mark.

James's preface names Milly as the heroine of *The Wings of the Dove*, but then goes on to confess that it is mainly the others who act. And indeed the first and the last words are Kate's and so are the great desires and the great retribution. In the tragic economy of the novel, Milly's part is that of victim, Ophelia or Desdemona. Hers is the kind of dual innocence which acquits her of any blame for her fate and at the same time makes that fate not improbable in the nature of things. Partly by reason of her function, partly because she is an undeveloped American girl by nature, Milly is not very closely studied. If, as Edmund Wilson says, "she is quite real at the core of the cloudy integument with which James has swathed her about," she is real in a special sense. As the restrictions of Renaissance court life gave Shakespeare his types of ideal innocence, his girl victims, so the very freedom of American life gave James his so different ones. With her red hair and beautiful pallor, her inconspicuously perfect dresses in black or white, Milly is a more exquisite Daisy Miller, a Daisy not so much refined of her bad manners as raised above all question of manners in a narrow sense. But she shares with Daisy the fact that she is a creature of possibilities; that her money, which so largely defines her for other people, means little to herself; that her will to live is relative to her capacity to love and be loved, her power to overcome her too privileged isolation. In short, precisely because her manners are not at issue here, Milly is free to figure in a large way the uncreated conscience of her race. She plays the "princess" to everyone's fancy, although she does so in a rented palace many times too large for her small self and meager court. And she is "the heir of all the ages," as James calls her in the preface, not merely because of the accumulated wealth of the world which is already hers, but also because of the heritage of suffering and responsibility which must be hers as well if she is ever to be complete.

In the long run, however, *The Wings of the Dove* quite transcends the international theme; Milly's death has a transfiguring effect on this as well as on the principal characters. It is true, as Kate says, that she has stretched her wings. Hers is not, like Daisy's, a case of disappointed love turning into a will to die; nor is it simply her death, the pity of it, that sanctifies her. It is what she does before she dies. By leaving the money to Densher she makes clear that her love for him has survived her knowledge of the plot, that she respects their mutual passion, and that in these generosities she has had at last her own experience of love. But the transfiguration is not entirely the work of Milly. Kate and Densher also contribute to the occasion by rising to it with so much feeling and awareness. Their falling apart constitutes their recognition of the power of love, which in their treachery they have debased. And theirs is the harder part, for they must go on living like another, and alas a divided, Adam and Eve.

The reviews of *The Wings of the Dove*, like those of *The Ambassadors* a year later, were hardly more than respectful and neither book reached any wide public. James's reputation was still suffering from the injury done it by *The Awkward Age* and *The Sacred Fount*. Howells and Conrad might defend him in perceptive essays; and Elisabeth Luther Cary might publish, in 1905, the first book-length study of his writings. For most readers the work of these years was "darkest James," as the American critic Frank Moore Colby observed in an essay of 1904. He thinks, said Colby, that "when he has made a motive he has made a man"; "nobody sins because nobody has anything to sin with"; "there are chapters like wonderful games of solitaire, broken by no human sound save his own chuckle when he takes some mysterious trick or makes a move that he says is 'beautiful.' " Colby's epigrams were acute and he was without real malice. He admired the earlier James and professed to see signs of recovery in *The Wings of the Dove*. But his reasons betray his prejudices, which were those of so many other readers as well. Quoting a passage descriptive of a squalid meal at the house of Kate's poor sister, he remarks that *The Wings of the Dove* "deals with conditions as well as people." And we are left to suppose that "conditions," to be recognizable, must be those of the frankly poor. Howells was more observant. "As for social conditions, predicaments, orders of things," he wrote, "where shall we find the like of the wonders wrought in *The Awkward Age?*" And the big magazines were beginning to be closed to James. *The Ambassadors*, rejected by *Harper's*, appeared in *The North American Review*, of which Howells was now the editor. *The Wings of the Dove* and *The Golden Bowl* failed of magazine publication altogether, as did three of James's chief tales: "The Birthplace," "The Beast in the Jungle," and "The Altar of the Dead." But if his reputation was deteriorating, so, very likely, were the standards of the popular periodicals— the age of the "little magazine" was at hand. Meanwhile he could at least always get published between book covers; and *The Golden Bowl*, issued in that form the year following *The Ambassadors*, was for James almost a success.

The Golden Bowl was to be his last long novel, and in it he returned with all his energy to the familiar themes of love and survival in an international situation. We know from the notebooks that the novel originated, as usual, in what then—in 1892—seemed to be merely a good idea for a short tale. James had heard of a girl and her widower-father who, though greatly attached to one another, decided each to marry, and who were then dismayed to discover that their respective partners were having an affair. This remained the central situation of *The Golden Bowl* as it was finally written; but meanwhile James greatly complicated the story and brought to bear on it all the mythologizing tendencies of his later mind. Maggie Verver, an American girl married to an Italian prince, is a princess in fact rather than, like Milly, by virtue of a metaphor; and her story is the story of how she comes in time to be emotionally equal to her position. This she does by overcoming the several forces that threaten her marriage. Together they constitute the symbolic flaw in the golden bowl of her wedded life; and the most obvious of them is the intrigue carried on by the Prince and Maggie's best friend Charlotte Stant, who although formerly intimate with the Prince unknown to the Ververs, has married Maggie's father. As Stephen Spender remarks in his notable study of *The Golden Bowl*; "Maggie is not in the position of Milly or Strether, who have only to live according to their lights, and then to lose everything. In James's other books he has convinced us that a part of life, of the *real* life of a human being, as apart from the performance of an automaton, is the power to choose to die. The question James has not yet answered is whether it is possible in the modern world to choose to live: and Maggie triumphantly answers it for him."

Triumphantly for James, no doubt, but whether triumphantly for the reader is the disturbing question about *The Golden Bowl*, which is the large problem child among

James's writings as "The Turn of the Screw" is the small one. How did he intend us to feel about the Ververs, father and daughter? Are they to be understood as sharing to some extent in the guilt of their partners? "The *subject* is really the pathetic simplicity and good faith of the father and daughter in their abandonment," James noted in 1892; and in the writing of the novel he seems to have tried to preserve this emphasis, unpromising as it would appear to be for a complex moral drama. To her confidante Fanny Assingham, Maggie continues to assert her solidarity with her father and their joint innocence of any fault. Moreover, as if it had not been sufficiently proved to them that they cannot hope to "collect" lovers as they collect works of art, Maggie and her father continue to the last to think of the Prince and Charlotte as among their "important pieces." To be sure, the Ververs have done no overt wrong; in a court of law they would be acquitted as Charlotte and the Prince would not be. In dramatic terms, however, they would seem to be implicated by reason of everything that they are, everything that makes their fascinating characters. The salient thing about them is the peculiar self-sufficiency they enjoy in their possession of enormous wealth, their mutual joy in buying precious art, their all-embracing love for one another. They always gaily refer to their relationship as a kind of marriage; and their actual marriages are both arranged with their own convenience in view. And we must conclude that the novelist in James collided with the moral idealist in him. He seems to have wanted to relieve Maggie of all original fault in order to enhance her triumph in the free exercise of love. But, as the situation was set up, he could not help observing her and her father on their weak and even their sinister side as well as on the side of their force and charm. Something of the false exaltation of an Olive Chancellor or a Rosie Muniment creeps into Maggie's tones and gestures when, at the end, she is demonstrating her newly acquired "majesty." And Ferner Nuhn is right in observing that she retains to the last something of the child playing house or the little American girl playing royalty.

But the Ververs, once they are relieved of their impossibly heroic role, become very human and the book itself becomes extremely interesting—James's chief chronicle of naked suffering. In novels, including many of his own, suffering is generally the privilege of poor or middling people. In *The Golden Bowl* people suffer and are rich, suffer in intimate consequence of *being* rich. Their distress is bound up with their luxurious settings and highly representative conditions: the great English houses which Prince Amerigo, of an ancient Italian family, inhabits with the Ververs. They themselves hold in a kind of vassalage a place beyond the Mississippi called American City, they have a million a year, and Mr. Verver is said to be one of the world's best-known collectors. "Set against this great historical and geographical tradition," Spender observes, "there is the strangely insulated, shut-off life of the actors. The two married couples, on this immense stage, in their admired and plausible surroundings, are yet living a life which is grotesquely at odds with their happy setting of envied appearance, and unsuited to the standards of the tradition to which they are trying to conform. They are perpetually at the edge of something quite sordid: of the divorce court, the reported evidence of servants, and love letters printed in the news. The struggle of the Ververs is a struggle to make the picture fit the frame; they are constantly struggling to make their lives worthy of their dead surroundings."

In his notebooks James refers to some wealthy American of his acquaintance as "the old *grand-seigneur* in a new bottle"; and it is this that the Ververs are quite sincerely trying to be. Not all the American barons of their time were robber barons, and this father and daughter embody the good faith of the best of them. Even at their best, however, the new barons were a precarious institution, in essential contradiction with the democracy. As individuals they were doomed even in their prime to a considerable eccentricity. As a class they were destined to prompt eclipse, though not extinction, by economic depressions and reforms; and in being eclipsed they left all over the Hudson Valley, the Berkshires, the Carolinas, California, and elsewhere the pretentious relics of their transient experiments in manorial living—the Brook Farms, let us say, of the rich. In the Ververs James caught some of this mixed pathos and self-indulgence, although the class was still intact in his time, and although, in trying to make the Ververs represent the best, he freed them of the usual burden of bad taste and eclectic philanthropy. Maggie and her father doubtless exemplify his ideal program for the class. Their first concern is with the moral well-being of themselves and those close to them. Their only public enterprise consists in the buying of works of art for exportation to American City, where they plan to build a museum for the enlightenment of the inhabitants, apt as those same inhabitants are to laugh at them. For the rest they are devotees of the private life, they are even addicts of it. As Americans, above all Americans of the West, they have no society proportionate to their wealth, and tend to huddle together, even at first shrinking from attendance at London parties. On their respective *sposi*, the worldly sociable Prince and Charlotte, they impose a curious quadrille-like pattern of existence, which consists in their regularly exchanging partners and now and then coming together, the four of them, over cards or dinner, with two trusted friends, Colonel and Mrs. Assingham, usually present as spectators. Their being partners in solitude is for the Ververs their distinction, their pathos, and their original sin. In the scale of their money and the adventurous life it would ostensibly open to them, they are shown as perennially shrunken and isolated. "The word 'small' is constantly associated with Maggie," notes Mr. Spender, "and it is she who in one of her moments of greatest exaltation realizes that her father was 'simply a great and deep and high little man, and that to love him with tenderness was not to be distinguished, a whit, from loving him with pride.' One remembers him always, with his dim smile, his quiet, very youthful manner, in the unassuming little scene; gazing at a 'piece' in his collection, or wandering vaguely about his garden." Jim Pocock of *The Ambassadors* is described as a businessman of "the new school"—"small and fat and constantly facetious, straw-colored and destitute of marks, he would have been practically indistinguishable had not his preference for light-gray clothes, for white hats, for very big cigars and very little stories, done what it could for his identity." Adam Verver is to Jim Pocock as the "tycoon" to the smaller businessman. His refinement is far greater but his identity is no less in question, and he too is forever fondling a cigar. He is also—for James spares us nothing—sexually impotent or sterile; he and Charlotte cannot, as she tells the Prince, have a child. Whatever else this may imply, it seems irresistibly to be the penalty of his somewhat morbid intimacy with his daughter; and Maggie, while she promptly bears a child, lives in unmistakable fear of the Prince's sexuality: it is the climax of her triumph when she can at last freely surrender to him, "touch him, taste him, smell him, kiss him, hold him."

In contrast to the Ververs, as Spender goes on to say, "the people they marry are, in a modern, almost a journalistic sense, suited to the public life . . . everything about Charlotte and the Prince is on the grand scale. As Maggie says when she recommends Charlotte to her father, 'I may be as good, but I'm not so great—and that's what we're talking about. She has a great imagination. She has, in every way, a great attitude. She has above all a great conscience.'" Of course Maggie is at this point ignorant of her friend's real nature. Like all James's major characters, Charlotte shows a strong feeling for beautiful behavior; but a conscience she never had, and it is a sign of the inexorable realism of the novel that she never acquires one. Nor, clever and charming though she is, does she have any insight into her own motives, not to mention those of other people. Her great fault lies in her strange egotistical unawareness. She has given up the Prince because they are too poor to marry; but as soon as he is engaged to her old friend she rushes overseas to be present at the wedding, tries to force on him mementoes of their old intimacy, seeks a place near him by marrying Mr. Verver. All unconsciously, in short, she is resolved to break down his scruples and resume the affair. And one rainy day when she has come to keep him company in Maggie's absence, she succeeds. As we read the novel, Maggie and her father are much at fault in all this: they are too fond of each other and leave the other pair too much together. Yet James cannot be said to have been of the devil's party without knowing it. Maggie's fault does not make Charlotte's justification: it merely makes her opportunity. And it is as an unconscious opportunist that Charlotte is at once so appealing and so appalling. She is much more that very pervasive type than she is the traditional "adventuress" living by her wits and trying to improve her social position. It is not position or even money that she wants, for such desires would argue a certain stability in her. She wants possession of the Prince and the pleasure of dominating other people's lives. Her place then is not with the highly practical Mme. Merle; nor, in her capacity for self-deception and her total incapacity for tragedy, is it with Kate Croy; it is rather with the insatiable Princess Casamassima. And when at the end she goes off to America with Mr. Verver, she goes as "a caged beast," tied to her husband by "a silken halter," and under the consoling misapprehension that Maggie's triumph over her has been the triumph of stupidity over intelligence.

Prince Amerigo is in something of Densher's position as between two feminine rivals; but he is a much more formidable creation, a man distinctly worth the battle, a real center of gravity. If he, like Densher, is rather passive, it is not because he is weak but because he is profoundly simple. Far removed from the bourgeois desires and exaltations of the Ververs and Charlotte Stant, their perpetual concern with success and failure, their belief that all trouble is from the willed arrangements of life rather than in the nature of things, the Prince occupies a middle ground where the trained elegance of the Italian noble comes together with the natural grace of the Italian peasant. He is *galantuomo* by virtue of a cultivation so thorough as to make the whole process nearly instinctive. As he has everything else a man should have, so he has a conscience, even if, given his happy complacency, it is less vigilant than that of the Ververs. No doubt he marries Maggie chiefly out of a need to be cherished and cared for; but he is eager to respect the Ververs in return for their care and to love in proportion as he is loved. Clearly too he is touched and aroused by Maggie with her strange terror of life, her virginal reluctance to show him how much she loves him, her willingness to put herself in the wrong by rattling on about how he is merely one of their *morceaux de musée*—will he travel about with them like their smaller pieces, "the things we take out and arrange as we can, to make the hotels we stay at and the houses we hire a little less ugly," or will he follow "the bigger and more cumbrous pieces" into the warehouse? But as time goes on and Maggie, still in awe of him and fearful of neglecting her father, actually neglects *him*, he cools off, becomes in Spender's phrase "politely but infinitely bored by the Ververs," and retires to his room with the *Times* and the *Figaro*. And as Charlotte, whom he admires in any case, is more and more thrust in his way, his scruples against having an affair with her vanish before his feeling that to refuse to do so is "to publish one as idiotic or incapable," as "supremely grotesque." He inevitably seeks order, and when he cannot find it with his wife he finds it with the next most natural thing, a mistress. Maggie, then, has only to assert herself, to make clear how much she loves him, to re-establish the original order, for him to find her attractive once more. Meanwhile she has grieved almost as much over his loss of repose, his obvious gloomy guilt, as over his infidelity itself.

And this inspired sentiment best proves her right to him; it shows she knows how to appreciate him. He has, it is true, little enough to say to her first or last. But he can take her in his arms and he can soothe her with his childlike profundities: "Everything's terrible, cara, in the heart of man."

Amerigo, with his melancholy wisdom, seems to catch up the whole spirit of *The Golden Bowl* better than Maggie in her triumph, whatever James may have intended. *Amor omnia vincit* is the ostensible lesson of the book; that sentiment certainly dictated the structure and movement, and nowhere in James is the scenic arrangement more powerful or the mind of the central observer—here partly the Prince but mainly Maggie—more effective in creating form. Yet what Glenway Wescott observed of James's novels in general is especially true of *The Golden Bowl:* "The psychic content is too great for its container of elegantly forged happenings: it all overflows and slops about and is magnificently wasted." The end, although formally more decisive than James usually attempted, is for that very reason rather question-begging. What will become of Charlotte when she is uncaged in American City? What then will become of American City? James saw these questions and, in the case of Maggie and the Prince, interestingly capitalized on them. There is a moment at the very end when Maggie, left alone for a moment after the departure of Charlotte and her father, experiences "an instant of terror." She has her triumph, her freedom, her restored order. "Only what *were* these things in the fact," what would she do with them?

The Prince promptly returns and wonderfully embraces her but her question rings on. We remember the woman in

The Waste Land with her "What shall we do? What shall we ever do?" And we feel that the really serious blemish in the lives of these people is the suffocating privacy forced upon them by their own sensitivity plus the low state of public enterprise. It is true, as Philip Rahv observes, that "there never was a writer so immersed in personal relations" as James was. And Maggie's final success with her marriage would seem to mean that solutions for the gravest problems may be found within the private life itself, without recourse to the courts or the church or even to any established morality. It is significant that the Prince and the Ververs are Catholics, and a priest appears briefly at their table. Yet the point is distinctly made that Maggie consults him not at all but settles everything for herself in what seems a flagrantly Protestant spirit. As she is her own priest, so she coins her own ethic out of her particular needs. In her feeling for her husband's intrigue with Charlotte there is no conventional horror of adultery, there is very little of judgment. And presumably it is out of a dread of being tempted into judgment, quite as much as out of a desire to spare each other, that Maggie and her father never mention between them the dereliction of their *sposi*.

But surely *The Golden Bowl* is an unsparing picture of the inevitable *strain* of the private life, the paralyzing effect of an existence in which right and wrong are entwined like roses on a tomb; in which the round of cards, the little dinner for six, the chance encounter on the terrace, the parley in the garden, are unbearably loaded with meaning; and in which nothing is ever really resolved except by death. All this makes *The Golden Bowl* as contemporary as last summer's week-end imbroglio. It is the source of the novel's peculiar atmosphere of horror, which envelops Maggie in particular. James's American girls have always been distinguished by the talent for life; even Milly was in this heroic line. But Maggie forges her triumph, such as it is, out of an original terror of life. As her father is always brooding in a solitude that seems to stretch out to eternity, so Maggie actively and dreadfully suffers; stuffs handkerchiefs in her mouth that she may not scream; sees herself as lying dead of a broken neck; fancies Charlotte's weary voice in the next room to be "the shriek of a soul in pain"; is visited by images of burglars "surprised in one of the thick-carpeted corridors of a house on a Sunday afternoon," of some "wild eastern caravan" bearing down on her out of the desert, "crude colors in the sun, fierce pipes in the air, high spears in the sky." Maggie of all James's characters is the most vividly susceptible to the presence of evil; she has a regular sensibility for it. And the evil is after all, as Spender suggests, "simply the evil of the modern world," the isolation of the sensitive and the loving, a condition for which "their only compensation is that by the use of their intelligence, by their ability to understand, to love and to suffer, they may to some extent atone." In all James's talk of American Princesses is there not some irony at the expense of these girls who can reign over no more than their small households and who must maintain their Urbinos in hotel suites or hired houses or in the fastnesses and among the sneering natives of American City? Maggie certainly demonstrates the potentialities of the private life; but such is James's impartial realism that she might also confess, with Maria Gostrey of *The Ambassadors*, that "the superiority you discern in me announces my futility." After all, the Louvre, scene of James's great dream, was once a real palace.

And what a distance the Jamesian novel has traveled

since the '70's, when the Warburtons and the Bellegardes, the Touchetts and the Wentworths, implied the existence of fairly stable systems of manners opening out into areas of public responsibility—systems so stable that the very drama of those early books arose from the spectacle of the relative incommensurability of the American and the European ones. In *The Golden Bowl* Americans and Europeans are united in the dismayed recognition of a quite different situation. What are incommensurable now are the moral life and that social entity which has always been so dear to James but which in *The Golden Bowl* has dwindled to a shadowy Italian ambassador, a superfluous priest, an empty and importunate pair named Assingham. How strange, then, to charge James, as has so often been done, with here ignoring the world, when his doing so makes just the point of the novel, is just his sacrificial tribute to the tragic actualities of his characters. How short-sighted to maintain that his long exile attenuated his energy and confused his point of view, when it was precisely his vantage point abroad that permitted him to combine the American moral energy with the hard wisdom of the good European, to keep bravely abreast of world developments however damaging they might be to his own theories and desires, and so to remain profoundly creative into his sixties.

Final Years

The Golden Bowl, beautifully printed by Scribner, astonished James by selling out four editions in the United States within a year. That, to be sure, was the year of his American visit, an event attended by some excitement in the newspapers and among the members, very numerous in those days, of women's literary clubs. It was, as he knew, rather because he was an expatriate than because he was an artist that he made good copy in America. Even then he was half amused and half gratified to be able to report to English friends that a "she-interviewer" from a New York paper rushed all the way to New Hampshire on the chance that he might be there; that he was taken by John Hay to see Theodore Roosevelt in the White House; that he lectured, chiefly on Balzac, to huge audiences in several cities, receiving as much as $500 for an appearance.

He had expected no such reception but he had long dreamed of a return. To his intimate nostalgia for the places of his youth was now added a European's interest in the strange country of Lincoln, Whitman, and Poe. The "inward romantic principle" now favored America, and brought him to such a pitch of expectation that William thought it advisable to warn him against possible disappointment. There were also practical reasons for the trip. A contract to write up his impressions for *Harper's* really instigated and partly financed it; and there was the scheme of a selected edition of his work to be discussed with Scribner. Above all, having exhausted the vein of the three great novels, he was in search of a new one.

Sailing in August 1904, he landed at Hoboken and left the same day for William's summer house at Chocorua, New Hampshire. There, reunited with his brother's family in "such *golden* September weather" and among the lakes and mountains of a rural New England whose charm was almost new to him, he spent the happiest weeks of the entire journey. He then went to Boston, where there were friends to see and scenes to revisit and where old memories again made the prose of his notebooks incandescent as they had done during his last sojourn twenty years before. "Oh, strange little intensities of history, of ineffaceability; oh, delicate little odd links in the long chain, kept unbroken for the fingers of one's tenderest touch! Sanctities, pieties, treasures, abysses." He traveled briefly to Salem, Concord, Newport, Cape Cod, and the Berkshires, noted the breakdown of the old New England agriculture, observed the presence everywhere of the immigrant intruder: in Salem an Italian of whom he asked directions had not heard of the House of the Seven Gables. But it was in New York, where he spent several weeks in the winter, that he experienced most powerfully the sense of dispossession by the alien multitudes. Old New York was almost consumed by slums and skyscrapers, and whatever beauty the city has since acquired was then only dimly discernible. He was to give

New York an elaborate analysis in *The American Scene*, but he actually found the place, as he told a friend, "appalling, fantastically charmless and dire." Thus far he was in familiar territory; but he had wanted most of all to explore places that were new to him. So, after stops at Philadelphia and Washington, he traveled southward to Florida, then cross-country to Chicago, Indianapolis, and California, where, spending some days at Coronado, he was more impressed than he had expected to be by the famous abundances of sun, fruit, and flowers. He had even planned a dash into Mexico, but this had to be abandoned for lack of time. Indeed the whole latter part of his trip was spoiled by frantic hurry and mounting impatience. He was soon sick of hotels and trains and lecture-halls. The huge American spectacle, surveyed at such a pace, proved less and less decipherable. He longed for England, the privacy of Lamb House, the comfort of daily work. His impressions were already too many and too intense and he needed "to return to England . . . as a saturated sponge and wring myself out there." Out of this frenzied homecoming, however, came *The American Scene*, one of his inestimable books and one of the great American documents.

Back in Lamb House in the late summer of 1905, he found his impressions harder to write up than he had anticipated, and his work on them was interrupted by problems connected with the New York Edition. *The American Scene* did not appear in book form until 1907 and even then it ended with his report on Florida: the West he reserved for a second volume which never got written.

In the detail of sentence and paragraph, *The American Scene* is intensely wrought; but the design of the whole is casual, allowing "the restless analyst," as the author calls himself, a large freedom. To a degree he follows his actual movements in America and makes out of them what capital he can in the way of organization. Starting with a poignant glance at what remains of the New York of his childhood, he establishes himself in his human identity as a revenant. But although this identity continues to yield touching overtones, it is quickly submerged when, shifting to the garish summer villas along the New Jersey shore, he sees the necessity of coping with an America irrevocably changed. Here "the very *donnée* of the piece" gets formulated: the book will investigate the consequences of "the great adventure of a society reaching out into the apparent void for the amenities, the consummations, after having earnestly gathered in so many of the preparations and necessities." New societies, he confesses, may be more interesting than old ones, especially if they are "backed" by unlimited funds and an inexhaustible will for self-improvement.

All these considerations give rise to the ostensible subject of *The American Scene*, the parts of it that deal with the arts, ceremonies, and other tangible signs of a republic in pursuit of the amenities. And James is an acute observer of these things, even though he is often inhumanly limited, as when his thoughts on the Negroes are confined to the question of their potential as a servant class. But the book has also a kind of latent subject. This makes itself felt once James has moved, as he does with another abrupt shift, from the New Jersey shore to the mother wilderness of New England; it continues to resound as he returns to New York for a longer look, only to fade out as he travels south. This subject consists in his search for buried clues to the secret life of the country, the human reality within the shifting and impalpable forms. Where may the imagination, as distinct from the appraising intelligence, hope to rest and feed? In pursuit of an answer he limits his impulse towards merely personal feeling, saving that for his memoirs and his late cycle of American stories. He suppresses both his memories and his more intimate revulsions—strong as these obviously were in some cases—in his artist's search for the objectively significant. And it is this effort which makes *The American Scene* so remarkably forward-looking, a kind of source book of later American writing, full of the unborn spirits of poems by Hart Crane and plays by Eugene O'Neill.

The American Scene is uneven. On the South, James can do little more than add a grace of phrase, and now and then a penetrating glimpse, to fairly routine observations. He is convinced of some lurking tragic fascination in the region, but the evidences of it escape him in his rapid survey of the architecture and scenery. As we have noted, he had no imagination for the pure exotic. He could never simply "ride away," like the woman in Lawrence's story or the boat in Rimbaud's poem. What really *lived* for him, in an imaginative unity transcending geography, was a universe composed of Rome, Paris, England, and eastern America; and no part of it was finally stranger to the rest. Even the early "A Passionate Pilgrim" turned on an act of intimate possession, the inheritance of an English country house by an American. Thus the greatness of *The American Scene* is all in the chapters on New York, the Hudson Valley, and New England—places his mind had once possessed and might therefore hope now to repossess. And although he writes elaborately throughout, it is in these chapters that the prose is best supported by complexity of feeling.

Because he is now more at home everywhere, he no longer, in *The American Scene*, talks about the "provincial" or looks for the picturesque in expected places. Rather, his mind *creates* the picturesque by virtue of its own enterprise. Drawing on its huge store of experience, it turns up a constant wealth of images suggestive of a haunting incongruity. This ranges from the occasional humor of such phrases as "verandas of contemplation," or "the law of the increasing invisibility of [New York] churches," or "the original sin of the longitudinal avenues," to a strategy of major discovery, by which the legendary is engendered before the reader's eyes. Thus in New England "the village street and the lonely farm and the hillside cabin . . . twitched with a grim effect the thinness of their mantle, shook out of its folds such crudity and levity as they might, and borrowed, for dignity, a shade of the darkness of Cenci-drama, of monstrous legend, of old Greek tragedy." Thus in the passage already quoted (page 237) on New York Harbor the "vision of energy" first materializes in a cheerful scattered lyricism of water and light, of whistles and breeze-borne cries; these then freeze abruptly into a single ominous effect, "a diffused, wasted clamor of *detonations*"; and at last the various sounds and sights, the rhythms of traffic by bridge and ferry, become inextricable parts of "some steel-souled machine-room of brandished arms and hammering fists and opening and closing jaws." And thus, in the admirable lines on Concord Bridge, that historic site is approached by way of a glimpse of "the sleepy, meadowy flood" of the Concord River: "It had watched the Fight, it now confesses, without a quickening of its current, and it draws along the woods and the orchards and the fields with the purr of a mild domesticated cat who rubs against the family and the furniture." But the river is not indifferent—it is only mild as the Fight was mild, and because, for the rest, it is in the presence of "the exquisite melancholy of the inexpressible." What this may be James then suggests in language gone vividly bare for the occasion: "It lies too deep, as it always so lies where the ground has borne the weight of the short simple act, intense and unconscious, that was to determine the event, determine the future in the way we call immortally."

The year 1907, which witnessed the appearance of *The American Scene*, also brought the first volumes of *The New York Edition of the Novels and Tales of Henry James*. Scribner in New York undertook to arrange copyrights and produce the 24 handsome volumes, and Macmillan sponsored the Edition in England. The rest was left to James, including the choice of photographic frontispieces, which, executed by A. L. Coburn, represented street scenes appropriate to the text.

Helping Coburn to track down good subjects—for instance, a curio shop similar to the one where Maggie acquires the golden bowl—seems to have been James's one unqualified pleasure in his task as self-editor. For although the Edition began as hardly more than a gesture in defiance of oblivion or a broad hint at intelligent readers, it soon turned, as James's undertakings so often did, into something rich and strange—and so exhausting, in this case, that he never fully recovered from the effects. Before he was done he had reread large portions of his work; carefully selected some of it and painfully rejected the rest; revised minutely most of the chosen pieces; arranged them in a loose unity which, according to Mr. Edel, is designedly reminiscent of the Comédie Humaine; and written a series of elaborate prefaces. In short, as James said, he had re-dreamed his career.

But the James of the Edition was a stern dreamer. In-deed, with his reminiscences, his judgments, and his ad-vice, he is rather the vigilant patriarch presiding over the ultimate *conseil de famille.* He selects, revises, and pref-aces his writings almost exclusively from his viewpoint as the ripe author of *The Golden Bowl.* And when, in the pref-ace to that novel, where the general problems of the edi-tion are discussed, he laments the inexpertness of much of his earlier work, we perceive that his idea of expertness is defined entirely by his later complexities and not at all by the ironic economy of a *Washington Square,* expertly ren-dered though that economy looks to us. Time, it is true, has made the Edition seem precious, a distinctive part of the whole *œuvre;* but some of the questions about it raised by his contemporaries, including his friends, are still lively. Why did he so underrate his earlier work as to omit *Wash-ington Square* and *The Europeans,* while giving two fat volumes to *The Tragic Muse* and devoting space to such overwrought later pieces as "Julia Bride" and "The Friends of the Friends"? (*The Bostonians* was left out less by James's wish than by that of the publisher, and with the un-derstanding that it might come in later if the success of the Edition warranted its expansion.) Again, do not his prefaces make the writing of fiction sound too much like a problem in mechanics? And, finally, did he not revise so relent-lessly as to spoil the original freshness of his stories, es-pecially the early ones? Now the excluded works may al-ways be read elsewhere, and the prefaces read or not as we please; so it is the rewriting which has always produced the most fascinated discussion. But the question is hardly one of principle nor is it unique with James. Revision is common practice among writers, and the rights and wrongs of it are a matter of tact and degree. In reworking his prose for the Edition, James sometimes spoiled but he also in most cases improved. Newman of *The American* certainly needed *more* raciness of speech and not less, which is what he got; but in return for this, the few carefully interpolated images made his reflections much more vivid. And in general only the revision of books composed prior to *The Portrait of a Lady* is seriously suspect. With that novel the style was already rich, and James's alterations, confined as they were to matters of verbal detail, gave color and point to many an ineffectual passage.

The making of the Edition was an act of self-criticism for him; and "to criticise," he said, "is to appreciate, to appropriate, to take intellectual possession, to establish in fine a relation with the criticised thing and make it one's own." The rewriting of his stories was perhaps the least part of this process. For his readers, at any rate, his selections and groupings are of greater import; and to discover, for example, "The Beast in the Jungle" next to "The Altar of the Dead" in a volume largely given over to similar tales is to learn much about his themes and their progression from work to work and period to period. In this way he could reveal something of the inner content of his writings without the pedantic self-exposure which might have resulted had he chosen to be more explicit on this subject in his prefaces.

And it was the prefaces that were the most ambitious feature of the Edition. Like *The American Scene*, they are a kind of last testament on a matter of the greatest importance to James; and they too push intensity of feeling and richness of image as far as traditional English prose would seem to allow. Possibly there is an excess of detail and amenity, although James's capacity to turn theory into resounding phrase is here at its greatest, not to mention his power to insinuate, ingratiate, and divert. Like all good critics he has his peculiar stresses for which allowance must be made. There is certainly too much harping on the indispensableness of the central observer, as if this unifying device were Unity in person; and anyone who took the prefaces as a program for novel-writing would doubtless find them stultifying. But to take them thus would be to mistake James's purposes. As R. P. Blackmur observes in his fine study of the prefaces, they are more dramatic than pedagogic in spirit. Each of them is "the story of a story," telling as a rule how the idea for the piece came to him, where and when he wrote it, and how he went about detecting and solving the various problems entailed in its execution. The discussion of these problems is very exhaustive but it is never merely mechanical. Craft is studied and celebrated by James because he believes it to be the essence of creation, and because the mastery of it "renews in the modern alchemist something like the old dream of the secret of life." This conviction unifies the various aspects, theoretical and personal, of the prefaces, makes vivid most of the technicalities, and impels him irresistibly from the case to the general precept. We may feel, as we open the preface to *The Wings of the Dove*, that his concern over the dangers to good taste involved in presenting "a sick young woman" is relevant only to his own sensibilities; but as we read on, the problem of the dying heroine gives way to large reflections on death as a theme for the artist—"let him deal with the sickest of the sick, it is still by the act of living that they appeal to him"; and leads finally into a statement, invaluable for the understanding of *The Wings of the Dove,* of the relation of Milly's death to the fate of the other characers and to those "communities of doom" which make up the novel's deepest tones. But the prefaces propose no final interpretations of the novels and it is of course right that they should not. We are left free to develop their suggestions and even occasionally to differ on a point of emphasis or appraisal. On the general implications of James's art they are also reticent, though far less so. Their focus now and then expands to include some philosophic or introspective comment of great beauty and interest—on romance and realism, on intelligence in literature, on art and personality, on the American girl as topic and symbol, on the recalcitrance for him of the "Downtown" subject. With their baroque surface, their strange idiom, and their high seriousness, the prefaces have remained and will perhaps always remain closed to all but a few readers. For the uninitiated, however, this is a loss. Really to give ourselves up to the prefaces, and to go along with their distinctive rationale, is to see what Mr. Blackmur means by calling them "the most sustained and I think the most eloquent and original pieces of literary criticism in existence."

"I sat for a long while with the closed volume [of *The American*] in my hand going over the preface in my mind and thinking—that is how it began, that's how it was done." So Joseph Conrad, his greatest disciple, wrote to James on receiving the first volumes of the Edition. Such tributes were few, however, and worst of all the Edition refused to sell. This laboriously prepared smoke-signal failed to effect his rescue from the wilderness of neglect and in failing only deepened his solitude. His doom, as he felt, had been pronounced for his lifetime. Yet he believed as invincibly as ever in a post-mortem fame, and there were numerous signs of it even then. Unexpected testimonials continued to reach him—from the historian Trevelyan, from a learned member of the Juridical Society of Edinburgh, from a group of Cambridge undergraduates, total strangers to him, whose invitation to spend a week end with them at the University he gaily accepted—Rupert Brooke was one of them. And it seems to have been in the years following *The Golden Bowl* that his prestige as a public figure increased so immensely and that some of his deepest friendships, including those with Edith Wharton and Hugh Walpole, came into being. Those were also the years of official honors. Harvard awarded him a degree in 1911, Oxford one in 1912; and in 1916, shortly before his death, the British government conferred on him the Order of Merit. But the best of these distinctions came in 1913 when a fund was raised among 270 of his English friends to celebrate his seventieth birthday by presenting him with a golden bowl and commissioning Sargent to do his portrait. The occasion was a tribute to him in his dual capacity as a writer and a social figure. "I was drawn to London long years ago as by the sense, felt from still earlier, of all the interest and association I should find here," he said in a letter of thanks to the subscribers, "and I now see how my faith was to sink deeper foundations than I could presume ever to measure—how my justification was both stoutly to grow and wisely to wait. It is so wonderful indeed to me as I count up your numerous and various, your dear and distinguished friendly names, taking in all they recall and represent, that I permit myself to feel at once highly successful and extremely proud." The Sargent portrait was duly painted and publicly hung; and although, in a strange eruption of the arbitrary, it was in 1914 severely mutilated by some suffragette with a knife, it was soon repaired and now hangs in the National Portrait Gallery.

If he completed no more long novels after *The Golden Bowl*, that was not, we may be sure, because of the state of his reputation. Even such great energies as his had presumably spent themselves in the immense efforts of the years 1900-1909; and while he continued to dream of a new creative period, and worked at the two fragments of novels already mentioned, he was to produce nothing of moment after 1909 except his memoirs. The despair that always took hold of him when he was inactive made his remaining years intermittently uneasy and probably accounted, as much as anything, for some of his troubles and activities. For one thing, the storm-flag of the theater again waved briefly, from 1907 to 1910. Asked for a play by Forbes-Robertson, he revised an old work into a piece called *The High Bid*, which the famous actor then performed with some success. The London audiences were pleased and the reviewers charming. Max Beerbohm wrote that "little though Mr. James can on the stage give us of his great art, even that little has a quality which no other man can give us: an inalienable magic." Almost as excited as he had been in 1891, James again treated his correspondents to unconvincing cries of jolly cynicism and hollow hope and at once set about writing or reworking further plays, dictating them to Theodora Bosanquet, the remarkable woman who was now his secretary. One of these, a curtain-raiser entitled *The Saloon*, which he adapted from his story "Owen Wingrave," was performed in 1911 to an indifferent world. Meanwhile the American producer Charles Frohman, planning a repertory season in London, invited him to submit something along with such proven playwrights as Shaw, Galsworthy, and Barrie. James was gratified to be in this company and promptly wrote *The Outcry*, only to see his hopes for it give way by degrees before a flood of casting difficulties and required excisions. *The Outcry* is a poor play, and to read it today is to wonder how it reached even the cutting and casting stage, or ever so much as took root in the fastidious mind of Henry James. Like the other pieces of these years, all equally unfortunate, it cannot be blamed on his old age, unless the impulse that made him write for the stage at all may be attributed to a kind of recurrent senility induced by the exhaustion now and then of his novel-writing powers.

And now, in 1910, when he was 67, old age was upon him in fact. While still at work on *The Outcry* he became very ill and was presently bedridden for many weeks and a near invalid for the remainder of that year. There were grave organic disorders, but he suffered most, as he told Desmond MacCarthy, from "the spiral of depression which . . . compelled him step after step, night after night, day after day, to descend. He would, he thought, never have recovered had it not been for a life-line thrown to him by his brother William." It appears to have been at this time that, as his physician later testified, he seriously debated suicide with William, who with his wife had hastened overseas to be near him. But William was also unwell, and when he was taken that summer to Nauheim his health rapidly gave way and it was soon clear that he was dying. Disabled though he still was himself, Henry could not tolerate separation and so accompanied the William Jameses back to America where they went at once to the New Hampshire home. There, after a week of suspense and pain, William James died on August 26. "I sit heavily stricken and in darkness," James wrote to T. S. Perry, "—for from far back in dimmest childhood he had been my ideal Elder Brother, and I still, through all the years, saw in him, even as a small timorous boy yet, my protector, my backer, my authority and my pride. His extinction changes the face of life for me—besides the mere missing of his inexhaustible company and personality, originality, the whole unspeakably vivid and beautiful presence of him. And his noble intellectual vitality was still but at its climax—he had still two or three ardent purposes and plans. He had cast them away, however, at the end—I mean that, dreadfully suffering, he wanted only to die."

Strangely, their brother Robertson died the same month, and Henry now found himself the single survivor of the original family. He remained for a year in the United States, keeping close to William's wife and children and recovering slowly from grief and illness. By September 1911 he was well enough to return to England, which he was not to leave again. Living partly at Lamb House, but more in London, where he presently took rooms in Cheyne Walk in view of the Thames, he began the memoirs on which so much of our knowledge of his early life depends. His strength was not what it had been and he worked painfully, publishing *A Small Boy and Others* in 1913 and its sequel, *Notes of a Son and Brother*, the following year. Mrs. William James had proposed the undertaking to him, and he seems at first to have had in mind a memorial of his brother. For whatever reason—perhaps because the beloved William proved impenetrable to analysis, perhaps in obedience to the old exigencies of the point of view and the old habit of the central observer—he made himself his real if exceedingly modest hero. The venture would be difficult, he knew, "but if I bring it off it will be exquisite and unique." And in its gravely tremulous way it is—his last notable performance. His surviving friends in America naturally read the volumes with great interest, among them Henry Adams, who was moved by them to address to him what James described as a "melancholy outpouring" full of "unmitigated blackness." He replied that Adams had mistaken the purpose of the memoirs, which was to exhibit not the despair that issues in silence but the hope that goes on talking and doing. "I still find my consciousness interesting—under *cultivation* of the interest. Cultivate it *with* me, dear Henry—that's what I hoped to make you do —to cultivate yours for all that it has in common with mine. *Why* mine yields an interest I don't know that I can tell you. . . . It's, I suppose, because I am that queer monster, the artist, an obstinate finality, an inexhaustible sensibility." And he concluded by saying that he would still *do* because doing was "an act of life."

And how much he could still do was shown when the war of 1914 precipitated his final act of life. He was not of course among those observers who had foreseen a world war. He assimilated the news, however, with the assurance of one long familiar with the latent violence of modern life; and on August 5th he addressed to Howard Sturgis what has become a classic account of the war's moral impact: "The plunge of civilization into this abyss of blood and darkness by the wanton feat of those two infamous autocrats is a thing that so gives away the whole long age during which we have supposed the world to be, with whatever abatement, gradually bettering, that to have to take it all now for what the treacherous years were all the while really making for and meaning is too tragic for any words."

He survived some two and a half years of the war and was strenuously and variously active in England's cause. Except that he surprised everyone by his energy, and felt his Americanism as a peculiar stress, the story of his opinions and emotions was largely that of the many other active patriots whose concern for the fate of civilization, however real in itself, was strangely, as it seems now, untempered by any knowledge of the complex moral implications of world imperialism. On the one hand he had never had any love for Germany; and on the other he had consistently envisaged the British Empire as the necessary if sometimes bad core of the world order. He was fired, moreover, by a special sense of obligation to the country that had so long harbored him and by a passion to make up for his own country's hesitation in coming to England's aid. No doubt, too, he was active with the intensity of one who, long confined to his study, mindful of his own enforced absence from the Civil War of his youth, discovered now a release for desires and faculties long unexercised. His war letters, to which Percy Lubbock gave so much space in his collection, are not among James's best; like Proust's Mme. Verdurin in her military phase, he rejoiced too much in the belated privilege of saying "we." He was not, however, insensitive to the horror of war, the menace to Paris, the deprivations of the Belgians, the loss of friends and the sons of friends, the anguish of the wounded soldiers who thronged the London hospitals and whom he visited day after day with gifts and encouragement. He was not unaware of the comic side of his embattled role, as when, with what must have been a calculated magniloquence, he remarked to Ford Madox Ford, about to depart for the front, *"Tu vas te battre pour le pays de Madame de Staël."* Nor did he finally hang back from a step which would have horrified him in other circumstances and on which even now he had brooded anxiously for many months. Indignant at American neutrality, and eager to do the thing that would best express his devotion to England, he renounced his American citizenship; on July 26, 1915, sponsored by the Prime Minister among others, he was naturalized as a British subject. "Civis Britannicus sum," he wrote to Gosse that day, adding, however, that "the odd thing is that nothing seems to have happened and I don't feel a bit different."

He had not much time left to ponder his new status. He suffered now from a bad heart—made worse, perhaps, by his wartime exertions. A. C. Benson, who lunched with him in the spring of 1915, noted that "he looks ill, he changes colour, he is dark under the eyes—but he was in a cheerful and pontifical mood. He ate a plentiful meal of veal and pudding but spoke to me very gravely of his physical condition and his chronic angina. . . . We went down together and he made a most affectionate farewell. He is slower and more *soigneux* in utterance than ever, but leaves a deep impression of majesty, beauty and greatness." By November he had failed considerably: "the past year," he wrote to Walpole, "has made me feel twenty years older, and, frankly, as if my knell had rung." On December 2nd he had a stroke, and is said to have told a friend that as he collapsed he heard a voice exclaiming: "So here it is at last, the distinguished thing!" There was a second stroke, then a brief rally, then a slow sinking. Mrs. William James, with two of her children, crossed the seas of war to be with him. He was sometimes conscious for moments; but gradually and with little pain he wasted away and on February 28, 1916, he died.

Two memorial services were held in London. But he had asked that his ashes—for the body was cremated— should be returned to the family burial place in his native country. And so they were brought at last to the Cambridge cemetery, which, as we know from his notebook, he had visited one day in 1904 and which had wrung from him these surpassing lines, so rich in the characteristic passion and idiom of Henry James: "Isn't the highest deepest note of the whole thing the never-to-be-lost memory of that evening hour at Mount Auburn—at the Cambridge Cemetery when I took my way alone—after much waiting for the favouring hour—to that unspeakable group of graves. It was late, in November; the trees all bare, the dusk to fall early, the air all still (at Cambridge, in general, *so* still), with the western sky more and more turning to that terrible, deadly, pure polar pink that shows behind American winter woods. But I can't go over this—I can only, oh, so gently, so tenderly, brush it and breathe upon it—breathe upon it and brush it. It was the moment; it was the hour; it was the blessed flood of emotion that broke out at the touch of one's sudden *vision* and carried me away. I seemed then to know why I had done this; I seemed then to know why I had *come*—and to feel how not to have come would have been miserably, horribly to miss it. It made everything right—it made everything priceless. The moon was there, early, white and young, and seemed reflected in the white face of the great empty Stadium, forming one of the boundaries of Soldiers' Field, that looked over at me, stared over at me, through the clear twilight, from across the Charles. Everything was there, everything *came*; the recognition, stillness, the strangeness, the pity and the sanctity and the terror, the breath-catching passion and the divine relief of tears. William's inspired transcript, on the exquisite little Florentine urn of Alice's ashes, William's divine gift to us, and to her, of the Dantean lines—

> *Dopo lungo exilio e martiro*
> *Viene a questa pace—*

took me so at the throat by its penetrating *rightness*, that it was as if one sank down on one's knees in a kind of anguish of gratitude before something for which one had waited with a long, deep *ache*. But why do I write of the all unutterable and the all abysmal? Why does my pen not drop from my hand on approaching the infinite pity and tragedy of all the past? It does, poor helpless pen, with what it meets of the ineffable, what it meets of the cold Medusa-face of life, of all the life *lived*, on every side. *Basta, basta!*"

General Index

Index of Works